RETHINKING THE UNIVERSITY

Rethinking the University

Structure, Critique, Vocation

Soo Tian Lee

COUNTERPRESS
OXFORD

First published 2018
Counterpress, Oxford
http://counterpress.org.uk

© 2018 Soo Tian Lee

Rights to publish and sell this book in print, electronic, and all other forms and media are exclusively licensed to Counterpress Limited. An electronic version of this book is available under a Creative Commons Attribution-NonCommercial (CC-BY-NC 4.0) International license via the Counterpress website:

http://counterpress.org.uk

ISBN: 978-1-910761-06-9 (paperback)

Typeset in 10.5 on 12.5 pt Sabon

Cover by SUGAHTANK design
www.behance.net/SUGAHTANK

Global print and distribution by Ingram

To Malik Ajani (1974–2017)

In memoriam

Acknowledgements

This book originated from my doctoral research at Birkbeck, University of London. Like a PhD thesis, a book is similar to a hearty pot of stew in that it manifests in physical form an infinite amount of relations between things in the world. Of these, only a select few can be spoken of, due to their gentle distinction within the complex whole.

I am grateful to the directors of Counterpress for their rock-solid support and encouragement throughout the process of revising the thesis-turned-manuscript.

I would like to thank profusely Peter Fitzpatrick for so kindly encouraging me to begin my doctoral journey and for overseeing its development for the first six years. His passion for the academic adventure, combined with his matchless rigour and precision, pushed me to seek better questions and deeper answers where my initial guesses failed.

I am greatly indebted to Nathan Moore for shepherding my thesis through its final year and a half with his gracious yet penetrating examination of the working out of its main ideas. His readiness to engage with even its strangest twists and turns was a great assistance to this mercurial writer. Words are insufficient to express my thanks to him.

Joel Wainwright and Tristan McCowan, the examiners of my thesis, provided me with many helpful comments and suggestions to improve this text. I am aware that I have not done anything close to full justice to their thorough and meticulous feedback, and so I must shoulder full responsibility for all the deficiencies in what follows. I have endeavoured to correct the glaring errors that they pointed out, but may have fallen short as to the more nuanced aspects of their thoughtful input. I would be grateful if the reader could view this book not as a perfect statement on the subject, but rather a record of the investigations of a fallible researcher working within the constraints of his situation. I write these words on the feast day of Timothy and Titus, the companions of St Paul, and am reminded that, like them, I am but a follower of thinkers far greater than me.

The community of Birkbeck Law School was an incomparable sphere to pursue the romance of intellectual-creative enquiry within the context of political engagement, and vice versa. So many of its denizens—past and present—contributed to this research project. At key moments during troubled times, interventions from Elena Loizidou and Thanos Zartaloudis were crucial in saving it from complete shipwreck. In all times and seasons, however, I was blessed by friends and comrades such as Anastasia Tataryn, Başak Ertür, Carolina Olarte Olarte, Chris Lloyd, Enrique Prieto Rios, Erdem Erturk, Hannah Franzki, Kanika Sharma, Laura Lammasniemi, Lisa Wintersteiger, Lucy Finchett-Maddock, Marcus Matos, Mayur Suresh, Paola Pasquali, Richard Bowyer, Simon Behrman, Tara Mulqueen, and Victoria Ridler.

Beyond the immediate institutional context, Irina Chkhaidze has been a constant source of strength, inspiration, as well as just simple fun and honest companionship. Probing comments from the late Malik Ajani midway through my research years helped me realize that the line of argument I had been pursuing up to that point was a dead end. Ayman S likewise gave me invaluable advice at a crucial moment in the final stages. In Oxford, where I spent my final years as a PhD student, Marek Sullivan, Max Harris, and Christine Hobden were wonderful co-pilgrims on the journey of reflection, writing, and argument. I am also grateful for fellow thinker-activists whom I came to know during and after the student uprisings in 2010/11. This research project would not have come into being if not for the 'Save Middlesex Philosophy' campaign, and may not have survived without invigoration from the effort to 'Save Philosophy at Greenwich.' Special mentions are due to Isabeau D, Johann H, Malise R, Clarrie P, 'Sel' T, Lloyd D, Ellese E, Perry S, Saffron G, Jacob S, Richard B, Jacob B-R, and Rory R.

Many thanks to the communities of the London Catholic Worker and Oxford Catholic Worker, where I lived for most of the period of this research project, especially Martin, Conor, Ciaron, Susan, Miriam, Mena, and Clive. *Muchas gracias* also to Jonny and Jojo, my brothers presently in black and blue. The parish community of Cowley St John in East Oxford was a bastion of support on both mundane and on most difficult days, especially Ruth and Martin Conway, Sabina Alkire, John Hammock, and Fr Phil Ritchie.

Space unfortunately does not permit me to mention by name many of the wonderful friends who have been there for me in manifold ways during this 'Long Walk' that has often felt more like 'Wandering in the Wilderness.' I am comforted that you folks know who you are, even as I am aggrieved by not being able to thank you more explicitly.

Nevertheless, I cannot avoid mentioning Benessa Tiong, Koralie Wit, and Sarah Epstein.

None of this would have been possible if not for the unflagging support of my parents, Doreen Khoo and Lee Kok Tee, as well as my sisters, Lee Sze Yuen and Lydia Lee. A thousand thanks to them, jointly and severally, for their gracious cheering on, faithful prayers, and great patience with me, their not-always-easy-to-handle flesh and blood.

Lastly, special thanks to Hui-En, the penultimate force behind the completion of this project. To you, dearly beloved being of passion and compassion, unto the ages of ages.

Lee Soo Tian
Feast of Timothy and Titus 2018

Contents

Introduction 13
    A Karatanian Interrogation. 18
    The University Triad. 21
        Instrumentalism. 22
        Idealism. 23
        Community. 25
        The Three Perspectives. 25
        Bracketing 26

1. A University Not for Itself: The Rise of Instrumentalism in Higher Education. 31
    The University without (Its Own) Content 32
    Post-war Keynesianism and the Dawn of
    Economistic Instrumentalism. 35
        The Myth of the Two Ruptures. 37
        Keynes Contra Fabianism and Others:
        The Pattern of the Post-war Consensus. 41
        The Beginnings of Economistic Instrumentalism
        in the Post-war University. 47

2. Self-(Mis)understanding After the Fact: The Formation of the Idealist Conception of the Public University 53
    The University with a Single Unifying Ideal. 54
    The Public University and its Founding Myth. 58
        Robbins: Social Democrat in Neoliberal Clothing,
        or Vice Versa? 62
    Examining the Structural Place of the Public University. 72

3. Torn Between Common Life and Individualism: The Thorny Issue of Community ... 75

Community and its Discontents ... 77
The Post-war British University and Community ... 83
    Students and Community ... 83
    Non-Academic Staff and Community ... 90
    Academic Staff and Community ... 94
    The (Al)lure of Non-Substantialist Community ... 100
Prolegomena to an Associationist University ... 102

4. Singularity, Particularity, and Structural History: On Personal and Collective Vocations in a Plural University ... 110

On the Singular Person and the Specific Context ... 114
    Singularities Seeking Universality in a World of Particularities ... 115
Vocation ... 121
    The Invention of Vocation ... 123
    A Very Brief History of Vocation in the Christian Context ... 125
    Versions of Academic Klesis ... 132
Partiality and Integration in a Web of Pluralism and Exclusivism ... 140
    Charismata: The Counterpart that Provides Form to Klesis ... 143
Conclusion: Toward a Past-Future University ... 150

Appendix A: On the Reception of Karatani's Writings in the Anglophone World ... 159

Appendix B: Foucault's Genealogy and Karatani's Transcendental Retrospection Compared ... 162

The Starting Point and the Purpose ... 164
On Origins ... 166
The University: A Universal? ... 167
The Totality of the University ... 169

Appendix C: The Structure of the Book ... 172

Notes ... 177

Index ... 221

Introduction

> We should have the modesty to say to ourselves that, on the one hand, the time we live in is not the unique or fundamental or irruptive point in history where everything is completed and begun again. We must also have the modesty to say, on the other hand, that—even without this solemnity—the time we live in is very interesting; it needs to be analyzed and broken down, and that we would do well to ask ourselves, 'What is the nature of our present?'
> — Michel Foucault[1]

In this book, I endeavour to rethink the history of higher education in the United Kingdom from the end of the Second World War to the present day. Using a framework inspired by the work of the contemporary Japanese philosopher Kojin Karatani, I explore three distinct perspectives—instrumentalism, idealism, and community—which I argue form a triadic structure and which, when grasped, opens the way to a heterodox yet illuminating reading of the post-war British university. Although there has been and still is no shortage of lively discussion and debate with regard to higher education in Britain, my contention is that the various parties who engage in these tussles, whether in word or deed, often slip into old ruts worn deep by those who have come before them. To escape from these well-worn grooves is not easy, but I believe it is an essential task if the university's past, present, and future is to be considered anew. I hope this book contributes towards a move beyond this stagnation, which I argue characterizes the main channels of discourse surrounding higher education in the United Kingdom.

It is my belief that the academic writer who wades into the subject of higher education has to do so with great trepidation. In most spheres of scholarship, one's primary audience is normally limited to the blessed company who have taken up the same discipline or, in some cases, crossed over into one's broader area of study. Others in the academy or the well-read layperson may have a certain respect for one's work, but it is more often the case that they will examine one's writings with dispassionate distance, pass a muted remark such as, 'How very interesting,' and then move on to what is really commanding their attention at that given time. However, I have found in writing about the university that my ideas and analyses are often met with general interest, for most people alive in the world today have a stake of some sort in higher education. For some it is the experience of having gone to university or, as it may be, not gone to university. For others it is the desire that one's offspring receive a university degree. For still others it is the daily existential reality of work within the university, whether as a student, an academic or non-academic member of staff, or a high-level manager. Whatever the reason, while carrying out the research that resulted in this book, I found that I could rarely escape from a conversation about my studies without the other person fielding follow-up questions or even, in some cases, castigating me for not looking into her or his pet subtopic in the field, whether it be access to higher education for the working class or the medieval disputation.

The reader may ask: What possessed the author to throw his hat into a ring already brimming with formidable prizefighters? Was it simply to enter a 'healthy industry'? After all, in his guide to turning a PhD dissertation into a book, the academic and former publisher William Germano writes,

> there are a surprising number of books published within a five-year period, and even in a single twelve-month period, that have common concerns and aim at the same readership. The hundreds of books on 9/11 or the Islamic world are but the most dramatic contemporary example, though books on Shakespeare or Lincoln or race in America (*or what's wrong with higher ed*) are other subjects that seem inexhaustible.[2]

The publication of a book was the last thing on my mind when I switched the topic of my PhD from social movements in the Global South to higher education in the United Kingdom. The point of genesis for my decision was rather my personal involvement in the twelve-day occupation of the Mansion building at the Trent Park campus of Middlesex University in May 2010 by students and supporters as part of a campaign to rescue the university's philosophy department from closure. The university's management was justifying this course of action on the allegation that the department was being subsidized by other subjects. Campaigners alleged, in response, that the university's policy of requiring a contribution of 55% of the gross income of each department to the centre was only calculated as unmet due to, firstly, the amalgamation of Philosophy with the far poorer Religious Studies department and, secondly, management's decision to close Philosophy programmes ahead of the 2010–11 intake, in which the requirement would have been met according to the university's projected figures.[3] While holed up in the Mansion building with other student activists actively working to save the department, I found myself asking: What sort of higher education world are we in at present, in which a small but world-renowned department of philosophy can be shut down ostensibly for narrowly failing to meet a financial target, when in fact it was questionable methods of accounting by the very central administration that led to this failure on paper?

As a result of this sense of amazement, befuddlement, and indignation, the research project that led to this book was conceptualized. Rather than simply interrogating the university as it appeared to function in the contemporary moment, it seemed to me more fruitful to dig further back into history in order to understand how higher education in Britain shifted from a mythical 'back there' to its present position. The time period I eventually settled upon was from the close of the Second World War to the present. My choice of this period was not an arbitrary one, but rather based on the simple recognition that much of what most people take for granted in the contemporary British university—from the significant proportion of state-managed funding to the institutions that presently exist—can be traced back to these crucial seventy-plus years. I realized that if I wanted to understand the roots of what alarmed me in current British higher education, I would need to pay special attention to developments in the post-war years.

At this point it is worth noting a potential challenge to the basic foundation of this book, namely that there is—to borrow a phrase from Shakespeare— something rotten in the state of the university. A casual observer of British higher education might contest any suggestion that there is anything deeply wrong with the way things are and are going by citing, for example, the relatively robust figure of 2.28 million students studying for a degree in 2015–16. One could also note with approval that despite a dip in applications to universities in England by 18-year-olds in 2012, when the controversial tripling of the undergraduate tuition fee maximum to GBP 9,000 came into force, applications to universities from this very demographic have since grown steadily, reaching a record-breaking 37.9% in 2017. The tuition fee hike, which led to a wave of protest by students and allies, could be rationalized as an unexpected blessing to universities given that, despite saddling students with unprecedented amounts of debt, the policy has thus far safeguarded the levels of state-backed funding for higher education during this ongoing period of austerity and uncertainty following the 2008 financial crisis. Furthermore, famed British institutions such as Oxford, Cambridge, Imperial College, and University College London remain at or close to the top of various world university rankings, testament to the high quality of teaching, learning, and scholarship that is carried out in these places.

However, a closer look at British higher education beyond these cheery statistics and signs of apparent health will reveal some rather alarming features that have emerged since the most recent wave of reforms began in 2010. First of all, the complete withdrawal of non-tuition related funding in the arts, humanities, and social sciences for undergraduate studies beginning in 2012 has resulted in a massive upheaval in the disciplines falling under these categories. To cite an extreme case, in anticipation of this defunding, London Metropolitan University in 2011 slashed the number of its degree courses from 557 to 160, abolishing in the process not only various humanities offerings, but the only programme on Caribbean Studies in the country.

Other reforms such as the liberalization of the rules governing the area of private providers of higher education have given rise to legitimate fears that institutions which fail as a result of the cuts to public funding will be either forced to close or taken over by for-profit education corporations. Indeed, the 2016 White Paper, 'Success as a Knowledge Economy,' includes a section on 'market exit' where it is stated that 'the possibility of some [higher education] institutions choosing—or needing—to exit the market ... is a crucial part of a healthy, competitive and well-functioning market.'[4]

Even if one has the view that it is perfectly legitimate for universities to be based on for-profit models, the sort of corporation that would be scanning the terrain for failing institutions to take over should give one pause. One of these would be Apollo Education Group, Inc., a private equity-owned corporation based in Phoenix, Arizona, which operates a number of for-profit educational institutions including BPP University, headquartered in London and granted university status in 2013 despite opposition from—among others—the University and College Union, which represents teaching and research staff. Apollo's most infamous institution is the University of Phoenix in the United States, which at its peak in 2010 had 600,000 students worldwide, its gargantuan size the result of, inter alia, very loose admission requirements and an emphasis on distance learning. Given the numerous criticisms of the quality of its academic provisions,[5] the likelihood of refitted higher education institutions in the UK based on such a model is a truly frightening prospect. Even more repugnant is the case of the for-profit London School of Science and Technology, known to some of its students as the 'cashpoint college' or 'ATM' due to the fact that they could register for courses, access up to GBP 11,000 in grants and loans per year, and then not turn up for classes.

More broadly, there is much reason to deplore the encroachment of the state in the workings of universities in the United Kingdom, which despite being generally understood as 'public' bodies, are in fact not under direct state control.[6] One of the examples of tentacular state power and influence in the running of British universities today is the introduction of the Teaching Excellence Framework (TEF), a dubiously derived metric of teaching quality and impact, originally attached to a policy to permit universities that perform particularly well to increase their tuition fees beyond the ordinary limit. A sceptical mind cannot help but suspect another attempt to create differentiated fees in the higher education system to produce market-like dynamics, following the government's disappointment with the cartel-like decision by almost all universities, in the wake of the 2010 reforms, to simply continue charging the maximum amount of fees. Another potentially concerning development is the requirement for universities to comply with the government's 'Prevent' counter-terrorist programme, as it has forcefully created a culture of policing in universities as well as a climate of self-censorship and fear among innocent students who fit the stereotype or profile of a potential extremist, with the chief feature being adherence to the Muslim faith. Prevent has also led to infringements upon academic freedom due to paranoia when discussing Islam, for example in the reported case of a criminology lecturer who sent her course reading list to the police for appraisal as to whether anything in it was 'too critical.'[7]

Many of these questionable recent developments have their origin in the market-driven ideology subscribed to by Conservative Party ministers who have held the reins of university policy since May 2010, but it is possible that such phenomena are not temporary aberrations but rather part of the emergence of a 'new normal.' Hence, faced with Foucault's question in the epigraph above, 'What is the nature of our present?', I believe that an honest university denizen or observer can only say that there are significant dangers and threats either presently with us or on the horizon, even if these have yet to be implemented fully. Thus, it is possible to say that both sanguine readings based on prestige and positive statistics, on the one hand, and doom-laden pronouncements that simply focus on negative trends and symptoms, on the other, obscure the truer picture of a university that appears to be in good working condition but, in fact, has a number of crucial components in varying states of malfunction.

It is this diagnosis of the contemporary British university as akin to a machine that is, at first glance, whirring happily away, yet with numerous worrying faults and vulnerabilities visible upon closer inspection, that animates the analysis carried out in this book. However, readers who expect as a central feature a detailed, blow-by-blow analysis of what has happened in the last seven or so years will be disappointed. It is my conviction that the aforementioned elements of the British university in the present day—whether positive or negative—can best be employed not as the primary subject of analysis, but rather as a contextual impulse to drive an investigation of the deeper roots that lie underneath these clearly visible manifestations above the ground. In other words, one's concern for the present should drive one to look back at the past, in order to understand the British university as it has developed in the post-war period afresh.

A Karatanian Interrogation

Writing the history of a particular thing as it exists in a particular time may seem to be a relatively straightforward matter. One may think that it is just a matter of accumulating all the facts and constructing a narrative from them, using interpretation where necessary to bridge the gaps between the raw data. In the writing of this book, I have adopted amore complex methodology and theoretical point of departure based on Karatani's ideas. Due to the relative obscurity of his work not just among the general public in the English-speaking world but also in most academic circles in the United Kingdom—his influence upon Anglophone academia is far wider and deeper in the United States—it is worthwhile briefly laying out aspects of his theories that form the bedrock of this book (on the reception of Karatani's ideas in the Anglophone world, see Appendix A).

I am greatly indebted to two interrelated areas of Karatani's work that I believe are incredibly fertile but which, thus far, have been relatively neglected in the literature available in English. Both of these can be found most prominently in his studies on Kant in the 1990s. Although these Kantian investigations can be regarded more broadly as laying the theoretical foundations of his far better-known writings published since 2000, such as his ambitious and provocative books *Transcritique: On Kant and Marx* and *The Structure of World History:*

From Modes of Production to Modes of Exchange, I would argue that some elements from this phase of his work have not received the attention they deserve.

The first of these neglected strands I deploy is Karatani's historical-philosophical methodology, which he sometimes refers to as 'transcendental retrospection' (for a comparison of Foucault's 'genealogy' with Karatani's transcendental retrospection, see Appendix B). Taking as his starting point Kant's project of transcendental critique, he explains that

> the point of [such] critique is to reveal that what we take for granted as object is only a composite of a certain 'form' that is unknown to us. This is a sort of retrospection, but to an origin that can be grasped only transcendentally, not one that we imagine to be the cause of the effect known to us.[8]

Put simply, when approaching what one wishes to analyze—in the case of this book, the historical materials on post-war British higher education—one has to bear in mind that there are always underlying patterns and structures that one may not be able to detect from a straightforward reading or perception. To apprehend these patterns requires a 'transcendental' (but not, it must be emphasized, a 'transcendent') perspective—that is, a standpoint that cuts through the naked 'content' to explore what Karatani in a conference paper in 1993 calls a 'mode of recognition,' which can be understood as, to invoke a phrase from *Transcritique*, the 'unconscious structure that precedes and shapes experience.'[9]

What is this 'unconscious structure'? The example of Freudian psychoanalysis is offered by Karatani as an example that may be helpful to grasp what is spoken about here. Freud's theoretical framework, Karatani argues, can be understood as a metapsychology rather than an empirical psychology in that the psychical structure of id, ego, and superego advanced in it 'can be spoken of only as *figure*'—which is to say that they, like the Kantian conceptual triad, are not empirically verifiable objects but rather 'functions about which we can only *say* that they are at work.'[10] By simply 'saying' that they are at work, Karatani does not mean that these conceptual models are false or mere figments of one's imagination, but on the contrary, that as a *transcendental* structure they by definition lie outside of the boundaries of purely empirical perception and therefore serve as maps to study the field of play. Hence, it is by analyzing the *relations* between the elements at stake that a structure may emerge in a dialogue between empirical analysis and rational conceptualization. What emerges then can be understood as a figure that not only represents what conditions the state of things but which may also be used as a tool for interpretation and even intervention.

If transcendental retrospection provides this book's methodological background, the second specific portion from Karatani's readings of Kant in the 1990s, which I draw from especially, provides the conceptual starting point. This segment is his formulation of what he termed the 'triad of concepts' in Kant's writings, consisting of phenomenon, idea, and the thing-in-itself.[11] According to Karatani, this conceptual triad is not restricted to Kant's writings, but is rather a recurring theme or pattern in the history of human thought, affect, and life. The three terms form a 'relational structure' in which 'the name of each term is alterable ... but only insofar as [this] relational structure is maintained.'[12] It is this triadic structure which Karatani distils from Kant that I employ in this book to think through the British university in the post-war period.

My central undertaking is thus to re-examine the history of the university in post-war Britain through a *structural* understanding based on Karatani's conceptual triad. By using the word 'structural,' I denote a perspective in which events, policies, statements, and other such 'data' can be organized into a comprehensive framework that allows its user to grasp the patterns involved. By adopting such a strategy I mean to avoid two grave pitfalls that can compromise an analysis of the history of post-war British higher education. The first is an approach, which can perhaps be described as crude empiricism, in which any theoretical framework is seen as obstructing a straightforward, 'non-ideological' analysis of the matters at hand by distorting one's perception of them. I consider any such 'structureless' or piecemeal strategy seriously mistaken, for there is ultimately no practical way of meaningfully interpreting the vast quantity of data involved in a project such as this without at least some conceptual organization. I believe that structure is inevitable, and a comprehensive structure extremely helpful.

The second pitfall I wish to circumvent is that of lapsing into stale binaries in analysis, that is, allowing a simplistic 'either-or' framework to unconsciously or at least semi-consciously structure the arguments. One of the most prevalent ways in which this happens in debates surrounding the post-war and contemporary university is to pit 'public' education against its mortal enemies, commonly identified as 'privatization' or 'the market.' While I do not deny that such analyses have had their uses, it is my contention that they are today a dead end. Such binary thinking does not show a way forward, but rather keeps the debate stuck in the same back-and-forth arguments.

The structure of the university that will be elucidated and utilized in this book derives from the aforementioned conceptual triad. I would like to call it the 'university triad,' and it consists of three distinct perspectives which, I argue, have stuctured and continue to structure the post-war British university. These are instrumentalism, idealism, and community, which are related respectively to the Kantian concepts of phenomenon, idea, and thing-in-itself. It is my contention that approaching the history of British higher education through each of these perspectives will yield not only fresh individual insights but, more importantly, a framework enabling a new understanding of the debates surrounding university education in the United Kingdom and possibilities for future interventions.

Before I proceed to sketch the lineaments of this university triad, it should be noted that a second triad is used in this book, albeit only to frame the argument and narrative rather than as a conceptual tool. It can be termed the 'epistemic triad,' because it is concerned with the sort of knowledge being sought in the various parts of the book. Unlike the elements of the university triad, it lies largely beneath the surface of the argument, and can thus be described as 'infrastructural.' This epistemic triad, which pertains not to the post-war British university itself but rather my *analysis* of this university, complements the university triad which is 'superstructural' and appears explicitly in the arguments that follow. In other words, the former triad conditions the lines of argument pursued in each of the chapters, even while it leaves the spotlight and centre stage to the elements in the university triad. Knowledge of this underlying structure may be helpful, but is not absolutely necessary, to appreciate the arguments that are made in the chapters to follow. The reader who is interested in turning this book inside out to see, as it were, the stitches on the inside may refer to Appendix C for a diagram and explication of what lies beneath the manifestly visible narrative and argumentation.

The University Triad

A transcendental retrospection to investigate the British university of the present begins with this question: 'What is taken for granted—that is, appears self-evident to the point of being invisible—within its bounds?' It is argued that this largely unconscious 'mode of recognition' is none other than the underlying foundations of discourses and practices within the university. Hence, one way to understand the excavation of these foundations is to see it as a process of discerning questions. By examining the various arguments about the direction of higher education as well as practical policies within this sphere, I am trying to discern the questions these arguments and policies are trying to answer.

The structure expressed by these questions and answers is not one that is completely unique to the university, but in fact mirrors the Kantian conceptual triad of phenomenon, idea, and thing-in-itself that Karatani has identified and traced through other forms of transcendental critique such as Freudian metapsychology and Lacanian psychoanalysis.[13] This triad, he explains, is a 'relational structure' that brings traditional philosophical concepts together, and which, I would like to add, allows one who uses it to scrutinize the state of play with a lens that brings the various discrete elements into focus.[14]

Instrumentalism

In the university at present, much of the debate, both ongoing and in the recent past, has been delimited by a consequentialist question, which can be phrased generally as follows: 'What are the consequences of a particular university policy for the goals that we are aiming for?' It is this question that has been answered at different times in different ways, but has remained primary throughout the post-war era. Many commentators on university policy have focused on the difference between the various answers given to the question, whether the succession of those that became for a time hegemonic or their competitors, while neglecting to enquire into the very question being asked. In other words, much ink has been spilt comparing competing policies of university policy and governance, without recognizing that at the roots of many of these is a single question which, when unconsciously accepted, structures almost all the debate and action that follows.

To situate this question in the structure that is being reconstructed, I would like to argue that it corresponds to the Kantian notion of *phenomena* within Karatani's triad. In other words, it is focused on what appears to be the 'objective world'—that is, the world of *nature*—but which is, rather, the sum total of *sensible* intuitions grasped by the concepts of *understanding*. It is unsurprising that predominantly empirical studies focus on this part of the structure of the university, for when this *action-centric* approach is taken out of its relational structure, it falls on one side of the antinomy between empiricism and rationalism. An antinomy is a contradiction, whether real or apparent, between two principles, and in this case the perspective of instrumentalism lies squarely on the side represented by empiricism and the historical. Those who call for pragmatism within the university thus display their obsession with this instrumentalist question, and with the layer of the university that is phenomenal.

At this juncture it is important to note two matters. First of all, in and of itself, the instrumentalist question is without definite content. To recapitulate, its generic form is as follows: 'What are the *consequences* of a particular university policy for the *goals* that we are aiming for?' If one changes the goal(s) or *telos* that is being strived towards, the weighing up of the consequences—and hence the conclusion that is likely to be reached—changes dramatically.

Secondly, it should be noted that the nature of the Kantian conceptual triad, as Karatani formulates it, is that each of the three elements is indispensable. The rejection or abandonment of any one concept in the triad results in an imbalanced and faulty picture, with potentially serious consequences. One example that Karatani gives is the tossing aside of the thing-in-itself by some German Idealists and Romantics such as Fichte, with the result being 'a loss of the position from which to view Idea as *Schein* [i.e. illusion].'[15] Following on from this insight, it becomes clear that it is impossible to avoid asking the instrumentalist question at specific points. It is ultimately futile to imagine a university that does not in some way take into account the impact of its workings upon practical and 'external' matters such as the training of skilled labour.

Idealism

The instrumentalist question has never been the only one animating the workings of the university. Although consequentialism has played a large role—perhaps even the formative role—in higher education from its very beginnings, alongside it has existed another tradition focused upon the *ideals* (or ideas) of the university.

The question this tradition asks is: 'What overarching principle(s) should govern the university?' Among the answers to this question that have been mooted in times gone by (but also in the present) are liberal education, the pursuit of truth, and the glorification of God. At the present moment in the United Kingdom, one of the most notable answers to this question of the university is that of the vision of the 'public university,' which will be investigated in greater detail later.

As with the instrumentalist question, the idealist question is a form without a determinate content. It is an integral part of the underlying structure of the university, but depending on one's pedagogical, philosophical, and political positions, the exact form of the question and the answers that are 'found' will differ. Nevertheless, whether they are current or dated, popular or unpopular, hegemonic or marginal, all answers to the question of ideals correspond with the realm of the *idea* in Karatani's Kantian conceptual triad. In other words, it involves the faculties of *understanding* and *reason*, which cooperate to apprehend these ideas. This being so, when extracted from the relational structure, this *thought-centric* approach falls on the side of the aforementioned antinomy represented by rationalism and idealism. Those who call for principles within the university display their obsession with this question of ideals.

However, this link to the Kantian idea reveals that all ideals are ultimately illusions or *Schein*. Although pragmatists who are focused on the instrumentalist question may wish to dismiss these illusions as being impractical, it is instructive that Kant made a distinction between constitutive and regulative ideas. The former claim to be realizable in fact, and so can be linked to the Marxian '*ideal* to which reality [will] have to adjust itself,' whereas the latter 'constantly offers the ground to criticize reality' by being 'an index toward which people should gradually attempt to draw close.'[16] Regulative ideas, while being illusions, are *transcendental* (or necessary) illusions, in that they are things 'we cannot do without.'[17] Likewise, as has already been said, it is impossible to conceive of the university completely outside the bounds of instrumentalism.

Between instrumentalism and idealism there appears to be an antinomy, similar and related to the ones Kant faced with empiricism and rationalism and to the ones Marx faced with historicism and idealism. One temptation, which many succumb to, is to resolve the tension in one or the other direction, embracing one side and tossing out the other. Such a solution is, in fact, an illusion, for a formal denigration of either instrumentalism or idealism does not prevent hidden calculations or ideals from operating. In other words, as alluded to above, a militant instrumentalism inevitably produces ideals of its own, while a militant idealism cannot avoid making decisions based on instrumental goals at various points.

Another temptation is to create a 'third way' that attempts to surmount this antinomy by turning to aesthetics and the notion of an organic whole. As shall be seen, this is the path taken by the German Romantics and Hegel, a stance within the sphere of the university that may be termed 'community.'

Community

So far the perspectives or questions of instrumentalism and idealism have been described using largely Kantian terminology. There is, however, a third question that can be formulated using developments in German idealism following Kant. This can be referred to as the perspective of *community*, which is founded upon a particular conception of human life together and which in its classic social-political form tends to be bound up with the idea of the nation. In *The Structure of World History*, Karatani elucidates how the conception of the nation, which is analagous in the university triad to community, is related to the domains or faculties Kant also employed:

> In [Hegel's] logic, as in Herder's, the germ of reason is already present at the stage of sensibility, and subsequently it gradually unfolds through a process of self-realization. This means that while the nation (*Volk*) pertains to sensibility, it also belongs to the domain of reason, and hence it reaches its final realization in the form of the nation-state.[18]

In other words, whereas the perspective of instrumentalism arises from the confluence of sensibility and understanding, and idealism from that of understanding and reason, the perspective of community—according to certain German idealists—is a blend of *sensibility* and *reason*. This latter combination is heretical within the Kantian system, and Karatani takes great pains to disclaim its validity, arguing rather that what Herder and Hegel performed was an illusory synthesis of sensibility with reason and understanding through the faculty of the imagination.[19] Regardless of the orthodoxy of this argument within a broadly Kantian framework, the fact remains that such a position has been and can be staked in the wider scheme of things. Rather than simply deny it, it is better to accord it a place within the present frame of discussion. What may be termed the question of community is focused on the following matter: 'What is the impact of a particular university policy on the university community?' This is far from a straightforward enquiry, for as shall be seen later, there are competing visions of community that influence the answers that are reached.

The Three Perspectives

The discussion thus far can be summarized diagrammatically, see *figure 1*. As the diagram demonstrates, each of the three perspectives is linked to a major category of ethical thought. Instrumentalism is solidly consequentialist, idealism is deontological, while the question of community to correspond, in its most common forms, to a rather traditional form of virtue ethics. As Ivan Illich points out, virtue in the Greek *polis* was understood as 'fitting behaviour,' that is, 'the *ethos* ... appropriate to a certain *ethnos*, or people.'[20] This ancient conception of virtue could not conceive of an ethics that was not rooted in a people and, by extension, a place or soil. So the perspective of community does not overcome the antinomy of instrumentalism or idealism, but rather creates a third position that competes with both of them. Rather than a conflict of two laws (*anti-nomia*), here appears a tussle between three laws, for which one might coin the word *trichonomy*, from the Greek *tríkha* (divided into three parts) and *nomos* (law).

There is no easy resolution to this triadic tension. We have to persevere through it by dwelling in what Žižek, in his exegesis of Karatani's thought calls the 'parallax gap,' which is the uncomfortable space between two seemingly conflicting viewpoints. In such a gap, one is confronted with neither simply analyzing phenomena nor debating ideas, but the uncomfortable space of what Karatani has termed the 'transcendental topos' for transcritique. Karatani's more recent concept of 'transcritique' involves accepting the 'pronounced parallax' that results from trying to avoid the optical delusion of a single standpoint, and instead moving back and forth between the poles of the antinomy. Hence, unlike community, the parallax gap or transcendental topos is not an alternative 'positionality' but a mere interstice where there is no imaginary synthesis between or escape from the opposed forces, but only the persistence of the trichonomy in the constant confrontation between pragmatic concerns, principled ideas, and communal aesthetics. To dwell in this space is to accept a vocation that involves moving between the various poles in order to find a manner of navigating the ternary of instrumentalism-community-idealism.

Bracketing

Having outlined the three main elements of the proposed discursive-practical structure of the university, it will be helpful to explore what it means exactly to be a 'question' within this structure. The latter's foundation is a perspective of 'pronounced parallax,' which allows us to view a particular thing in its multiple facets, and has been described by Karatani as a practice of 'bracketing.'

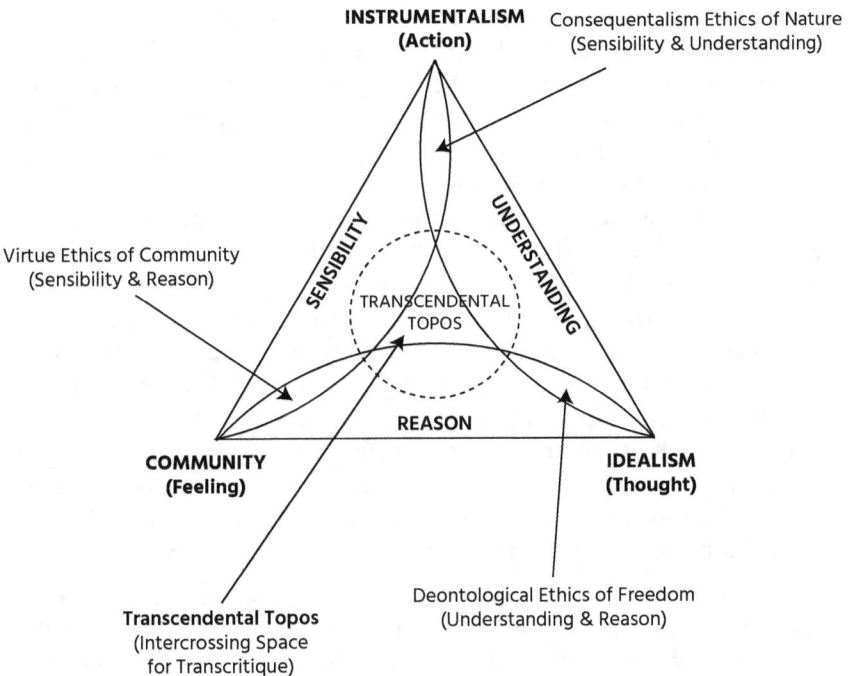

Figure 1

It is true that bracketing has a post-Kantian lineage in that it was first deployed by Husserl to refer to the phenomenological suspension of judgement about the natural world in order to focus on the contents of mental experience. This development of Husserl's was itself premised on Kant's distinction between noumena and phenomena, and it certainly describes well Kant's operation in *The Critique of Judgment* where he argues that when it comes to matters of taste we have to place to one side concerns that do not pertain to the aesthetic domain. He illustrates this in a vivid passage in which he gives examples of wrong-headed responses to a question about whether a palace is beautiful, such as ranting against the vanity of the rich and influential or declaring that such luxury would be unwanted even on a deserted island. These may be valid arguments when discussing a palace in general terms, but irrelevant to an assessment of its beauty. In other words, an aesthetic analysis becomes clouded if one attempts to engage at the same time with matters ethical, political, or idiosyncratic bordering on irrelevancy. To critique the political message of a film, for example, is a task that is separate from a judgement of the qualities of its cinematography. However, it is not the case that any of these stances 'assumes priority over all other criteria. What counts here is not simply bracketing but also un-bracketing.'[21] Such is the movement of parallax: examining the contours of each domain by temporarily suspending the others.

Bracketing is not simply investigating particular domains—such as cognition, ethics, aesthetics, or economics—as if they predated the act of investigation. Instead, it is the very operation of bracketing that brings these domains into being. In the words of Karatani:

> Modern science was established by bracketing moral and aesthetic judgments. Only at this moment did the 'object' appear. Machiavelli came to be known as the father of modern political science precisely because he discovered the domain of politics by bracketing morality.[22]

How does all this apply to the investigations in this book? The argument I am making is that each of the three questions of the university arise when the other two are bracketed. For example, instrumentalist calculations—which are often justified by a deceivingly simple phrase such as 'let's be realistic here'—can only be made by pushing aside issues of ideals and community and it is this bracketing procedure that creates the instrumentalist perspective in the first place. Likewise, the idealist position is summoned into being when one insists that principles are to trump all other considerations. Finally, the perspective that privileges the community in evaluating a particular course of action has to suspend instrumentalist and idealist matters.

Of course, in actual practice, these three questions often intermingle, or at least are ordered in some hierarchy of importance: 'x should come first, and then y, and finally z.' Although this is possible in a sense, because shuttling from one question to the next in some fixed order could be seen as a variety of the practice of transcritique, it is tempting to regard this procedure as being more stable than it is in reality. The reality of parallax means that one cannot view one's subject matter from multiple perspectives at the same time—after all, each of us has only one pair of eyes. This limitation explains why, for example, those who privilege an instrumentalist perspective simply cannot see 'eye to eye' with those who privilege an idealist perspective.

Beyond this, it also explains how people who consider themselves 'principled' can swiftly turn into 'pragmatists' when placed in a different context, as the different viewpoints can be adopted in a manner akin to switching between spectacles of various tints and lenses. It is for this reason that cases of academics with clearly conflicted loyalties can be found, such as that of Craig Calhoun, who served as the President of the London School of Economics 2012–16. In November 2011, Calhoun wrote an article for the 'Possible Futures' blog of the Social Science Research Council—of which he was the president at the time—criticizing the eviction of various Occupy groups by city and university authorities across the United States. In this piece, the decisions of leaders such as New York Mayor Michael Bloomberg and the presidents of Harvard and UC Berkeley to call in the police to dismantle protest camps were criticized as 'reminiscent of the Chinese government ousting protestors from Tiananmen Square' and a 'disturbing' development in 'ostensibly democratic America.'[23]

Fast-forward a few years, and we find Calhoun, as President of the London School of Economics, supporting the eviction of student occupiers due to, among other things, the disruption of a lecture which led to the management stating that they were left with no other option other than to put an end to the occupation. Although Calhoun stated in a letter to the occupiers that he was 'personally sorry to have reached this point,' does that alter the fact that he ended up mirroring the actions of the authorities he criticized back in 2011, who 'thought it was more important to maintain public order than to allow ... particular citizens to exercise public voice'?[24] It can be argued that in this case, Calhoun switched from viewing protests of this sort from an idealist perspective to an instrumentalist one. Even though he had not publicly disowned his earlier statements with regard to the Occupy camps, his new job as head of the LSE meant that he had to bracket those views.

In the chapters that follow, I will examine each of the three perspectives of the university in turn using the mechanism of bracketing. Although they are intimately connected, it is impossible for us to grasp the relations between them without this procedure, one that isolates the key elements of each perspective to understand its essence and dynamic place in the triad. At the beginning of chapter V of Book 1 of Charles Dickens's *Hard Times*, the narrator says to the reader, 'Let us strike the key-note ... before pursuing our tune.'[25] Having attempted in this introduction to strike such a note—or, rather, a series of introductory notes that perhaps can be described as a *motif*—we can now begin to rehearse the long angular tune that is the history of higher education in post-war Britain.

1

A University Not for Itself: The Rise of Instrumentalism in Higher Education

> A cow can pretend that it exists not for itself but for man. Man can pretend that he exists for humanity. Humanity can pretend that it exists in order to sustain ontological reality. ... Thus the meaning of existence is tossed about from one level of reality to another.
>
> — Egon Bondy[1]

In a BBC Radio 3 programme in 2000, the intellectual historian Stefan Collini explored the awkwardness—or perhaps even the absurdity—of higher education institutions like his own University of Cambridge having glossy mission statements by imagining a hypothetical 'mission statement' for a medieval monastery:

> There'd no doubt be one bar graph showing the increasing number of souls prayed for per annum, and another showing the declining value of the tithe; there'd perhaps be a picture of a saintly elderly monk painstakingly illuminating a manuscript, and certainly pictures of younger monks happily planting vegetables and brewing beer; and of course there'd be a statement by the prior about the efficiency gains that had been made by starting matins earlier and ending vespers later. But wouldn't all that leave you with just the teensiest suspicion that something rather important about monasteries was being omitted or misrepresented here?[2]

This quote comes from the published version of Collini's radio addresses, from a 2012 collection, released in the waning ferment of the 2010–11 reforms under the Conservative-Liberal Democrat coalition and titled *What Are Universities For?* The book's title poses a deceivingly simple question, but, as with many such queries, a multitude of answers can be (and have been) proffered in response to it. Collini's tongue-in-cheek monastery mission statement, framed as an analogy to contemporary higher education captures an important aspect of recent developments in this age-old debate, namely the sidelining of purposes for the university intrinsic to the university itself. The medieval monastery, like the contemporary university, was a hive of activity, but much of it could not be properly understood without an immersion into the deep *ethos* upon which it was founded. What Collini describes is a perspective that would result from a steely-eyed corporate consultant being transported through time to this cenobitic community in the Middle Ages. Yet, without grasping the foundation of the contemplative community in the cycle of worship offered multiple times a day—known as the Work of God (*opus Dei*)—one would be simply distracted by the many other activities which may seem far more interesting or 'useful' from the hegemonic viewpoints today, but which were in fact incidental rather than essential.

As was set out in the previous chapter, the starting point of our genealogical enquiry is the present-day actuality of the university, and not an idealized form. We have to accept that in the case of much top-down higher education policy—whether at the level of elected government or individual institutions—the dominant framework in which decisions are made is one where the university's reason for being is found not in itself but rather its instrumental functions. This is the instrumentalist viewpoint that forms the logical starting point of our investigation in this chapter. We shall first define and outline the essence of this perspective before exploring its surge to prominence in the post-war period and its centrality until the present day.

The University without (Its Own) Content

An instrumentalist perspective of higher education can be defined as an approach whereby the primary measure of the value or desirability of a particular university policy or a particular set of practices in the sphere of higher education is its consequences for the specific goals that have been predetermined. The crude version operates as follows: if the policy or set of practices advances these goals, then it is to be favoured; if it has minimal positive effect upon or, worse still, hinders these goals, then it is to be rejected or at least seriously called into question.[3]

Hence, the essence of instrumentalism in higher education, in its most extreme form, is that the university is merely an instrument to further certain ends. It therefore does not have intrinsic value, that is, it exists not for itself but for whatever goals we may wish to set for it. The end result of the purest version of this viewpoint is that the university is emptied of whatever *raison d'être* it may have been seen as having, becoming a *university without (its own) content.*

In his seminal work, *The University in Ruins*, published soon after his untimely death in 1996, Bill Readings diagnosed in the university of the time a condition very similar to what we have named instrumentalism, albeit using his own terminology. According to Readings, for most of the history of the modern university, its operations had been characterized by being tied to what he called a 'referent,' which was 'a specific set of things or ideas' that pulsated at the heart of the institution.[4] The predominant referent, whose definitive statement was made in the nineteenth century by Alexander von Humboldt, was that of culture. The university, through its activities of research and teaching, was 'linked to the destiny of the nation-state by virtue of its role as producer, protector, and inculcator of an idea of national culture.'[5]

But since the 1960s, Readings argues, the ideology of culture has been gradually displaced from the heart of the university, and in its place we now have a discourse of 'excellence.'[6] This new central idea of excellence at first appears to be something of substance, since there seems to be no shortage of methods of measuring it. However, it is precisely due to this limitless multiplicity of ways of measuring excellence that it is revealed as having no content of its own. This content-free (non-)referent is particularly slippery, for as Readings puts it:

> What gets taught or researched matters less than the fact that it be excellently taught and researched. ... 'Excellence' is like the cash-nexus in that it has no *content*; it is hence neither true nor false, neither ignorant nor self-conscious. It may be unjust, but we cannot seek its injustice in terms of a regime of truth or self-knowledge. Its rule does not carry with it an automatic political or cultural orientation, for it is not determined in relation to any identifiable instance of political power.[7]

Indeed, this non-referent of excellence is something we cannot oppose without looking odd or at least giving the appearance of mere cynicism. Thus, 'we all agree upon it because it is not an ideology, in the sense that it has no external referent or internal content.'[8] If the pursuit of excellence in higher education sounds vague, even vacuous sub-divisions of such excellence are often no less ambiguous, as Readings demonstrates with the following example:

> Cornell University Parking Services recently received an award for 'excellence in parking.' What this meant was that they had achieved

a remarkable level of efficiency in *restricting* motor vehicle access. ... [E]xcellence could just as well have meant making people's lives easier by increasing the number of parking spaces available ... The issue here is not the merits of either option but the fact that excellence can function equally well as an evaluative criterion on either side of the issue of what constitutes 'excellence in parking,' because excellence has no content to call its own.[9]

The underlying emptiness in the notion of excellence brings us to a deeper understanding of instrumentalism that may not be obvious in the more simplistic form that was outlined at the start of this section, namely the fact that even if one selects an apparently clear goal to be pursued in higher education policy and practice, such as the facilitation of economic growth or simply being one of the 'top universities' in the country, one's progress towards that end cannot actually be determined other than through extremely crude metrics that provide an inadequate or deceptive picture of what is supposedly being measured. *Pace* Readings, however, what he identifies as the discourse of excellence does not, in the British context, have its point of invention in the 1960s, but as we shall see later in this chapter, already arose in recognizable form in the immediate post-war period.

Hence, the irony is that even as instrumentalism attempts to evacuate the 'soul' of the university so that external and measurable considerations may take first place, the mechanisms of measurement intended to steer the ship of higher education towards these goals will likely turn out to be far less empirically rigorous than they appear at first sight.

It is important to note that the absence of specific content has not prevented particular forms of content from overtaking others and muscling their way into a central position. Although it is theoretically true that 'excellence' in a particular situation can be determined in multiple ways, more often than not it is instrumentalist agendas of an economistic kind that have become generalized, that is, the sort of excellence that has been pursued has been that which complies with the demands of the sources of one's funding, whether a consumer market, a bureaucratic apparatus, or something else. Indeed, where there is an apparent vacuum of sorts, it is the most reductionist forms of ideology and practice that easily fill the space.

Returning to the broader picture, in the history of the post-war British university, the instrumentalist perspective has never attained—or, at least, has yet to attain—such a degree of hegemony as to bring about a complete emptying of the university's inner *raison d'être* as in the hypothetical extreme we have just briefly described. Instead, it has coexisted alongside idealist perspectives of many kinds, as well as, to a less obvious extent, perspectives focused on the university community. As we have seen, this coexistence has as its paradoxical partner the peculiar condition in which each type of perspective can only be employed at any given moment to the exclusion of the others.

It is quite clear the wind of instrumentalism has been blowing strongly in our direction for some time and with apparently ever-increasing ferocity. Wherever we turn in the university today, we find instrumentalist concerns of all kinds: research is not only to be rated and ranked, but is rewarded if it has 'impact'; teaching is measured not by any intrinsic qualities but according to student satisfaction; the funding system is designed in order to drive costs down while driving 'quality' up through the operation of market rationality; and so on. Although we, to quote a bard of the 1960s, 'don't need a weatherman to know which way the wind blows,'[10] we might want to know why this particular stiff gale has been howling at us so incessantly, as well as where it comes from and when it began. For this, some meteorological history may be helpful and so it is to this history that we now turn.

Post-war Keynesianism and the Dawn of Economistic Instrumentalism

According to one common narrative of post-war higher education, the period from the first Attlee government until circa 1979–81 was one in which the vision of a 'public university' reigned and government funding was provided to realize such a vision, with 'public' here seen as the antithesis of the gradual 'marketization' or 'privatization' that followed. Various versions of this thesis can be found across the literature. To give just a few examples, A. H. Halsey wrote that the supply of public monies for university expansion were reduced 'for the first time, at least in living memory' by 'a monetarist, market-oriented government.'[11] Maurice Kogan and Stephen Hanney, while recognizing the problems of this narrative, nevertheless identified the year 1981 as the starting point of 'a period of change in which the finance, government and substantive content of higher education was subjected to ... radical changes.'[12] Finally, in a recent study triggered by the latest wave of higher education reform under the Conservative-Liberal Democrat Coalition, Roger Brown and Helen Carasso have stated that the 'process of marketization may be seen to have commenced with the Thatcher Government's announcement in November 1979 that, from the following academic year, students from overseas would no longer enjoy a fee subsidy.'[13]

The picture that emerges from a reading of these texts can be described as follows: we first have a gradually expanding public university imbued with the values of the post-war consensus, brought into being by the first Attlee government but subsequently honoured by governments both Tory and Labour, which consisted of a collectivist politics whose central pillars were a welfare state and a mixed economy;[14] this was brought to an end by a rupture with this consensus during the first Thatcher government that set in train the move towards a 'neoliberal university.'

This relatively uncomplicated narrative of what happened and how we got here can lead to rather problematic political conclusions as to what sort of university we ought to be fighting for (see chapter three). In brief, if there were two great breaks in the history of the post-war university, and if we find the second break the dawn of a ghastly marketized and privatized system, then it is far too easy to conclude that the solution is to return to the public values seen as exemplifying the first break, thus overlooking—or even ignoring—what Matthew Charles has identified as 'a fundamental contradiction [that] exists between capitalism (and not merely its *neo*liberal version) and a *mass*, modern and [truly] public [i.e. popular][15] higher education system.'[16]

Hence, in the next section of this chapter, an alternative story of the development of the contemporary university will be put forward, which contests the ostensible break between a 'public university' of the post-war consensus and a 'neoliberal university' of the Thatcher and post-Thatcher period that is still our present. The narrative will show that the elements of the neoliberal university that proponents of a welfare statist public university find most abhorrent in fact originated in the immediate post-war period itself. In other words, there was no paradise followed by a fall, because the seeds of the fall were already sown in the very making of paradise.

Before we proceed, it should be noted that although state investment in higher education overlaps partially with both the welfare state and economic planning, and hence with the history and debates of those aspects of post-war reconstruction, it contains specificities that make it a *sui generis* case of sorts. While public funding of post-war higher education can be considered part of the wider effort to reduce inequality in British society through the slow but steady opening up of a hitherto elitist institution, it was not originally conceived as an essential or even a secondary element of the 'cradle to the grave' welfare state that arose out of the Beveridge Report. With regard to the five 'giant evils' that Beveridge diagnosed as plaguing Britain at the time, it is possible to subsume the expansion of higher education as an attack upon ignorance.[17] Nevertheless, although Beveridge was most concerned with the form of ignorance that would prevent citizens from fully participating in the institutions of democracy, given the more pressing problems in the provision of primary and secondary education, the issue of university expansion—or, in contemporary idiom, widening participation in higher education—was clearly not seen as a priority and received no discussion.[18] The primary impetus for such an expansion would come from a different source, namely the Barlow Report, discussed further below, which made the case in the language of economic competitiveness rather than welfare. Regardless of all this, the more recent and ongoing changes to university funding and regulation have been and are associated, in the eyes of many of its critics, with what is seen as the wider dismantling of the post-war welfare state.

Likewise, the injection of public funding into the university system in the post-war period was in no sense directly associated—in the minds of those in the government, the civil service, or indeed the public at large—with the wider effort towards nationalization. However, there are certain parallels between the post-war university funding system and the policies of the first Attlee government which involved the expansion of public ownership as well as attempts to introduce elements of state planning within the British economy. It was these parallels that led to John Carswell's comment that the widening of the University Grant Committee's terms of reference and accompanying changes to the composition of its personnel in 1946 could be considered a 'quiet measure of nationalization.'[19] These partial links to the welfare state and national policy complicate any discussion of developments in the British university since the Second World War, but have to be accommodated rather than dodged. Having clarified this matter, it is time to begin our alternative narrative of the post-war British university.

The Myth of the Two Ruptures

Although our focus is on the university of post-war Britain, it is impossible to examine its development without situating it within the wider context, in related and interpenetrating spheres such as the social, the economic, and the political, that is, the 'network of alliances, communications, and points of support' of which Foucault wrote.[20] As the historian of British higher education Michael Shattock opined in a discussion of how best to periodize the post-war university's history into a coherent narrative,

> perhaps the most reliable interpretation is that the development of British higher education closely mirrors the development of post-War British history, political, economic and social. In other words, its development should not be seen as a [specific] progression, as such, but as a reflection of wider currents of economic and social change.[21]

Having made this bold pronouncement at the outset of his extremely detailed chronicle of higher education policy since 1945, Shattock nevertheless restricts his engagement with the wider scene of post-war Britain to brief calculated forays, keeping the technicalities of higher education always at the centre. We will be less cautious and more promiscuous than the accounts that have been hitherto provided by scholars of higher education, such as W. A. C. Stewart's *Higher Education in Post-war Britain*.[22] In so being, we shall devote some space here to the broader picture before zooming back into the specific sphere of higher education.

In many ways, the strength of what we may call the dominant 'two ruptures' understanding of the post-war university outlined above is that it dovetails with a wider narrative of British society that can be seen, in what is arguably one of its starkest forms, in Ken Loach's documentary *The Spirit of '45*.[23] The storytelling force of this particularly strident statement of the view of the post-war period as divided into a broadly social democratic period followed by a neoliberal long revolution was succinctly captured in a review in the *Irish Times*, which pointed out that 'the film allows in no dissenting voices. Forget thesis, antithesis and synthesis. This is thesis, thesis and more thesis.'[24]

The film provides a visual chronicle of the policies of the Labour government led by Clement Attlee, from its 1945 landslide victory to its extension in state policy of the wartime system of centralized governance to peacetime. This resulted in, inter alia, the creation of the National Health Service, a vigorous programme of housing development, the expansion of social security and the nationalization of sectors including the transportation system, the mining of resources, and the provision of electricity. Through interviews with people who lived through the war and the post-war social democratic reforms, we hear stories of working-class folk who felt their struggles in the preceding decades had finally borne fruit. From usually tough miners weeping underground when told of the results of the general election to doctors joyfully announcing to patients that they no longer had to go without medical treatment due to lack of means, the electrifying circumstances of the time for many is recalled in moving image.

The mood shifts to a much bleaker tone in the last third of the film as it deals with the Thatcher period and what has followed. Following footage of Margaret Thatcher quoting St Francis of Assisi outside 10 Downing Street after her election victory, the first words of the next interviewee, consultant radiologist and public healthcare campaigner Dr Jacky Davis, are, 'Along came Thatcher, and suddenly it was all about the individual. You know, the important thing was let's get rich and it's all about me.'[25] The remainder of the film tracks developments such as the privatization of various industries, the dismantling of trade union power and identity, as well as the rise of outsourcing, before ending for an impassioned plea, juxtaposing the words of interviewees with footage of Clement Attlee's first victory speech, to return to the collectivist ideals represented by '1945.'

The Spirit of '45 is useful to us as an example of the 'two ruptures narrative' at its purest. It thus opens the way to questioning the narrative as a whole, a task which is less straightforward with more sophisticated versions of the story. It would be a mistake, though, to consider our operation here to be erecting Loach's film as a straw man. Not only is the film, with its embodied interviews, clearly far from made of straw, in its approximation to a Weberian ideal type, it effectively represents others in its tradition.[26]

To return, now, to one of the problems of the film which was gestured towards at the beginning of the last paragraph, the straightforward depiction of the Attlee government as enacting a socialist programme obscures the deeper reality of the changes in British society at the time. It is undoubtedly true that in the minds of many in the Labour Party of the time, as well as many of their supporters, what they were doing was nothing less than building socialism within a framework of representative democracy. In his speech at the celebration of the Labour landslide victory at Methodist Central Hall in the evening after the government had been formed, Attlee declared, to loud cheers, what seemed to be an obvious fact: it was 'the first time in the history of [the United Kingdom] that a Labour movement with a *socialist* policy' had been elected with a working majority.[27]

In fact, what was eventually rolled out after the election was an amalgamation of some elements of 'supply side' socialism with a broader framework that can be more accurately described as Keynesian. Hence, it can be said that the post-war Attlee government was in its actual policies closer to the liberal socialism of John Maynard Keynes, rather than the proletarian socialism of Karl Marx that was more influential even among non-Communist socialists on the Continent, the technocratic Fabian socialism of Beatrice and Sidney Webb, or even the ethical socialism of R. H. Tawney so beloved by early British Labour figures such as Keir Hardie. This is despite the fact that, by most accounts, Attlee himself identified with the latter tradition.[28] The key point for us here is that Keynes's version of socialism was far more instrumentalist than its 'competitors.' Whereas the guild socialism of thinkers such as G. D. H. Cole had broader ideals such as industrial democracy and the ethical socialists were concerned with a renewal of human conscience, the liberal socialism of Keynes placed at its heart the issue of efficiency. In his 1924/1926 lecture, 'The End of Laissez-Faire,' he argued that 'capitalism, wisely managed, can probably be more efficient for attaining economic ends than any alternative system yet in sight.'[29]

To advance the argument that the only socialism the Attlee government brought about was one of a Keynesian variety, it is necessary for us to focus on the actual content and effects of the policies in question, rather than the more strident and purist rhetoric that preceded, accompanied, and subsequently justified them. After all, the gap between intentions and results in politics is often closer to a canyon than a comfortable margin. This rather banal truism, however, may be enlightened by an interpretation of Nietzsche's dictum that 'the deed is everything.'[30] A more recent translation of the passage from which the phrase comes from renders it as follows: 'There is no "being" behind the deed, its effect and what becomes of it; "the doer" is invented as an after-thought,—the doing is everything.'[31] According to Robert M. Pippin, 'Nietzsche is not denying that *there is* a subject of the deed. He is just asserting that it is not *separate*, distinct from the activity itself; it is "in" the deed. ... [As he writes in] *Thus Spoke Zarathustra*: "I wish *your* self were in the deed like the mother is in the child."'[32] The lesson we may draw is this:

> Intention formation and articulation are always temporally fluid, altering and transformable 'on the go,' as it were, as events in a project unfold. I may start out engaged in a project understanding my intention as X, and over time, come to understand that this first characterization was not really an accurate or a full description of what I intended; it must have been Y, or later perhaps Z. And there is no way to confirm the certainty of one's 'real' purpose except in the deed actually performed. My subjective construal at any time before or during the deed has no privileged authority. The deed *alone* can show who one is, what one is

actually committed to, despite what one sincerely avows.³³

The stated intentions and official sources of inspiration for the Attlee government's policies that laid the foundations of the British university after the war and the rest of the post-war consensus are less important than an analysis of their deeds and what such analysis reveals of the vision and actuality of socialism contained within them.³⁴

Keynes Contra Fabianism and others: The Pattern of the Post-war Consensus

Harold Lever, the barrister and Labour Party politician, stated the following in an article in *Tribune* in 1949:

> Two schools of thought are battling for the allegiance of the Labour Party. Both schools believe that Labour's political and economic aims can only be achieved by Socialist planning. One School ... insists that our plans must be more or less permanently based upon direct physical control of the country's production and consumption ... but the second school would rely mainly on the use of budgetary and other financial measures ... to achieve the plans with the minimum of physical controls.³⁵

Here we have, in summary, the two main strands of Labour thought upon the question of planning and nationalization. The former can be traced back to, inter alia, the Fabianism of Beatrice and Sidney Webb whereas the latter finds its genesis in the liberal socialist ideas of thinkers such as James Meade, who themselves draw their strength in a large measure from the ideas of Keynes.³⁶ In his survey of ideas and practices of political economy in the British Labour movement from 1884 to the 2000s, Noel Thompson argues that although senior figures in the Attlee government such as Stafford Cripps, the Chancellor of the Exchequer, and Attlee himself favoured a more direct microeconomic form of planning that would take place in tandem with a strongly nationalized system of industry and other forms of state intervention, the constellation of circumstances and early decisions in which the Labour Party's 1945 manifesto was to be played out (including the weak form, institutionally speaking, of nationalization chosen, involving an emphasis on tripartite consensus between management, trade unions, and government as well as a lack of willingness by the government to pursue the deep institutional reforms required for centralized planning) resulted in the ascendency of the macroeconomic demand management approach ultimately premised upon Keynesianism.³⁷ The end result was that, in his evocative turn of phrase, 'instead of the pure milk of socialism, [the Labour Party] had resorted to offering a semi-skimmed variety.'[38]

Most of us are familiar with nationalization and planning of the centralized form, partly due to its relatively simple logic: egalitarian public property replaces inegalitarian private property, while rational planning replaces the irrational market. The actual intricacies of putting this logic into action are, of course, far more complicated, but the essence of the vision is clear. With regard to liberal socialism, however, complications arise even in attempting to describe it in brief. To say that the market can be employed for the achievement of socialist objectives is an interesting proposition but one which flew directly against the mainstream of left-wing thought in the nineteenth century and at least the first half of the twentieth. Yet it was this marriage of markets and social justice that was to triumph over both laissez-faire and state socialism in the three decades after the war. In the British scene, there were a number of writers who beginning in the 1920s onward espoused varieties of this perspective, including J. A. Hobson, John Strachey, and Oswald Mosley. The specifics of their respective proposals for a liberal socialism varied to a considerable extent, which enlivened the debates on the British left in the 1920s and 1930s. However, the intellectual force of liberal socialism, when it was actually incorporated into the post-war consensus, was undoubtedly that of Keynes.[39] It is for this reason that in this section we shall focus on Keynes's writings on what, in a 1924 article, he termed a 'true socialism of the future'; that is, a 'politico-economic evolution' grounded upon 'co-operation between private initiative and the public exchequer.'[40]

It may come to some as a surprise that Keynes ever espoused socialism, even one of a liberal variety, given the conventional view of him as the saviour of capitalism. This conventional view is, in part, quite correct. Keynes did not have a problem with capitalism per se, but only with what he saw as the problems of its laissez-faire variety. It is also true that he was not primarily concerned with equity in how capitalism functioned, but rather with efficiency. Faced with the bipolar disorder of boom and bust in capitalism, his primary prescription was counter-cyclical monetary and fiscal policy, which would function akin to mood-stabilizing drugs, 'abolishing slumps,' and keeping the economy 'permanently in a quasi-boom.'[41] After all, given a choice, only the most gung-ho of manic depressives prefer to retain their wild mood swings. Most, like Keynes, prefer a policy that allows for the evasion of crushing depressions, even if it means sacrificing the joyful exuberance of manic periods. After all, a steady state of 'quasi-boom' is, in theory and when realized in practice, more efficient than a mercurial sequence of bubbles and crashes.

While it is also the case that Keynes was, in some ways, concerned with issues of equity and social justice, these were always secondary to efficiency. In 'The End of Laissez-Faire,' he takes his distance from '*doctrinaire State* socialism ... not because it seeks to engage men's altruistic impulses in the service of society, or because it departs from laissez-faire, or because it takes away from man's natural liberty to make a million, or because it has courage for bold experiments'; indeed, he states that he applauds 'all these things.'[42] What he took issue with was rather its irrelevance, as he saw it, to the economic problems of the time. State socialism, in his view, was 'little better than a dusty survival of a plan to meet the problems of fifty years ago, based on a misunderstanding of what someone said a hundred years ago.'[43] In other words, it was incapable of achieving its aims and so failed the test of instrumentalist efficiency. For Keynes, visions of socialism other than his own were not to be rejected because they sacrificed a particular understanding of individual liberty, nor was laissez-faire to be rejected because of its economic injustice. They were both to be rejected because they were too ideological, and were thus, practically speaking, ineffective instruments for the goals they sought to bring about.

Hence, while Keynes's liberal socialism shared with other versions of the creed the general belief that the private and the public could be harmonized towards an effective realization of socially just aims, its particularity lay in the fact that pragmatism trumped idealism at every point in which they came into conflict. An integral part of this pragmatism was a technocratic perspective, whereby persons of expertise were to oversee the workings of a complex machinery of state and quasi-state institutions. In his address to the Liberal Summer School in 1925, he spoke the following words that were not included in the version published at the time:

> I believe that in the future, more than ever, questions about the economic framework of society will be far and away the most important of political issues. I believe that the right solution will involve *intellectual and scientific elements* which must above the heads of the vast majority of more or less illiterate voters. Now, in a democracy, every party alike has to depend on this mass of ill-understanding voters, and no party will attain power unless it can win the confidence of those by persuading them in a general way that it intends to promote their interests or that it intends to gratify their passions. ... [However,] [w]ith strong leadership

the *technique*, as distinguished from the main principles, of policy could still be dictated above.[44]

Here we have one of the interesting characteristics of the instrumentalist perspective, namely its association with elitism. Instrumentalism as a whole, due to its obsession with efficiency and results, often leads to top-down and indeed anti-democratic procedures for formulating and executing policy. It is important to note, however, that although Keynes's ideal system was not micromanagement by state bureaucrats via directed planning, the combination of centralized and decentralized management he advocated could only be successfully carried out by those deemed to be experts. All this was certainly the case with the institutional model of nationalization that the Attlee government put into place, and likewise for the structure of the post-war university, with its central organ in terms of planning and coordination being the technocratic University Grants Committee and its successors, and its partners being the ranks of management in each higher education institution.

The conception of nationalization theorized by the Fabians was grounded on the idea that the 'taking over of the great centralized industries'[45] would enable 'the substitution of consciously regulated co-ordination among the units of each organism for their internecine competition.'[46] This was public ownership and planning of a decidedly statist sort. Keynes did not believe such a system was the right one, and in the interests of efficiency supported a rather different form of public enterprise founded upon the 'management by public boards with statutory powers (along the lines of 'semi-autonomous' corporations).'[47] Although the public board or corporation is linked most notably to the Labour politician Herbert Morrison, who famously made the case for such a model of nationalization in his 1933 book, *Socialisation and Transport*,[48] Keynes had already been putting a similar case from the latter half of the 1920s. Keynes's conception of the 'semi-autonomous corporation' was a middle way of sorts in between centralized statism and laissez-faire, anchored on an idea of the 'public,' which, as will be discussed further below, was wider than the standard idea of the state and yet very much detached from the profit principle.[49] In a 1927 lecture entitled 'The Public and the Private Concern,' Keynes argued for the management of public enterprise by boards at a distance from the political elements of the state, comprised of those 'chosen solely for their business capacity' and 'adequately remunerated,' thus combining 'the advantages of public ownership and responsibility' with 'the technical methods of management which private enterprise had evolved as the most efficient for large-scale affairs.'[50] It was this vision that was ultimately to prevail in the post-war consensus, rather than that of many other writers who considered themselves true socialists.

It has already been stated that while there were parallels between the establishment of post-war instrumentalism in the universities and wider efforts at nationalization, there were also obvious divergences. In no sense was there the establishment of a National Universities Board under which regional boards carried out their work. However, it is instructive that in one of his earliest public pieces on the subject, Keynes identified the universities as one of the two already existing examples of institutions in Britain that embodied his 'socialism of the future.'[51] Like his other primary example, the Bank of England, despite their legal status as private entities, they had 'immense prestige and historical tradition,' but did not 'in fact [work] for private profit,' and had 'no interest whatever except the public good' while being 'detached from the wayward influence of politics.'[52] It should be noted that despite Keynes's likening of the universities to the Bank of England, their respective fates were to be rather different in post-war Britain, at least in legal status. While the former remained independent, the latter was nationalized by the Attlee government in 1946.

Despite their status as private bodies, the universities in the post-war period became even more part of the state, according to Keynes's definition of the term. Robert Skidelsky has argued that for Keynes, the state was *not* 'a synonym for the "government of the day",' or 'those institutions which are conventionally located in the "public sector"' but rather the 'network of institutions whose stake in the proper functioning of the economy and society was so deep and extensive that their corporate actions were not determined by motives of short-term profit maximization.'[53] How does a private institution, driven by short-term profit maximization transform into a public one, according to Keynes? To explain this, Skidelsky quotes Keynes's letter of 26 March 1925 to *The Times*, already referred to above, in which the latter argued: 'when a corporation, devised by private resources, has reached a certain age and a certain size, it *socialises* itself, or falls into decay.'[54]

It is telling that Skidelsky ends the preceding quote with the following comment by Keynes: 'As time goes on not a few of the institutions which were individualistic experiments are socializing themselves. But none, perhaps, except the Bank of England—*and (should I add?)* The Times *newspaper*—has yet completed the process.'[55] Although probably written tongue-in-cheek and so different to his other two examples of the universities and the Bank of England, Keynes's regard for *The Times* as a public institution, even laying aside the elitist perspective from which it springs, still speaks to our times. For we live, after all, in the era of the British press in which the 1981 acquisition of the newspaper by Rupert Murdoch's News UK (formerly known as News International) and its subsequent deployment for not only short-term profit maximization but also political manoeuvring has completely taken it out of Keynes's definition of what it means for an entity to have a 'public' character, which, we should remember, had as its two pillars transcendence beyond the profit motive into the realm of the public good and freedom from the pernicious influence of politics.

In the tale of Keynes's third example of an institution prefiguring his 'socialism of the future,' we may draw a lesson that also applies to his second example and our subject of interest: the university. This lesson is that any entity appearing to transcend narrow interests can easily revert to a focus on the bottom line, especially when at risk of bankruptcy and closure. The financial difficulties that led to the Thomson Corporation selling *The Times* to News International mirror the present consumer-oriented turn of the British university, imperilled as many of the individual institutions of the latter are in terms of funding, particularly since the latest round of reforms beginning in 2010 under the watch of former Universities Minister David Willetts. So long as we live in a social formation where capitalism predominates, an orientation towards the common can only take place in a situation of financial stability, and therefore it is of immense importance how any institution is funded. The more it is dependent on a single source—whether a private owner or the state—the more susceptible it is to being thrown into a crisis when that source begins to run dry.

Dependence on a primary external source for one's funding is also the crux of a focus on instrumentalism. In the days where money flowed from the University Grants Committee and its successors, the university, despite its officially independent status and significant degree of autonomy, had to ultimately toe the line whenever its funding was at stake. This it did quite readily so long as its broader independence was respected, for example with regard to the earmarked grants for specific fields of study in the 1947–52 quinquennium,[56] but as greater pressures built up from the 1980s onwards, the character of its operations began to change. The nature of research, in particular, was transformed with the advent of the Research Assessment Exercise. With each rise in fees and concomitant decrease of state funding, instrumentalist policy has shifted to pleasing the university's new source of sustenance: the student-consumer, whose most potent individual threat is to simply take its custom elsewhere and whose heftiest collective weapon is the National Student Survey, with its potential impact on choice of future consumers. But we are getting ahead of ourselves. Before we can speak of the development of instrumentalism in the post-war university, we must first chronicle its emergence into the limelight.

The Beginnings of Economistic Instrumentalism in the Post-war University

It is often said that it is during times of crisis—that is, the moments characterized by extraordinary circumstances—that seismic shifts in policy are made possible. In the case of the gradually increasing role of state funding in the sphere of higher education, it was the Second World War that provided the ideal environment for its ascendency, as well as the instrumentalist ethos that both accompanied and outlived it.

Prior to the outbreak of war, only 30% of the recurrent income of universities came from government coffers, while as for capital grants, state funds channelled to universities made up only GBP 500,000 between 1923–9 as compared to the GBP 3,320,000 in endowments during the same period.[57] Turning to the first quinquennium after the war, we find that the sum of recurrent grants alone from the Treasury to the universities in 1950–1 was triple the figure in 1945–6, that is, GBP 15,222,408 as compared to GBP 5,149,000.[58] By the end of the 1940s, funding from the government made up 63.9% of the entire income of universities, in contrast to just 35.8% between 1938–9.[59]

This sea change in the higher education funding landscape was in part an unintentional product of the war, a historical period as contingent as any other. The war had led to the deterioration of university education through both damage to infrastructure from the Battle of Britain as well as the dispersal of academics and students either throughout the armed forces and other branches of national service or, in the case of those who did not serve, around the country. However, by the end of the war, the national mood had shifted significantly enough that what was to follow during the period of reconstruction could in no true sense be described as unintentional. In December 1945, the Attlee government appointed a committee and gave it the task of assessing the state of higher education, particularly in relation to the provision of 'man-power' for scientific research and advancement. In May 1946, the report of the committee was released, officially titled *Scientific Man-Power* but colloquially known as the Barlow Report after its chair, Sir Alan Barlow, who was at the time the Second Secretary to the Treasury.[60] On the first page of the report the Committee declared:

> We do not think that it is necessary to preface our report by stating at length the case for developing our scientific resources. ... By way of introduction, therefore, we confine ourselves to pointing out that least of all nations can Great Britain afford to neglect whatever benefits the scientists can confer upon her. If we are to maintain our position in the world and restore and improve our standard of living, we have no alternative but to strive for that scientific achievement without which our trade will wither, our Colonial Empire will remain undeveloped and our lives and freedom will be at the mercy of a potential aggressor.[61]

In December 1946, seven months after the Barlow Report was published, the Parliamentary and Scientific Committee—an unofficial and rather large body composed of Parliamentarians and representatives from the scientific world—published a report of its own. The document supported almost all the recommendations of the Barlow Committee, and its summary ended with the following words in capitals:

> THE REQUIRED EXPANSION OF THE UNIVERSITIES WILL ONLY BE ACHIEVED—AND ACHIEVED IN TIME—IF GOVERNMENT HELP IS FORTHCOMING ON A BOLD AND GENEROUS SCALE—AND WITHOUT DELAY. FINANCIAL ASSISTANCE ALONE HOWEVER WILL NOT SUFFICE UNDER PRESENT CONDITIONS. ... WITHOUT SUCH HELP WE CAN NEVER SECURE THAT RAPID AND SUSTAINED INCREASE IN SCIENTIFIC MAN-POWER WHICH IS SO VITAL TO THE WELL-BEING AND PROSPERITY OF THE BRITISH COMMONWEALTH IN THE YEARS THAT LIE AHEAD.[62]

Returning to the Barlow Report, it argued that bold measures were necessary in order to achieve an 'immediate aim' of 'doubl[ing] the present output [of scientific researchers], giving us roughly 5,000 newly qualified scientists per annum at the earliest possible moment.'[63] Apart from radically expanding the already-existing universities, the Barlow Committee pressed for the establishment of 'at least one new university' and for the upgrading of the five university colleges that existed at the time (Exeter, Hull, Leicester, Nottingham and Southampton) to full university status 'at the earliest possible date.'[64]

By what means were recommendations such as those in the Barlow Report to be implemented? With regard to the financial assistance to be channelled to the universities, it was the University Grants Committee

(UGC) which was to preside over its disbursement. The UGC has already been mentioned a few times thus far, but here it may be helpful to explore its origins. Unlike most of the public university systems that developed in other parts of the Western world, British higher education managed to maintain a formal separation between individual university administrations and the state. Aside from the government's role in approving the establishment of universities and university colleges through Royal Charters, the first significant link between the everyday workings of the government and the universities came with the establishment of the UGC in 1919. The UGC was essentially a top-down creation of the Liberal government in the period immediately after the end of the First World War.[65] Although it was widely acknowledged that the existing resources of the universities at that historical juncture were exhausted to a point that could be described as a 'financial crisis,'[66] it was particular political figures in the government—most notably in the Board of Education—and not the management or academics of higher education institutions who took the lead in the chain of events that led to the formation of the UGC.[67]

Impelled by the post-WWI situation, the UGC was set up to advise the government on the distribution of public monies to the various self-governing universities.[68] In the words of the Barlow Committee, it 'was originally intended to be a somewhat passive body whose main function was to criticize proposals put forward by the universities and which was not itself expected to make any attempt to suggest possible developments involving expenditure to university authorities.'[69] While the Barlow Committee recognized, with some pleasure, that 'the [UGC] has not in fact been content to accept so passive a role,' the Committee's opinion was that, given the challenges facing post-WWII Britain, the time had come for the UGC to 'increasingly concern itself with *positive university policy*' and thus it was 'desirable for this purpose to revise its terms of reference and strengthen its machinery.'[70]

On 30 July 1946, Hugh Dalton, the Chancellor of the Exchequer announced in Parliament the new terms of reference that the UGC was to adhere to. The most important amendment was worded as follows: the Committee was 'to assist, in consultation with the universities and other bodies concerned, *the preparation and execution of such plans for the development of the universities as may from time to time be required in order to ensure that they are fully adequate to national needs*.'[71] However, the UGC, in its own account of the period, went at lengths to counter the view held by some that 'the principles of central planning and of academic autonomy' were 'irreconcilable opposites.'[72]

Here we can see how a significant part of the impetus behind the UGC was a growing faith in centralization or, at the least, greater coordination or planning which we have already discussed in the previous section of this chapter. Indeed, although Keynes championed the universities as an example of his 'socialism of the future,' for his vision to truly be incarnated, the individual institutions had to be augmented by the strengthening of this semi-independent state body. With this blended system of centralized and decentralized management by experts, the task that was set out by Keynes and his co-authors in Book Two of the 1928 Liberal Party report *Britain's Industrial Future* could be fulfilled. This task was that 'of guiding existing tendencies into a right direction and getting the best of all worlds, harmonizing individual liberty with the general good, and personal initiative with a common plan.'[73] Nevertheless, when faith in a common plan started to fade, or at least morphed into its neoliberal version whereby central government would set out the framework in which individual institutions would operate (and indeed, compete), the strong flavour of instrumentalism did not subside.

The most significant aspect of the expansion of the UGC's work is the fact that it created a situation whereby the universities were increasingly beholden to state finance. This was fine while university-state relations were cordial, the economy was healthy, and the principles of the postwar consensus held sway. However, the British economy experienced a gradual slowdown from the 1950s onwards, as evinced by its decline in gross domestic product from seventh in the world in 1950, to ninth in 1960, to eighteenth in 1970, to twentieth in 1975. Various theories have been offered for this slow but steady decline, including the competitive advantages of other nations such as a larger proportion of agricultural and self-employed labour moving into the industrial workforce as well as the opportunity of the defeated Axis countries to rethink and revamp their economic strategies.[74] As Britain began to face further difficulties from the 1970s onwards, it was only a matter of time before an ideological realignment would take place. The financial drivers for this shift can be linked to the circumstances surrounding the 1973–4 oil crisis and what followed,[75] while its ideological component was the rise of a neoliberal rationality beginning in the Thatcher period and continuing under New Labour.

If the centralization of university funding had not taken place in the 1940s and 1950s, the impact of the shift in state policy with regard to the welfare state and public services from the 1980s onwards may not have been as significant within the sphere of higher education as they were in actuality. In other words, the rise of state funding managed by the UGC was a necessary if not sufficient condition for the process that led to a shift in the dominant form of instrumentalism in the neoliberal period. Economic progress and the needs of society were now to be served by an extension of the consumer mentality within the sub-sphere of teaching and the mechanisms of technical measurement within the sub-sphere of research within the wider sphere of the university. Nevertheless, the form of instrumentalism was preserved, if not the content.

Nowhere within the Barlow Report, other reports of its time, or in the records of their implementation by the Attlee government was there any mention of or even the hint of a sentiment towards the creation of a publicly funded university system that would serve ideals such as Deweyan democracy by—in the words of the *Manifesto* of the UK Campaign for the Public University—'the development of a public' with 'the capacity for full participation.'[76] Equally absent is any notion of a public university that would expand the ranks of a university-educated 'middle class' and that would, to quote the American academic Christopher Newfield, 'have interesting work, economic security, and the ability to lead satisfying and insightful lives in that personal and collective social development advanced side by side.'[77] It is thus manifestly clear that the foundation of the post-war university was the service of an instrumentalist aim that lay outside the boundaries of higher education itself, namely economic progress. In the eyes of the Barlow Committee, it was to do so by training scientists and other experts who were indispensable to developing the post-war economy; in other words, its task was not the fostering of citizens for democracy, the facilitation of social mobility, or even 'widening participation,' but rather the training of what has more latterly become known as human capital.[78] From whence, then, came these conceptions of the public university that contemporary idealists so stridently defend, if not from its practical origins? This puzzling question is the subject of the next chapter.

It is important to note here that the various *raison d'être* supplied by proponents of a 'public university' are themselves not devoid of instrumentalism. After all, the tasks of forming citizens or widening the net of those who are to benefit from higher education are also, strictly speaking, exterior to the internalities of the university—that is, teaching and research. Indeed, it cannot be overemphasized that the three questions of instrumentalism, idealism, and community are always engaged at any time, although due to the pronounced parallax it is impossible to grasp them as a harmonious whole. The essential thing to be discerned is not whether elements of these three are present—because they will always be, even if some are obscured—but rather which of the three is *dominant*. The difference between a vision of the public university and a vision of a university subordinated to economic imperatives is that the former emphasizes an ideal, while the latter emphasizes instrumentalist aims and calculation, necessarily bracketing other domains in order to attain these emphases.

Returning to our narrative, throughout the Conservative hold upon the reins of government in the 1950s, the system of higher education developed during the Attlee government was not tampered with or reorientated. In fact, following a marked surge from GBP 16,600,113 between 1951–2 to GBP 20,000,000 between 1952–3, the annual recurrent grant managed by the UGC continued to rise steadily and by the end of the decade stood at GBP 34,350,000 (1959–60).[79] When urged in a written question from a Labour MP in 1953 to form a Royal Commission on the role of universities, Prime Minister Winston Churchill responded that he saw 'no reason to be dissatisfied with the way in which *the needs of society have been met by the universities.*'[80] Indeed, in the wider sphere of social policy the Keynesian consensus too continued to hold; however, within higher education the specific message was clear: the universities were serving the instrumental purposes for which government funding was provided, and thus the status quo was to be affirmed and perpetuated. At the end of the day, instrumentalism was and remains to this day a widely accepted framework in which much dispute occurs over its technicalities, but not the principle in itself.

2

Self-(Mis)understanding After the Fact: The Formation of the Idealist Conception of the Public University

> If we want to spare ourselves the painful roundabout route through the misrecognition, we miss the Truth itself: only the 'working-through' of the misrecognition allows us to accede to the true nature of the other.
> — Slavoj Žižek[1]

'If I wanted a market, I would go to Billingsgate, not a university!' Such was the statement written on a placard at one of the early demonstrations I attended in London against the rise of the cap for British and EU undergraduate tuition fees in late 2010. The sentiment expressed there was clearly founded on the idea that university education should be a sphere for neither profit-making market operations, such as would be appropriate at the famous Billingsgate Fish Market in the city, nor perhaps even pseudo-market-like mechanisms within a quasi-public sector. While the laconic genre of the placard did not allow its author to state what she thought higher education should be premised upon, the context of the protest would indicate that it was highly likely that its carrier believed in an ideal of the university as a place of learning governed by its own principles, and not those of capitalist exchange relations.

Having explored the contours of the instrumentalist perspective in the previous chapter, this chapter picks up on another trend in our present conjuncture, namely the affirmation of an approach to higher education that valiantly stands opposed to instrumentalism, particularly of the neoliberal variety. Grounded on firm principles rather than calculations of an instrumentalist sort, this approach can be called 'idealism,' and it is this that drives sentiments such as the one animating the placard discussed above. The first section of this chapter is devoted to mapping out the general contours of such an idealist perspective. Following this, the second section focuses on the most prominent of the many varieties of an idealist conception of the university in present debates in the United Kingdom, namely the vision of the *public university*. In the final section, we examine in greater detail the place of the idealist perspective within the structure of the post-war British university.

The University with a Single Unifying Ideal

An approach to higher education founded upon an idealist perspective involves the identification of an overarching ideal by which theory and practice within the university is to be judged. Speaking simplistically, any substantive policy or set of practices conforming to or at least advancing this central principle or model is to be favoured, while policies or sets of practices detracting from it are to be resisted.

Whereas the instrumentalist perspective discussed in the preceding chapter empties the university of its own content and measures higher education policy primarily by its effects upon specific, predetermined goals, the idealist perspective is premised upon an opposing dynamic. Its supporters are firm believers in the unique place and mission of the university, even if they disagree with each other as to the specificities of such a place and mission. They are thus united in their resentment towards any enslavement of the institution to what they consider externalities, such as attempts to quantify contributions to economic growth and cost-benefit analyses grounded upon methodological individualism. This is not to say that all idealist perspectives are categorically opposed to such externalities, but they consider them to be secondary at best, and hence disapprove of the instrumentalist's constant recourse to such calculations in attempting to evaluate higher education theory and practice.

While idealist perspectives often do justify themselves, at least in part, with arguments of the university's contribution to wider society, they are often phrased in high-minded terms such as culture, collective intelligence, or the common good. However, for the most pronounced idealists, even these are seen as concessions to an instrumentalist mentality focused on practicalities rather than pure principles. Hence, while the obsession of instrumentalists with empirical statistics is quite conspicuous, it should be noted that moderate idealists are not opposed in principle to quantification per se, but the figures they favour are those measuring the advance or retreat of their ideals, such as rates of participation in higher education for those with a democratic vision of the university. In the end, the essence of the idealist approach is the belief in a *single unifying ideal* for the university, premised upon rational conceptualization rather than empirical pragmatism. Indeed, it is this emphasis on rational principles that distinguishes it from perspectives grounded upon community, because although idealism and community share a certainty about the uniqueness of the university, their respective grounds for this belief are very distinct. Idealists focus on abstract principles and are therefore thought-centric. Conversely, those who focus on what makes the university a community unlike any other and the manner in which this specialness can be maintained are accordingly feeling-centric.

There have been innumerable manifestations of the idealist perspective throughout the history of the university, even if many have drawn their sustenance from a few key sources in history, including the Greek notion of *paideia*, the Roman idea of *liberalia studia*, the *studia humanitatis* of medieval Europe, and the German conception of *Bildung*. A few classic and recent examples may be illustrative here. John Henry Newman's famous defence of a humanistic ideal of liberal education in *The Idea of a University* needs little introduction.[2] More recently, Bill Readings, in *The University of Ruins*, charts a narrative of the modern university ideal from Kant's university of reason to Humboldt's university of culture.[3] Finally, Derrida, writing in one of the cyclical crises of the humanities, formulated his ideal of 'The University Without Condition.'[4]

What unites all these different versions of idealism is that they occupy the space of the idea or transcendental illusion in the conceptual triad that Karatani derives from Kant.[5] Constructed upon and governed by first principles, the ideal is akin to a majestic castle raised in the domain of the rational mind.[6] Nevertheless, every ideal can, in the final instance, be categorized under one of two headings also derived from Kant, namely *constitutive* or *regulative* ideas.[7] In Karatani's words:

> To explain this distinction, Kant used the difference between mathematical proportionality and philosophical analogy. In mathematics, if three terms are given, a fourth can be determined: this is an instance of the [constitutive]. In speculative [i.e. regulative] thought, on the other hand, the fourth term cannot be derived a priori. But speculative thought provides us with an index as we search through experience for something that might serve as the fourth term. ... To put this in simple terms, we see the [constitutive] use of reason at work in its classic form with Jacobinism (i.e., Robespierre): the violent remaking of society based on reason. By contrast, the regulative use of reason works to draw people ever closer to some index, even as that index always remains at some distance.[8]

In other words, a constitutive idea is one whose adherent believes can be actualized in its purity, whereas a regulative idea is one which serves primarily as a horizon to move towards, a guide to channel its adherent's efforts. Although both involve deep commitment, the former's dogmatism lies in clear contrast to the latter's openness. Karatani makes a link between this Kantian-inspired distinction and a passage in *The German Ideology* which he attributes to Marx rather than Engels:

> Communism for us is not a *state of affairs* which is to be established, an *ideal* to which reality [will] have to adjust itself. We call communism the *real* movement which abolishes the present state of things. The conditions of this movement result from the now existing premise.[9]

The failure of mainstream Marxists to pay heed to this key passage led them to adopt a constitutive use of reason, a choice with grave consequences particularly in the twentieth century.[10]

On the left wing of politics, the struggle between constitutive and regulative forms of ideas has, of course, not been unique to Marxism. Anarchists, too, have grappled with this problem, especially following the gradual ebbing away of revolutionary anarchism as a mass movement in the twentieth century. In the British context, a fiery debate raged in the pages of the anarchist journals *Freedom* and *Anarchy* from the mid 1950s to the early 1960s about the possibility of achieving a fully anarchist society. On one side were those who wished to maintain a revolutionary stance that made the establishment of such a society as the central aim, in other words, anarchism as a constitutive idea. On the other side were those such as George Molnar who proclaimed that, given the fact that the tenets of anarchism were unlikely to ever achieve universal assent, any fully anarchist society would be an imposition and thus contradictory to the essence of anarchism itself. All that anarchists could and should do is live in 'permanent opposition' to mainstream society.[11] This latter position effectively threw out the idea of an anarchist society altogether, leaving only the possibility of pockets of principled resistance in the interstices of societies indelibly opposed to anarchism.

George Woodcock took an intermediate position, arguing that since anarchism as a mass political movement in the form envisaged by Bakunin and Kropotkin appeared no longer tenable, anarchists therefore had to 'abandon all social, economic and organizational dogmatism' and instead work to nurture 'the various positive tendencies that emerge in society almost spontaneously' in order to 'transform them into a trend towards growing liberation from the trammels of the state.'[12] Building on Woodcock's argument between the two poles, Colin Ward staked out a position resembling anarchism as a regulative idea, arguing that it should be treated 'not as an aim to be realized but as a yardstick, a measurement or means of assessing reality.'[13] Stuart White sees Ward's position as involving both elements of the dichotomy subsequently formulated by Murray Bookchin between social anarchism and lifestyle anarchism, contending that Ward 'refuses to choose between them.'[14] 'Beyond the episodes of "permanent protest",' White writes, 'in which anarchy is fleetingly grabbed and enjoyed, there is a need for a social vision: a working, always provisional conception of a different kind of society towards which the anarchist should work.'[15] More generally, and particularly on an experiential level, it can be argued that a regulative idea arises from a transcritical oscillation between a constitutive idea and its abandonment, rather than a fixed and stable third position. Affirming a regulative idea involves a longing, however brief, for it to be actualized in a constitutive manner as well as a sense of loss, however fleeting, when such a longing is released, thus returning the idea to the status of an index to guide and evaluate one's efforts.

This book contends that adopting a constitutive approach to ideas does not always mean an attempt to remake the entire world according to a radical blueprint, such as with Jacobinism and Stalinism. The various forms of totalitarianism that we have seen in history and continue to struggle with in the present certainly form one tradition of constitutive thinking. There is also a strand of constitutive idealism in which a more 'moderate' ideal is taken up, and what seems on the surface to be a less ambitious blueprint often leads to a greater confidence that it may actually be implemented. The form of mainstream social democracy ascendent from the second half of the twentieth century, discussed in the preceding chapter, is one instance of this tendency, but the same can be said of other non-utopian visions that attempt to realize certain ideals while accommodating themselves to the really existing conditions of the contemporary socio-economic-political matrix, which is well described by, even if not wholly reducible to, what Karatani has termed the Borromean knot of Capital-Nation-State, a system of interlocking elements sometimes appearing to be opposed but which in reality stabilize each other.[16]

One such constitutive idea in the sphere of higher education is that of the public university. In our present conjuncture where the dominant trajectory in higher education policy—at both the levels of the state as well as individual institutions—appear to be strongly leaning towards 'privatized' values, affirming the public character of higher education is, in one sense, a valiant, principled response. Nevertheless, there is much that the vision of the public university does not question, such as the idea of the omnicompetent modern state, the ideology of meritocracy, the assumption that education is best carried out through large institutions, and the embedding in the last instance of the university within the circuits of capital; in other words, the foundations upon which mainstream social democracy has been constructed over the past half-century or so. These capitulations to the modern state appear at first as a further hindrance to the constitutive idea of the public university mounting a totalizing challenge to the regnant instrumentalist order, but in fact illustrate the truth that pure idealism is impossible. Unlike instrumentalism, which may be expressed in near total forms by straightforwardly bracketing ideals and community—although, as was pointed out in the previous chapter, not without inevitably creating pseudo-ideals and pseudo-communal structures—the realization of idealism (as well as community) is always circumscribed by the bare facts of material and practical limitations. In other words, even those most committed to a particular idealist approach are inevitably restricted by the necessity of unbracketing practicalities at various points.

In other words, if we return to *figure 1* in the previous chapter, there are areas that are, in practice, near impossible to dwell within. These inaccessible spaces of pure idealism or community are depicted in *figure 2* on the following page. Having outlined the basics of the idealist perspective in the university, we can now turn to evaluating the specific constitutive idea of the public university. The best way to begin is to trace its points of invention, and it is to this task that we now turn.

The Public University and its Founding Myth

The slow yet steady neoliberalizing 'reforms' to British higher education that have taken place over the last few decades have been given various labels, but one of the most widespread is that of 'privatization,' linked as the term is to the wider Thatcherite reforms in the state and economy from the 1980s to the present. Its invocation brings us to the famous dichotomies, the old yet constantly shifting battle lines that have structured political and economic thought since the dawn of industrial capitalism and liberal democracy in the West: public versus private, state versus market, left versus right, 'equality' versus 'liberty,' and so on. In this perceived tug of war, any move towards one side is followed by clarion calls across what appears to be the great divide to reaffirm the other side, regain any lost ground, and, if possible, attempt

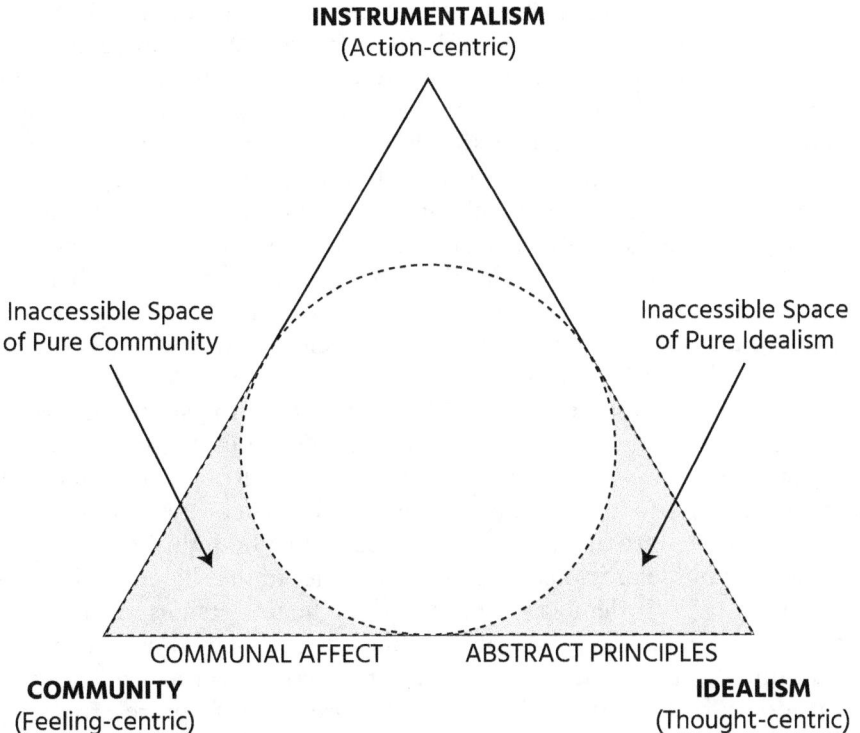

Figure 2

to retake the advantage.

It is no wonder that the ascendency of values linked to private interests over public goods in the sphere of the university have led to a counter-movement that aims to defend the vision of a 'public university.' The dichotomy posed is problematic, not least because it all too easily traps us within the allied dualisms already mentioned, thus foreclosing alternative ways of thinking through the problem. One example of such an alternative perspective, draws from a more medieval understanding of the public/private distinction, in which the two are far from being diametrically opposed but are instead complementary due to the distinction between possession and use.[17] Even more crucially, the nature of the historical and contemporary ideal and actuality of 'the public' in the United Kingdom is left unexamined, leading to a fuzzy conception primarily premised upon a negation of forms of privatization that introduce the profit motive and business models in thought and organization. In other words, even if one has a strong distaste for profit-driven private initiatives in the sphere of higher education, one should be wary of such aversions driving one into the arms of 'the public,' if one is not clear about what affirming such a public really entails.

To begin, the concept of a public university, for some, has been bound up with questions of property and ownership. In the 1960s, the educationist and later polytechnic director Eric Robinson advocated the outright nationalization of the universities (in contrast to the postwar 'quiet measure of nationalization' described by John Carswell and referred to in the previous chapter) as he believed that higher education could not be truly democratized so long as the universities remained in private ownership and control and thus outside the realms of rational planning on a national scale.[18] For others who wish to preserve the autonomy of the university from the state, what is more crucial is simply public funding. A third view is that a general orientation towards the public good over private interests is all that being 'public' involves. As we have seen, this was the view of Keynes, who exalted the British university as a quintessential part of the public, and indeed the state as he understood it. To repeat the words of Keynesian scholar Robert Skidelsky, the state was, for Keynes, the 'network of institutions whose stake in the proper functioning of the economy and society was so deep and extensive that their corporate actions were not determined by motives of short-term profit maximization' (Skidelsky 1997, 434). It is at times easy to forget that Keynes was writing about how the university embodied his vision of liberal socialism in the late 1920s, when the large-scale injections of state funding of the post-war period were still some years away. It is possible on this third account of 'the public' to have a university primarily funded by private means and yet be considered a public institution.

For many contemporary advocates of the public university vision, this Keynesian definition of what it means for an institution to have a public character will not do. For John Holmwood, inspired by John Dewey, the university's 'fundamental role for culture and for public life' comes from the idea of being 'an instrument for "collective intelligence".'[19] A truly public university is 'at the service of the public' and has 'social justice at its heart'; if it is not so, then it is 'just another private corporation in which a corporate economy has become a corporate society.'[20] State funding, according to this strand of thought, is crucial to maintaining the actuality of the former public-minded idea and preventing it from degenerating into the latter 'corporate-dominated' model. The Robbins Report of 1963 is seen as a harbinger of mass higher education and democratization,[21] as well as a prophetic text to be returned to in these neoliberal times.[22] Holmwood states that 'to argue for the public university and its social mission is not to look back to a "golden age" of the university before mass higher education, but to embrace the very principles associated with the development of mass higher education.'[23] This statement by Holmwood notwithstanding, it must be pointed out that for many proponents of the public university, there is indeed a 'golden age,' namely the period from the 1962 Education Act, which instituted compulsory local authority grants for fees and living expenses for all those obtaining a place in higher education, until 1973 when the gradual rollback of funding began.[24]

This 'long decade' from 1962-73 can be analysed as the higher education component of what educationist Brian Simon termed 'the breakout' in education of the 1960s.[25] This relatively compressed period of time saw drastic changes to the higher education landscape. No fewer than twenty new universities were created, the population of students in higher education more than doubled as a result of supportive state policy and rising interest in university degrees, from 217,000 between 1962-3 to 463,000 between 1971-2,[26] and the controversial 'binary policy' separating the 'autonomous' university sector from the 'public'—that is, local authority-controlled—institutions was promulgated by the Labour government, leading to the establishment of thirty polytechnics,[27] hailed by socialist educationist Eric Robinson as 'people's universities.'[28]

These practical developments were nothing short of monumental for the institutional structure of higher education in the decades to come, but their legacy is more than matched by a single report commissioned by the Tory government in 1961 and published in 1963, namely the already much-mentioned 'Report on Higher Education' chaired by the eminent economist Lord (Lionel) Robbins. These two elements of the breakout of the long decade, the practice and the theory, were closely interrelated yet not equivalent, for there were a number of significant divergences between the two, such as the report's clear preference for a 'unitary system' of higher education that was negated by the aforementioned 'binary policy.' But the meeting of the two streams produced a rushing river that has been immortalized in the history of supporters of mass higher education according to progressive and democratic principles of a particular social democratic sort, under which those in the tradition of the 'public university' ideal can be subsumed.

Here we see the various threads from which the ideal of the public university was and is knitted, which essentially draws from the side of the infamous dichotomies that favours the public over the private, the state over the market, equality over liberty, and so on. On the other side of these divides, we find, of course, the elements dovetailing more smoothly with the instrumentalist visions we examined in the previous chapter. In our present higher education conjuncture, we could add to these binaries the Robbins Report against the Browne Report, the Alternative White Paper produced by academic critics against the government's own 2011 White Paper on Higher Education, and so on.

However, the link that a narrative such as Holmwood's asserts between a professed democratic conception of mass higher education, which one might call 'the public university,' and the Robbins Report is actually far more complicated than it first appears. After all, the fact that the higher education blueprint most celebrated by British social democrats in the post-war period originated from the pen of a well-known neoliberal economist and member of the Mont Pelerin Society is one that should make us pause and reflect. We shall now examine this incongruous confluence of social democracy and neoliberalism, the putative (proto-)manifesto of the public university ideal.

Robbins: Social Democrat in Neoliberal Clothing, or Vice Versa?

In an interview with Robbins not long before he died, the educationist and historian of higher education Peter Scott enquired as to how, as a member of the establishment and a right-wing economist, he ended up endorsing the progressive cause of higher education expansion. Robbins replied that his perspective on the importance of such an expansion originated from a conversation he had on the subject with a London School of Economics colleague, the renowned ethical socialist R. H. Tawney. Tawney, who had spent some of the war years in the United States, had said to him: 'You could never overestimate how much America had benefited from the fact that so many of her people had had at least the smell of a higher education.'[29]

Given that this explanation for Robbins's progressivism in higher education came straight from the horse's mouth, it may seem harsh to opine somewhat cynically, as philosopher-sociologist Steve Fuller did in a letter to the *Times Higher Education*, that Robbins's real motives were in fact consistent with his wider intellectual positions. According to Fuller, the true spirit of the Robbins Report was what we know today as 'human capital development,'[30] in which the ancient universities such as Oxford and Cambridge could be regarded as 'intellectual protectionists that imposed artificially high barriers to student entry.'[31] Robbins's solution, Fuller argues, was to support the establishment of competing institutions that were focused on 'contemporary subjects'—that is, new products in the 'market'—but without a decrease in quality.[32]

Fuller's theory may seem uncharitable, but it is far from unsubstantiated. Placing aside his apparent repetition of the common misassumption that the Robbins Report was the driving force behind all the 'plate-glass universities' of the 1960s—seven of these had in fact already been approved in the late 1950s[33]—the fact that Robbins had consistently argued against the ethical and political philosophy of the welfare state throughout his career makes it difficult for us to conclude that he had negated those views in the area of higher education policy merely from a single enlightening comment from Tawney. Another explanation must be found for the apparent about-turn of the man who argued in his influential text, *An Essay on the Nature and Significance of Economic Science*, that 'social utility' is 'interesting as a development of an ethical postulate' but 'entirely foreign to the assumptions of a scientific Economics.'[34] Fuller's brief letter is a gesture in the right direction, but we have to journey further for an answer that may fully satisfy.

A suitable place to begin our investigation is the very text of the widely lauded Robbins Principle:

> Throughout our Report we have assumed as an axiom that courses of higher education should be available for all those who are qualified by ability and attainment to pursue them and who wish to do so. What

type of education they should get and in what kind of institution are questions we consider later on; and the criterion by which capacity is to be judged is clearly a question on which there may be a variety of opinions. But on the general principle as we have stated it we hope there will be little dispute.[35]

Robbins then goes on to say that if this axiom is challenged, there are two grounds upon which it may be vindicated. Firstly, 'conceiving education as a *means*,' it is clear, Robbins says that 'modern societies [cannot] achieve their aims of economic growth and higher cultural standards without making the most of the talents of their citizens,' especially 'if we are to compete with other highly developed countries in an era of rapid technological and social advance.'[36] Such language is redolent of the 1946 Barlow Report on *Scientific Man-Power*, discussed in chapter two, and thus lends an instrumentalist twist to the Robbins Principle, revealing a clear element of continuity with the economic utilitarianism of the immediate post-war period.[37] Nevertheless, it is the next section of the Report that may provide a backbone for an idealist reading:

> But beyond that, education ministers intimately to ultimate ends, in developing man's capacity to understand, to contemplate and to create. And it is a characteristic of the aspirations of this age to feel that, where there is capacity to pursue such activities, there that capacity should be fostered. The good society desires equality of opportunity for its citizens to become not merely good producers but also good men and women.[38]

Such language certainly resounds to a certain extent with the progressive humanism contained in the words of Tawney, which Robbins related to Scott. Still, there is a distinct transposition in key, for Tawney's phrase, 'how much America had benefited,' still revolves around a conception of social utility similar to that which Robbins rubbished in his famous monograph, whereas Robbins's words appear to transcend—or, rather, descend from—the level of collective interest, entering the sphere of the intellectual, artistic, and perhaps even spiritual development of individual human beings.

When we examine the text of Robbins's report, we see the collective good that Tawney spoke of takes on an unsurprisingly economistic flavour, while the humanistic ideal is one that is focused squarely on the individual. The progressive tone with which this key portion of the report has been rehearsed in the last half-century now seems to have been a creative reworking rather than a faithful representation. The explicit use of the term 'equality of opportunity,' as well as the references to providing for and fostering capacity where it exists, evinces a meritocratic ideal beloved of technocrats of all political colours and many right-wing individualists.

Nonetheless, all of this provides us only with clues of Robbins's underlying loyalty to right-wing economic and social ideas. The Robbins Report was a manifesto of both continuity and rupture with the higher education policy of the post-war order up to the point of its publication. The element of continuity was in its instrumentalist concern with economic growth, but this thread was not emphasized in many later readings of the report. The true rupture, however, did not involve the statement of a progressive vision of the public university, but rather a marginalist or 'Jevonian' revolution in higher education policy.

The term 'Jevonian revolution' has become associated with the Marxist economist Maurice Dobb.[39] In his 1973 work *Theories of Value and Distribution since Adam Smith*, Dobb employed it to analyze William Stanley Jevons's development of the marginal utility theory of value as a specifically British version of the wider 'marginal revolution' also associated with the Austrian economists such as Carl Menger and the French economist Léon Walras.[40] According to Dobb, the impact of Jevons's intervention was to move economic analysis away from the emphasis of the classical school on 'costs incurred in *production*'—which were 'rooted in conditions and circumstances of production'—and instead 'toward *demand* and final *consumption*; placing the stress on the capacity of what emerged from the production-line to contribute to the satisfaction of the desires, wants, needs of consumers.'[41] It is also rather instructive for our purposes that back in 1936, Robbins himself delivered a paper to mark the centenary of Jevons's birth in which he appraised his intellectual ancestor's 'great idea, the idea that the origin of the objective exchange values of the market was to be traced to the subjective valuations of individuals,' arguing that it 'shifted the whole emphasis of analysis in such a way as to deserve the name of *revolution*.'[42]

The pre-existing paradigm of post-war higher education policy before the publication of the Robbins Report was based on calculations of the number of personnel needed for specific jobs, especially scientists. The Barlow Report and others written in the 1940s and 1950s were based on this model, whereby the number of higher education graduates required in particular fields were estimated in order to determine the number of places and amount of funding to be made available. Robbins unsurprisingly rejected this model, given its production-centric foundations that were the mainstay of central planning. In a recent article to mark the fiftieth anniversary of the report's publication, Claus Moser, the statistician who led Robbins's research team recollected, 'Lionel said that all the studies there have ever been about how many people in a particular job are needed by society were always wrong.'[43] The correct question according to this view is not, 'How many scientists do we need to "produce"?' but rather, 'How many people are qualified to attend university, and would like to do so?'[44] Rephrasing the latter in crude economic terms: what is the consumer demand for university education as a product, and how could it be most effectively satisfied? The answer that the Robbins Committee arrived at in 1963 was, of course, expansion.

In other words, the Jevonian revolution that the Robbins Report enacts effectively converts the position of students from being the product or commodity in question—that is, a system where graduates are the object of planned calculation by the state and its related bodies—to being the consumer of the commodity of higher education qualifications. The protagonist of university policy shifts from the top-down state, which attempts to determine the demand for graduates, to the individual potential graduate whose demand for a degree is what matters. The 2011 White Paper much maligned by many in the academy and left-wing commentators turns out to have had a title firmly in the tradition of this reading of the Robbins revolution, namely *Students at the Heart of the System.*[45]

Thus, when contemporary campaigners for the public university urge for a return to the principles of the Robbins Report, they have taken a generous reading of the rhetoric— bordering on misinterpretation—for the real essence. The Browne Review and the coalition reforms to higher education in 2010 stand squarely in a more hidden, but more authentic strand of the Robbins Report, which was principally concerned with higher education as the satisfaction of a consumer demand, even if it was largely masked by an accompanying discourse that could be read in liberal humanistic terms. When seen through this light, the apparent perversity of the Robbins legacy being appropriated by David Willetts, the former Minister of Universities and key antagonist of proponents of the public university, in his 2013 pamphlet *Robbins Revisited: Bigger and Better Higher Education* no longer seems so sacrilegious.[46] Indeed, Willetts quite rightly imputes Robbins's approach to higher education expansion, which 'put the aspirations of the student for more education centre stage,' to 'his training as a neo-classical economist sceptical of central plans.'[47]

Some of Willetts's arguments in the pamphlet are worthy of closer analysis, not least because they tell us something of the mind of the man who oversaw the rise of the fee cap for undergraduates to GBP 9,000, but also because they illuminate a deeper issue, which is how the tension between instrumentalism and idealism is conceived by many. In particular, with regard to Robbins's ideas on learning, which shaped the policy content of the report, Willetts states that he 'achieved a perfect equipoise between utilitarian arguments and confident appeals to underlying value.'[48] Here we find the rather commonsensical belief that instrumentalism and idealism are merely conflicting tendencies that require a balance to be struck between them. However, according to the transcritical perspective laid out in the preceding chapters (particularly in the last part of chapter one) striking such a balance is impossible due to the fact that one is unable to view the university from these two opposing perspectives at once. Any apparent 'equipoise' attained is in fact an illusion that hides either the subordination of one to the other, a frenetic transposition that allows for conflicting interpretations, or both.

It is argued that Robbins's ostensible balancing act within the dichotomy between instrumentalism and idealism is a case whereby both rhetorical transposition and effective subordination are present but obscured. The first, Robbins's oscillation, is unsurprising due to his own subjective position as both a neoliberal economist and an academic schooled in the traditions of the British university. In a strange enactment of transcritical motion, the former role compels him at certain points to take an instrumentalist perspective that favours utility, productivity, and other economistic measurements, while the latter leads him to switch at other points to an idealist vision founded upon 'ultimate ends.'[49] It is crucial that we recognize that these perspectives, contra Willetts, do not meet elegantly in the middle or even coalesce in some form of stable synthesis, but remain incongruous and opposed. Their tension-filled cohabitation, however, is what has led to the emergence of two divergent lineages of the Robbins's legacy. Most academics and the liberal-minded have latched onto his defence of higher education as an intrinsic good, forming what may be termed an 'Idealist Robbins' in no small part in their own image, while ignoring the evidence of economistic utilitarianism that has provided the basis for a counter-tradition, which we may call the 'Instrumentalist Robbins.'

This leads one to ask: Which of these two, then, is the 'true Robbins'? Is it the high-minded rhetoric the report was couched in or the policy-minded reality the report brought about? The answer proposed in this book is that *both* can be said to be true, because if we are to dig beneath the surface where economistic utilitarianism and humanistic education appear antinomically opposed in the British university, we will find that their roots are actually intertwined. In other words, what is a real contradiction on one level turns out to be connected at a deeper level. However, like most marriages throughout human history, this hidden matrimony is not one of equals, but involves a relationship of subordination. In this case, the ultimate supremacy of instrumentalism within the knot can be traced to the fact that mainstream twentieth-century British socialism—the tradition that the supporters of the 'public university' consciously and unconsciously draw their sustenance from—chose to set its philosophical foundations upon the very Benthamite individualism that nourished the market liberalism it attempted to displace in the economic and political sphere.

This latter insight is one that David Marquand discussed at some length in his 1987 essay, 'Beyond Social Democracy.' After pointing out the Benthamite essence in the mainstream of British socialist thought in the twentieth century—with the honourable exception, among the central figures, of Tawney—he goes on to write:

> As Karl Polanyi showed, the 'great transformation' from agrarian to industrial society followed a parabola rather than a straight line. In the first, market-liberal, phase, the laws and customs which impeded the growth of a market economy were repealed or done away with. But before that phase had run its course, a reaction had set in; and in the second, interventionist, phase, new laws and customs were introduced to protect society from the consequences of the previous one. *In Britain, however, the reaction against full-blooded market liberalism took place under the same philosophical aegis—and, more importantly, in the same cultural framework—as had the movement towards it.* ... State intervention was tentative, hesitant and reactive; and although it was sometimes justified in other terms, the logic behind it was essentially utilitarian.[50]

This capitulation to the utilitarian framework of British social thought has greatly hobbled the development of alternatives to the market liberal position by demarcating the boundaries where thought and practice are allowed to operate according to an instrumentalist orthodoxy. In the sphere of the university we are concerned with, it is easy to see the playing out of this early decision to justify public expenditure on higher education primarily on economic terms. In the previous chapter we saw how the reforms to the British higher education system in the immediate post-war period originated in instrumentalist calculations to promote economic growth rather than any firmly held and/or rationally formulated ideals, thus disproving any claim that the British university of the immediate post-war period was founded upon a solidly humanistic or principled vision. Now our closer reading of the Robbins Report reveals an underlying instrumentalism that in the end overpowers its idealist outer shell. This discovery too goes against the grain of many dominant narratives of the post-war university which place the report on a towering pedestal.

At this point, a committed proponent of a resolutely idealist approach to higher education might declare, even object, slightly paraphrasing G. K. Chesterton, 'The ideal has not been tried and found wanting. It has been found difficult; and left untried.'[51] There is a sense in which this is true. A university founded upon a single unified ideal has never come into actuality, due to the practical and constant subordination of the ideal to the instrumental.[52] However, in the history of the post-war university, the coexistence of idealist discourse with instrumentalist reality created an illusion that the former was in the driving seat, particularly in the minds of those predisposed towards it such as academics and others of a progressive bent. As shall be discussed further in chapter four, it is often the case that one's overall inclinations within the university triad, which often correspond to one's material location within the institution, shape one's interpretation of ongoing developments in the field. It was thus possible for idealists to formulate the constitutive idea of the public university, even though it did not correspond to reality. Of course, from the perspective of the politicians and civil servants who formulated higher education policy in Whitehall, the instrumentalist underpinnings of post-war university policy were never obscured, as a cursory glance through any White Paper or equivalent official document in the post-war period would demonstrate.

This phenomenon of observing a single chain of events and yet arriving at very different interpretations of what was and is going on can be explained by the failure of academics and bureaucrats to fully practise transcritical oscillation. The choice to persist in viewing the development of British higher education from a single perspective, even after becoming aware of other perspectives, has brought about the mutual self-deception on all sides. The degree of self-deception has been greater on the side of the idealists, culminating in the Robbins Report-thumping we have seen as of late in reaction to the overt neoliberal tone presently being employed by the government and those supporting its policies. To be precise, the idealists of the public university have not only deceived themselves, but have actually carried out an act of 'misrecognition,' to use a term of Žižek's. Žižek explores the concept of misrecognition throughout his oeuvre, drawing from, inter alia, Lacan, Althusser, and Spinoza, but fairly concise statements and examples can be found in chapter two of *The Sublime Object of Ideology*.[53] It should be pointed out that a large portion of his work on misrecognition involves the individual misrecognizing an element *of* herself, whereas what we are dealing with here is the idealist misrecognizing of the nature of the post-war university, that is, something (largely) *outside* herself. If traditional false consciousness is doing one thing while believing one is doing another, and contemporary self-deception or ideology is apparently seeing or doing one thing while tacitly knowing one is seeing or doing another, then misrecognition, in the instance we are dealing with here, is seeing one thing and giving it another name, only to realize at the end that what one understood by that other name is in fact the thing as it really is. Moreover, at the end of the process, one comes to realize that one's misrecognition has also contributed to producing the truth of the thing that one thought was present.

In the case of proponents of the public university, what they beheld was the expansion of British higher education for instrumentalist purposes from the end of the war until the early 1970s, but in their eyes what was being constructed was a system of democratic mass higher education. Since 1973, expansion has continued even as public funding has gradually ebbed away, and, in response, these adherents to the public university ideology have been critical of government policy, believing it to be a betrayal of the ideals of the public university. It is argued here that although the enlightening moment of *kenshō* has not yet arrived for many of these idealists, the deeper truth is that the public university was never anything more than the sunny side of instrumentalist university policy—that is, it is not that they saw a public university where one did not exist; rather, the public university was in fact the primarily ideological but also partially real counterpart to the hegemonic instrumentalism in the post-war higher education order.

Ideals such as the public university thus operate in a manner akin to the Tower of Babel in Franz Kafka's short story, 'The City Coat of Arms.' In this adaptation of the Biblical tale, a group of people gather as a community in order to build 'a tower that will reach to heaven.'[54] The grand project of a tower stretching to the heavens is what brings this community together, but various factors, including a fear of making errors as well as a cheery optimism about the progress of human knowledge and building technology, lead to very little actual construction work on the tower taking place. However, what does result is the building of a city for the workmen, even as the project of the tower persists as a unifying ideal for the various factions among the population. In Kafka's words: 'The idea, once seized in its magnitude, can never vanish again; so long as there are men on the earth there will be also the irresistible desire to complete the building.'[55]

It is also interesting that the narrator in the parable states that 'the second or third generation [of city dwellers] had already recognized the senselessness of building a heaven-reaching tower; but by that time everybody was too deeply involved to leave the city.'[56] Although the general paucity of invocations of the relatively moderate ideal of the public university in recent years may be an indication that it is regarded by many denizens of British higher education today as an unachievable project, the fact that it continues to be trotted out in times of trouble such as the ongoing reforms since 2010 shows that it continues to operate as a residual ideology that can never be completely erased from the British university unconscious.

Of course, one clear distinguishing feature of the public university ideal that sets it apart from Kafka's parable is the fact that while the Tower of Babel is an unrealized monument, there are some who argue that the public university as defined by its proponents actually existed during a putative golden age, for at least the 'long decade' from 1962–73 discussed above, if not from the immediate post-war period until 1973. For these city dwellers, the tower once stood proud and tall—or had been at least constructed sufficiently for use, even if there were still plans for further expansion—but was demolished by neoliberal saboteurs and remains to be rebuilt once again. As argued above, this view is founded upon a misrecognition, and it would be more accurate to say that what proponents of the public university ideal thought was a majestic tower to the heavens was, in fact, always a corporate skyscraper painted in gold, focused on instrumentalist aims even while decorated in a manner congruent with idealist propaganda. The grand vision was only attained in the imagination, and here Karatani's words are instructive:

> Plato did not capriciously pose the being of the *ideal*, or the foundation of knowledge. Indeed, he failed rather miserably in his attempt to implement his idea of the philosopher-king. Instead, Plato realized the impossible in the *imaginaire*: he made Socrates a martyr to this impossible-to-achieve idea ... All of this demonstrates the impossibility of the *being* of the *ideal* and yet, at the same time, it repeatedly invokes the *will to architecture* by asserting that the impossible, the *being* of the *ideal*, be realized. This *will to architecture* is the foundation of Western thought.[57]

How do we grapple with this persistent will to architecture—which can also be described as a drive towards construction and implementation—that is a daily reality? The answer is, once again, to approach ideals regulatively rather than constitutively. As was stated above, one adopts and feeds a regulative idea by oscillating transcritically between the temptation towards a constitutive idea and its abandonment. Just as the regulative idea of communism as 'the *real* movement which abolishes the present state of things' only comes into being by opting against the constitutive idea of communism as 'a *state of affairs* which is to be established, an *ideal* to which reality [will] have to adjust itself,'[58] a regulative approach to an ideal of the university involves giving up the dream of implementing a blueprint or actualizing a total vision, embracing instead the task of 'draw[ing] people ever closer to some index, even as that index always remains at some distance.'[59] This is, after all, the insight of Kant, who believed that the transcendental illusion or *Schein* cannot be done away with, but could be transformed into a regulative form.[60]

Examining the Structural Place of the Public University

In the previous section it was shown that the prime position given to the Robbins Report in the genealogy of the modern British public university as formulated by its proponents is, to say the least, highly questionable. Despite the alleged adherence of the architects of the post-war university order to a vision of higher education diametrically opposed to the presently hegemonic versions of instrumentalism, a closer inspection revealed that such a vision was never much more than the ideological supplement to a system that was, at its core, clearly instrumentalist from the very beginning. The place of the public university ideal within the structure of the post-war British university is nevertheless a relevant matter for our consideration, for to dismiss this ideal merely on the evidence of a flawed line of descent would be to commit what some epistemologists have termed the 'genetic fallacy' and thus sidestep the issue of its contemporary significance.[61]

As things presently stand, the ideal of the public university serves as a rallying point for those who wish to oppose the economistic forms of instrumentalism whose dominance in the sphere of higher education continues to increase. By reaffirming the broadly social democratic vision of the post-war consensus, projected onto the Robbins Report, campaigners for the public university enact a form of resistance towards the creeping neoliberalization of the British university.

It is at this point that Karatani's insight into the wider context in which the social democratic impulse takes place may prove instructive. In *Transcritique* he analyzes our present social formation as follows:

> One often hears the prediction that, thanks to the globalization of capital, the nation-state will disappear. ... But, no matter how international relations are reorganized and intensified, the state and nation won't disappear. When individual national economies are threatened by the global market (neoliberalism), they demand the protection (redistribution) of the state and/or bloc economy, at the same time as appealing to national cultural identity. So it is that any counteraction to capital must also be one targeted against the state and nation (community). The capitalist nation-state is fearless because of its trinity. The denial of one ends up being reabsorbed in the ring of the trinity by the power of the other two. This is because each of them, though appearing to be illusory, is based upon different principles of exchange. Therefore, when we take capitalism into consideration, we always have to include nation and state. And the counteraction against capitalism also has to be against nation-state. *In this light, social democracy does nothing to overcome the capitalist economy but is the last resort for the capitalist nation-state's survival.*[62]

While it would be ill-advised to simply transpose the dynamics that are active in the wider social formation into the more restricted and specific sphere of the British university, we can identify an analogous tendency in the latter whereby those who are discontent with our present day vicissitudes have turned to reasserting a social democratic vision of the university in order to counteract the accelerating developments towards a more neoliberalized system. However, if we accept Karatani's argument about the futility of attempting to re-establish social democracy given the underlying connection between capital and the state, then we have to recognize that fighting for a renewed public university is merely shifting from one articulation of an unjust university to another—with apparent victories on one side counterbalanced by losses on another—yet ultimately maintaining the overall structure. Hilaire Belloc's poem, 'On a Great Election,' captures this paradox in the patriarchal politics of the 1920s:

> The accursed power which stands on Privilege
> (And goes with Women, and Champagne and Bridge)
> Broke—and Democracy resumed her reign:
> (Which goes with Bridge, and Women and Champagne).[63]

Yet our analysis here of the university has so far involved only two elements, instrumentalism and idealism, whereas the conceptual triad discussed in the previous chapters involves a third element, namely community. Investigating this third factor is a crucial step towards breaking out of what seems like an unending struggle between the two titans discussed in this and the preceding chapter, a struggle that on one level looks to be a deadlock between diametrically opposed forces, but on another level can be understood as internecine strife between components of a greater whole.

3

Torn Between Common Life and Individualism: The Thorny Issue of Community

> As philosophers, we search below our feet because our generation has lost its grounding in both soil and virtue. By virtue, we mean that shape, order and direction of action informed by tradition, bounded by place, and qualified by choices made within the habitual reach of the actor; we mean practice mutually recognized as being good within a shared local culture that enhances the memories of a place.
>
> — Ivan Illich[1]

> What is evoked by world religions—whether that of Moses or of Jesus or some other—is a repressed exteriority that worked and still works as a power to deconstruct the community and communalized religion, even though it is soon reappropriated by the community. We find such thinking from the exterior in the pre-Socratics who worked in the communicative spaces of the Mediterranean Sea, which they look on as Verkehrsraum. Unlike Socrates, they were foreigners and stood in the space between communities. ... Heidegger decries the loss of being after Plato, but he himself is, in fact, a thinker belonging to the community that expels this kind of in-between being.
>
> — Kojin Karatani[2]

The rustic village and the cosmopolitan city are spatial figures that represent the two extremes of our contemporary experience of human community. In the first, everyone knows everyone else, and the presence of a stranger is swiftly recognized. A tangible communal, indeed parochial sense pervades the entire place, and for those who choose to dwell there, the dominant experience of belonging is that of holding things in common. In the second, neighbours often do not even know each other, and a stranger can slip past unnoticed. The spaces where people congregate are hives of often disconnected activity, even if in the same 'genre' such as sport or reading, and for those who opt to live in such places, belonging is ephemeral and difficult to pin down. The experience of openness, general freedom, and plurality is dominant and highly valued.³

The sociologist Ferdinand Tönnies uses the word *Gemeinschaft* (often translated as 'community') to denote the first state of affairs and *Gesellschaft* (often translated as 'society') to denote the second state of affairs.⁴ The epigraphs above from Ivan Illich and Karatani likewise capture the forces tending towards these two concepts, the former being an interiorizing dynamic forming and reinforcing what is shared, and the latter a deconstructive dynamic, arising from an exterior and calling into question the inward-facing nature of its opposite. Nevertheless, as it is with almost all such conflicting forces, they often coexist in a certain tension, rather than one reigning in unadulterated form. In this chapter we shall explore how they shape the dynamic of the third pole of the university triangle—community.

If the 1940s and 1950s formed a period whereby the instrumentalist foundations of the post-war university were laid down, and the 1960s and 1970s saw the rise of an illusory idealist conception of the public university, immortalized in the Robbins Report, the period from the 1980s until the present is particularly salient for examining the question of community. The shifts in policy during this period have resulted in a system of higher education that focuses increasingly on the individual—whether a member of the student body, academic staff, or non-academic staff—as the privileged site of academic life. This individualization of governance, and the concomitant rise of self-governance, raises in a particularly intense fashion the problem of alterity, that is, how those within the sphere of the university relate to each other, the other related spheres of society and indeed, by extension, the otherness present within themselves.

In the first section, we shall engage in a broader enquiry into the perspective of community, which is ultimately an attempt to grapple with the question of alterity, with some help from twinned concepts such as *Gemeinschaft* and *Gesellschaft*. In the second section, these ideas are put to the test within the context of the post-war British university, and, in particular, since the reforms of the early 1980s. This contextualized discussion is supplemented by juxtaposing developments over the last few decades with eerily similar instances from the earlier history of the university in Europe. The recent and present conditions experienced by students, academics, and non-academic staff are examined in turn, noting the impact of particular policies on the vibrancy or otherwise of community in its variegated forms. In the last section we begin to sketch out an alternative to the forms of community that the first and second sections explore, based on the judgement that they are ultimately insufficient for the situation we face in the contemporary British university.

Community and its Discontents

The issue of community is primarily concerned with the problematic of otherness, and can be taken in two main directions, both appearing to be equally valid yet fundamentally opposed. The first form of otherness is found and experienced within the context of proximity and commonality, manifesting itself as a life in community. To illuminate what is here meant by community, we might use rather the term *Gemeinschaft*, as formulated by the Tönnies in the following terms: 'All kinds of social coexistence that are familiar, comfortable and exclusive are to be understood as belonging to *Gemeinschaft*. ... [For example, in] *Gemeinschaft* we are united from the moment of our birth with our own folk for better or for worse.'[5] Here the other to be encountered is not primarily the absolute other but rather 'his brother [or sister] whom he hath seen,' the love of whom is established in the First Epistle of John as the first test towards the love of the one 'whom he hath not seen' (1 Jn. 4:20, KJV).[6] Moreover, even in a tight-knit group people are not carbon copies of each other.

Some may deride this conception of otherness as being insufficiently other, in that it necessarily involves a significant degree of common belonging, based upon aspects such as place, tradition, vocation, and shared ideology. Such is the position held by Karatani, hostile as he is towards what he considers communal spaces where rules are shared and the other can be 'interiorized within the self.'[7] His stance, however, can and should be understood, at least in part, as the result of his lifelong struggle against inward-looking trends in his native Japan.[8] Those who favour this form of otherness, such as Ivan Illich in many of his writings, argue that what they call 'vernacular' rootedness is essential in order to avoid the pitfalls of overly abstract modern society. Such a turn towards the vernacular is, in a sense, one possible response towards the standardizing and conformity-inducing aspects of modern technologized society, a response that looks back to move forward. In the 1990 'Declaration on Soil,' co-authored with Sigmar Groeneveld, Lee Hoinacki and other friends,[9] Illich argues for a revival of virtue in order to address the ecological crises we are still facing now. Virtue, they write, 'is traditionally found in labor, craft, dwelling and suffering supported, not by an abstract earth, environment or energy system, but by the particular soil these very actions have enriched with their traces.'[10]

The second form of otherness is focused on exteriority and difference, manifesting itself as an existence oriented towards spaces where alterity is central, such as cosmopolitan world society. The corresponding concept in Tönnies, opposing the aforementioned *Gemeinschaft*, is that of *Gesellschaft*, which he defines as follows: '*Gesellschaft* means life in the public sphere, in the outside world. ... We go out into *Gesellschaft* as if into a foreign land.'[11] On his part, Karatani argues that 'society should be clearly distinguished from community: the language spoken to the other will become social, dialogic, and polyphonic only if the other is an outsider to the community where a common set of rules is shared; the *dialogue within a "community" is merely a monologue*.'[12] If we are to follow this definition, the space for such dialogue—or, more expansively, for such intercourse or exchange—is necessarily at the interstices of established communities; that is, at what Karatani in his writings in the 1980s and 1990s calls a 'communicative' or 'intercrossing space,' drawing from the term *Verkehrsraum* found in Marx's early writings.[13] In his more recent output, Karatani does not make use of the term 'communicative space,' but the concept remains active even as it modulates, as is clear from his later discussion of the 'transcendental topos' where transcritique is possible,[14] as well as in many implicit references to similar 'in-between' spaces, such as in his discussion of 'intercourse and commerce' within world empires.[15]

Before we move on, it should be noted that it would be incorrect to pit Illich and Karatani against each other. While the target of each thinker's critique appears at first to be exactly what the other is putting forward, a more careful reading demonstrates that the abstract modern society that Illich lambasts is not in fact the transcendental topos of Karatani's transcritique, and neither is the inward-facing community that Karatani attacks equivalent to the form of being-together that Illich truly believes in. That is to say, Illich's apparently simple affirmation of *Gemeinschaft* was in fact a tactical move that does not fully represent the radical conception of human solidarity he developed in his late work, namely that of borderless yet embodied friendship based on Christian *agape*. Similarly, Karatani's advocacy of *Gesellschaft* was a manouevre he performed in the 1970s and 1980s in order to outflank Japanese insularity, but in his most recent work we find a far more nuanced idea of what an intercrossing space may look like. Thus, Illich's position is in fact more complex than is apparent in most of his popular writings, even if it is undeniable that the contents of the latter display a bias towards *Gemeinschaft*. Likewise, careful distinctions can and should be made between the various concepts that stress exteriority and difference in Karatani's thought. We shall turn to examine these matters in more detail in the final section of this chapter.

Returning to the main thread of our argument, the degree of conflict between the two conceptions of otherness is far from insignificant, as each harbours within itself a critique of the other. This two-sided critique is often latent or implicit, but can also quite easily become patent or explicit under the right conditions. At a deeper level, what is at stake is what we may call a meta-antinomy within the problematic of otherness, in which one is torn between belonging and withdrawal, or community and solitude. *Pace* Karatani and his withering critique, for a community tending towards *Gemeinschaft* to be healthy and stable, it cannot smother the subjects that are part of it with demands for total belonging and community, because some degree of withdrawal and solitude is necessary for these persons to maintain their personality or, shall we say, singularity.[16] Likewise, a community tending towards *Gesellschaft* that only encourages withdrawal, solitude, dispersion, and freedom will eventually turn into—if it is not already—an antisocial collection of individualistic monads. The phrase 'tending towards' is important, because as Jose Harris points out,

> the crucial question in any 'empirical' setting [is] not whether a particular individual, institution, idea or action belong[s] to 'Gemeinschaft' or 'Gesellschaft,' but where they [are] positioned on the continuum between the two,' because 'a human individual ... simultaneously experience[s] some degree of both *Wesenwille* [natural will] and *Kürwille* [rational will], spontaneity and calculation, 'selfhood' and 'personhood,' kinship ties and market forces.[17]

Upon reaching this point of the argument, it is inevitable to pause, indeed to hesitate, because what is involved is an entry into or at least a skirting around the edges of very old never-ending debates. To gesture to just one recent period of such intense academic skirmishes, towards the end of the last century, a series of books by reputable French and Italian philosophers entered, *sans* any evasion, this terrain of intellectual struggle. These texts include Jean-Luc Nancy's *The Inoperative Community*, Maurice Blanchot's *The Unavowable Community*, Giorgio Agamben's *The Coming Community*, and Roberto Esposito's *Communitas*. Taken together, they form an approach to community that we may term 'non-substantialist,' one of two matrices of interactions of *Gemeinschaft* and *Gesellschaft* that we will explore, the other being 'substantialist' community.

The general aim of these monographs was, in the recent words of Esposito gazing back in retrospect, to be

> radically deconstructive toward the way the concept-term [of community] had been used in twentieth-century philosophy as a whole—first by the German organicist sociology on *Gemeinschaft* (community), then by the various ethics of communication, and finally, by American neocommunitarianism.[18]

Despite their many divergences, what united these three strands of thought and made them ripe for deconstructive critique was 'a tendency—which could be defined as metaphysical—to conceive of community in a substantialist, subjective sense,' that is, 'as a *substance that connected certain individuals to each other through the sharing of a common identity*.'[19] For these continental philosophers, the most perverse, if not immediately noticeable, effect of positing such a substance was that, in Esposito's words, it converted community from being about the *common* to being rather about the *proper*, that is, 'what its members had in common was what was proper to them—that of being *proprietors* of their commonality.'[20] Moreover, Nancy argued the sort of organic community that many long(ed) for has never in fact existed, stating that

> *community has not taken place*, or rather, if it is indeed certain that humanity has known (or still knows, outside of the industrial world) social ties quite different from those familiar to us [in the modern West], community has never taken place along the lines of our projections of it.[21]

To put it simply, what we may call the ideal type of substantialist community is a matrix in which *Gemeinschaft* generally takes the lead, with its positing of organic belonging based on clear (if often invented) markers of identity such as geographical origin, language, or ethnicity. Nevertheless, there are also more overtly 'artificial' forms of substantialist community based on, for example creeds and ideologies. In such cases what is shared is to a much greater extent a matter of conscious adoption, but what is constant is the idea that the community is bound together by something—a property—they hold jointly, such as their shared religious, political, or philosophical persuasion. On the other hand, the ideal type of non-substantialist community can be said to be community formed under general conditions of *Gesellschaft*, in that it is the unknown, suspect, unruly, or even overtly hostile other—the one with whom one does not share some 'thing' such as nationality, race, or belief—to whom one opens oneself. In the words of Esposito,

> the common is not characterized by what is proper but by what is improper, or even more drastically, by the other; by a voiding, be it partial or whole, of property into its negative; by removing what is properly one's own that invests and decenters the proprietary subject, forcing him to take leave of himself, to alter himself.[22]

It must be acknowledged that the non-substantialist conception of community—whether termed as inoperative, unavowable, or coming—is particularly seductive in an age where the utter failures and indeed disasters of deploying the concept of community in the previous century are still not far from our minds. Yet, is there a sense in which we should resist the allure of such deconstructions today? Although we have quoted Karatani as endorsing *Gesellschaft* in his earlier work, in a 2003 lecture, he traces his being influenced in the 1970s and 1980s—the period in which he wrote works including *Architecture as Metaphor*—by the work of Derrida, before stating that 'deconstruction was meaningful under the binary opposition of the Cold War regime. It may be said that when the Soviet bloc collapsed, deconstruction lost its political meaning, and more often than not resulted in rhetorical techniques for equivocating.'[23] This argument is an explicit example of Karatani's aforementioned principle that 'critique is impossible without moves.' As will be discussed further below, Karatani's shift from speaking about intercrossing spaces to a transcendental topos is significant. Returning to the continental European expositions of non-substantialist community, it is noteworthy that the first text in this dialogue, namely Nancy's essay, 'The Inoperative Community,' was written in 1983, before the fall of twentieth century really existing socialism, and in fact begins with a consideration of the disappointment of 'real communism.'[24] Thus, if we are to follow Karatani's argument, at the point of emergence of this series of related texts, the critique shared by Nancy, Blanchot, Agamben, and Esposito of substantialist community had a particular relevance that we cannot assume today in the wider world, much less in the specific sphere of higher education in Britain today.[25]

Hence, the question that befalls us is this: Is the critique of substantialist community what the context of the contemporary British university requires, or at least would benefit from? Or would either an affirmation of substantialist community or an abandonment of a focus on community altogether in favour of a fully deconstructive

Gesellschaft—that is, one that does not even attempt to establish an attenuated form of community—be more appropriate? This is an action-centric question within the structure of the epistemic triangle, whereby the measure is neither truth, which guided our investigations in chapters two and three, nor authenticity, the focus of the next chapter, but rather *timeliness*, based on a reading of the context we are in. We previously glimpsed how rampant instrumentalism and illusory idealism have created an environment of university education that is antithetical to any strong formation of community, and in this chapter we shall examine this question in greater detail. At present, the concept of the university as a community is, if it appears at all, but a flimsy veneer covering some of the excesses of consequentialist and instrumentalist university policy and governance. This takes a few forms and we shall selectively map out the territory according to the impact of post-war policy, in particular since the 1980s, on students, academics, and non-academic staff.

At the risk of sounding like a music player set to repeat, we should preface our cartography by emphasizing once again that the deficiencies of a particular manifestation of community do not, in and of themselves, provide sufficient reason to abandon the concept altogether. The writer and popularizer of Eastern philosophy Alan Watts, in an early book meant as an immanent critique of the Christian tradition, wrote that 'the Church has always walked forward on extremes like a man on two legs, and you cannot walk by putting both legs forward at the same time.'[26] At the day's end, it is possible to justify, in the abstract, each of the approaches to the question of community briefly explored above, and thus, on one level, the crucial task is to determine which foot is the most appropriate one to put forward at a given time. After all, if the foot one settles on is in reality already ahead of the other (or other two, for we can imagine the university better as a three-legged creature), one is likely to lose one's balance and topple over.

However, if one views the three-legged university as being akin to Karatani's Capital-Nation-State, to maintain the former's balance is a conservative rather than a revolutionary operation, and so there is a sense in which a discernment of the *untimely* may be in fact more important for those who wish to see radical change. For there are two divergent poles in the discernment of what it is to be advanced in a particular time and place. Both involve sensing what the mood of the times is in a particular context, but the response of the first is to move along with it, while that of the second is to move against it. The first may be called a liberal approach, and the second a radical one. The

Victorian theologian William Inge captured the challenge of the former approach when he said that 'he who marries the spirit of the age will soon find himself a widower.'[27] The latter alternative was put forward forcefully by Nietzsche in his second *Untimely Meditation* where he counselled: 'If you want biographies, do not desire those which bear the legend "Herr So-and-So and his age," but those upon whose title page there would stand "a fighter against his age".'[28]

In both cases, one's stance is strongly determined by one's context, for if, in the abstract, one person has decided to say 'yes' and another person to say 'no' to whatever is hegemonic in the present day, then the actual content of their stances are essentially dependent on what exactly is the dominant position in a given place and time. Some may consider both these approaches too reactive, and indeed there are positions that appear to lie between the two, such as the 'moderate conservative' who merely reinterprets the tradition to which she has pledged herself in order to best engage the situation at hand, but does not have a strong desire to either be for or against the current. Such an outlook is radically different to the approaches that choose to affirm or negate the present state of things, for a different bracketing operation is at work. What is being privileged is no longer timeliness—which, it must be emphasized, includes also its inverted image of untimeliness—but a form of truth. Hence, in this chapter, we shall leave such cases to one side.

The Post-war British University and Community

It is now time to turn from abstractly considering the two approaches to handling alterity, namely the ideal types of substantialist community and non-substantialist community, comprised as they are of interactions between *Gemeinschaft* and *Gesellschaft*, to a more concrete analysis. This analysis will be carried out by addressing, in turn, the question of community as it is manifested within the distinct yet overlapping spheres in which students, non-academic staff, and academics work and dwell in the contemporary British university with reference to its history.

Students and Community

The first thing to be pointed out with regard to the condition of the contemporary British student is her role within the present system of university finance, which can be traced back to the 1966 decision by the Department of Education and Science (DES) under Anthony Crosland to raise international student fees from GBP 70 to GBP 250.[29] The DES justified their decision as being in line with a recommendation by the Robbins Committee to broaden the income base of universities, but it was pointed out by Lionel Elvin, director of the Institute of Education a member of the committee, that the original proposal was to increase the fees of all students, and not just international students.[30] J. M. Lee argues that the DES's decision was driven by the belief, not backed up by any hard evidence or even sustained argument, that wealthy European and American students should not benefit from highly subsidized British higher education, rather than the Robbins Committee's concern for creating multiple streams of income for the universities.[31] The German anti-Nazi theologian Martin Niemöller's famous phrase, 'first they came for ... and I did not speak out because I was not a ... ,' thankfully did not fully describe the response of students and academics of the time, as not only did student activists occupy buildings in protest, even the Committee of Vice-Chancellors and Principals issued a statement protesting the discriminatory effect of the decision and its negative impact on the universities' international character.[32] Nevertheless, these acts of resistance failed to reverse the decision, which was indeed in fact 'repeated' with a wider scope in the reforms under Willetts in 2010. If we use GDP per capita to measure income value, the increase of overseas students' fees in 1966 would be an increase from GBP 2,736 to GBP 9,773 in today's terms. Hence, forty-four years after a tripling of fees was imposed on international students, home students in British universities (with the partial exception of Scotland) received the same treatment, with the fee cap rising from GBP 3,000 to GBP 9,000.

As a result of these changes, contemporary higher education is increasingly dependent for its funding upon—and thus beholden to—student finance, while being regulated by and residually funded by the state.[33] In this sense, what has arisen is a system very much similar to the medieval universities, with the ironic twist being that it is highly unlikely that the architects of higher education reforms over the last four and a half decades consciously set out to revive elements from the university of the Middle Ages, but in their desire to create reform and progress, they have ended up producing repetitions.

Hence, it may be instructive for us to briefly examine some salient elements of the earliest days of the medieval university, relevant as they are for our time due to their particular blend of *Gemeinschaft* and *Gesellschaft*. Many today may be unaware that when the institutions that developed into the great universities first emerged in the High Middle Ages, fees from students were the only source of livelihood for the doctors of the *studium*.³⁴ Indeed, even though the University of Bologna is said to have been officially founded in 1088, there was little to distinguish the Bolognese law schools from previously existing private operations, run by masters for students who paid the agreed fees, until around the final two decades of the twelfth century, when a key development occurred.³⁵ This was the founding of the first *universitas* or guild of scholars with an elected rector by foreign students in the town, modelled on the other guilds that had begun to make headway into Italian cities.³⁶ It is particularly important to note that the first *universitas* or scholars guild in Europe, was founded in Bologna not by masters but rather by students. This led to the formation of a university controlled by students rather than—as developed later in Paris—by masters.³⁷ Although today the word university is used to describe most institutions of higher education, the medieval teaching organization managed by the *collegia doctorum* was in fact known as the *studium*, and in many places in Southern Europe this structure remained separate from that of the *universitates* or universities managed by students.³⁸

In order to best understand this phenomenon of the student-run university, we should examine its most outstanding example, namely the university that arose in Bologna. The purpose of the *universitas*, itself a federation of smaller organizations of students from specific localities, was 'to guarantee the mutual aid and protection of the students against the exactions of the local people and local authorities.'³⁹ The *universitates* were set up as a necessity within a political structure that did not accord legal rights to non-citizens, a category that most of the students in Bologna and other such universities fell under due to their foreign origin.⁴⁰ Some who believe strongly in the abstract concept of 'student power' may be tempted to see these forms of self-organization as a wholly beneficient development; however, the early history of the University of Bologna reveals a dark side to these historically realized forms of organized student power, as we shall see below.

The institution of salaries paid by the State was a slightly later but no less significant development, and was the result of an attempt to put a brake on the emerging trend of Bologna doctors being lured to teach in other towns upon being promised a salary.⁴¹ The first extant record of such a payment was in 1280, a sum of 150 *librae* to the Spanish canonist Garsias for a year's teaching, and here too it is important to note the power of the students, who negotiated the contract even though it was paid by the Bolognese Republic.⁴² At this moment in history, with the organized power of the *universitas* at a high point, and was recognized by the magistrates of Bologna, it did not matter a great deal whether the salary was paid by the City or by the *universitas* itself. What was certain was that in Bologna the students had usurped the power that in the universities of Northern Europe were held almost completely by the masters.[43] However, in their attempt to escape or at least improve their precarious existence as resident aliens, far from being 'the oppressed who, by freeing themselves, can free their oppressors,'[44] the student guild in Bologna became instead 'the new boss' who was 'same as the old boss.'[45] The following extended quote from Hastings Rashdall is helpful as a vivid illustration of the extent of the domination of the organized students exercised over their professors in those years:

> The Doctors were compelled, under pain of a ban which would have deprived them of pupils and income, to swear obedience to the Students' Rector and to obey any other regulations which the Universities might think fit to impose upon them. While not entitled to a vote in the University Congregation, the Professor was liable to 'privatio' or expulsion from a Society to whose privileges he had never been admitted. ... [A] Professor requiring leave of absence even for a single day was compelled to obtain it first from his own pupils and then from the Rectors and *Consilarii*: and if he proposed to leave the town, he was required to deposit a sum of money by way of security for his return. ... The Professor was obliged to begin his lecture when the bell of S. Peter's began to ring for mass, under a penalty of 20 *solidi* for each offence. ... Even in the actual conduct of his lectures the Doctor is regulated with the precision of a soldier on parade or a reader in a French public library. He is fined if he skips a Chapter or Decretal: he is forbidden to postpone a difficulty to the end of the Lecture lest such a liberty should be abused as a pretext for evading it altogether. ... The Law-texts were divided into portions known as *puncta* and the Doctor was required to have reached each *punctum* by a specified date. At the beginning of the academical year he was bound to deposit the sum of 10 Bologna pounds with a banker, who promised to deliver it up at the demand of the Rectors: for every day that the Doctor was behind time, a certain sum was deducted from his deposit by order of these officials.[46]

It is perhaps rather ironic that this excerpt mirrors Foucault's description of a key element of the guild apprenticeship that was the forerunner of the disciplinary apparatus known as the 'manufactory,' namely 'the relation of dependence on the master that is both individual and total.'[47] The irony, of course, is that at the University of Bologna, it was the masters who became for a time completely dependent upon the apprentices, a fact that resonates with the rather grim actuality of other ostensibly revolutionary regimes throughout history where an oppressed majority has gained the upper hand over the previously dominant minority. It is clear that all these instances have been a far cry from the Marxist ideal where, to quote Paulo Freire, the 'resolution of the oppressor-oppressed contradiction ... implies the disappearance of the oppressors as a dominant class.'[48]

The humanist Marxist critique of those such as Freire holds that

> it is therefore essential that the oppressed wage the struggle to resolve the contradiction in which they are caught; and the contradiction will be resolved by the appearance of the new man: neither oppressor nor oppressed, but man in the process of liberation. If the goal of the oppressed is to become fully human, they will not achieve their goal by merely reversing the terms of the contradiction, by simply changing poles.[49]

If we are to adopt this tenet of the humanist Marxists, then it is clear that the law students of Bologna did not set out to create and live out the existence of the new man, a figure for which some of us are still waiting, and may perhaps be doing so in vain.

The end of student power in Bologna and other universities in Southern Europe came about as a result of the communes taking on more and more of the duties of remunerating the professors via the fixed salaries that superseded individually paid fees.[50] This gradual change was perhaps summarized best by Alan B. Cobban: 'Student power, bereft of its economic teeth, fell a victim to communal politics. It lingered on in Italy as a movement without much substance: by 1500, it had been reduced to nullity.'[51]

At this point a clamouring voice may cry out with the question: What does this genealogical detour have to do with community in the postwar British university? The answer is simple and unsophisticated: the case of the Bolognese student *universitas* demonstrates that a university that is funded primarily by student fees can be presented as one that puts—to borrow the title from the 2011 White Paper published by the Department of Business Innovation and Skills—'students at the heart of the system,'[52] but in reality tends toward a condition where vulgar instrumentalism is the true beating heart of the institution. Such an instrumentalist core is incapable of building a just university or even creating a community that is not based on more than transient interests such as 'good teaching' and 'a great student experience.' Hence, the formation of a student-centred university, if lacking a wider ethical and political framework that may be part of a common pattern of life to check tendencies towards narcissistic self-service and self-enjoyment, will very likely lead not to freedom, but indeed unfreedom for all. For aside from the impact upon the conditions of academic and non-academic labour, the only freedom a student has under such an arrangement is that of the total consumer.

To return to the rebellious *universitates* of thirteenth- and fourteenth-century Southern Europe, it is clear that far from being idealists of the *soixante-huitard* variety, they were pragmatists whose primary reason for attending university was to gain the qualifications required for career advancement. Far from being the preserve of aristocrats interested primarily in a broad humanistic education, Cobban reminds us that 'the universities [of these two centuries] were, *par excellence*, centres for vocational training, gateways to lucrative careers, [and thus] those who attended them did so primarily from a sense of social urgency, from a need to realize professional ambition.'[53] In this sense, the twenty-first century British university has more in common with the medieval university than many of us realize. But there is one key element that differentiates the medieval student 'at the heart of the system' from his contemporary counterpart, namely that while the first exerted power over the masters and the city authorities through *collective* organization and action, the second does so through *individualized* mechanisms like the National Student Survey.[54] While such atomized forms of power have a cumulative effect that may be as formidable as the *universitates* of the Middle Ages, the central difference is that the latter promoted a more immediate and embodied sense of community than the former. The medieval scholars could still be regarded, more or less, as consumers, but they believed in banding together as associations of consumers, whereas the contemporary student-consumer primarily acts in isolation, in line with monadic liberal philosophy.

The student-controlled *universitas* may appear at first sight to have been a straightforwardly substantialist community strongly tending towards *Gemeinschaft*, as its members shared not only a common experience and identity as apprentice scholars, but lived in the same locality. Nevertheless, this apparent stability is counteracted by the fact that the strongest weapon the *universitas* wielded against one of its chief rivals, the communal authorities, was not fuzzy notions such as prestige but rather the very real threat of secession.[55] Hastings Rashdall points out that this bargaining chip was unique to the *universitas* as opposed to the other guilds in the medieval commune, for the latter

> were composed of citizens, who never thought of disputing the authority of the city-government, and who could not put themselves beyond its

jurisdiction without losing both property and status. The Universities were composed of aliens, who refused to recognize the authority of the State in which they lived when it conflicted with the allegiance which they had sworn to their own artificial commonwealth.[56]

The essentially nomadic character of the scholars meant they could uproot themselves at any time and move the operations of the university elsewhere, leaving the commune bereft of sources of income and status. This *mobilitas loci*, which actively militated against the development of deep ties to a particular place (and which can be seen as evidence of *Gesellschaft*-tending relations within a generally *Gemeinschaft*-oriented wider environment), was largely destroyed along with the organized power of students as the university developed a 'more ordered, sedentary character' in the fourteenth and fifteenth centuries.[57]

If the endowment of various chairs and construction of permanent colleges and buildings have led to a definitively sedentary core of the university, the continued fact that it provides only a temporary home for most who enter as students means that a nomadic undercurrent still flows strongly beneath the seemingly solid superstructure. While the political-legal environment in which students in British universities carry out their studies no longer necessitates anything close to the student-dominated *universitates*, the return of the university to having student fees as a primary source of funding threatens to deepen the elements of self-seeking and 'thin community'[58] instrumentalism, the previous historical incidence of which we have briefly explored in the case of the Bolognese *universitas*, but which has also been steadily growing in the post-war period. We cannot, of course, use the word 'antisocial' to describe these trends, for if we understand the social through the lens of *Gesellschaft* or even Karatani's earlier conception of communicative spaces, the free-flowing and weakly bonded elements of medieval and contemporary student life is indeed constitutive of such 'social' or 'thin' communal connections.

Does this rise in looser *Gesellschaft* bonds indicate—or at least create the conditions for—a growth of non-substantialist community within the university student body? It is difficult to answer this question conclusively at this point. To start with, it can be argued that the possibility of non-substantialist community tends to arise upon the failure and/or disillusionment with substantialist community, which takes place not only within the boundaries of a particular sphere such as the university but also in the wider 'social imaginary,' to borrow a term from Charles Taylor.[59] We have already mentioned evidence of the latter in the work of Karatani and the continental theorists of non-substantialist community in the 1980s and 1990s, in which they point out the flaws of the substantialist model. The shrivelling of a substantialist conception at a particular point of space-time, however, does not automatically lead to the growth of a non-substantialist alternative, for it is equally possible that the disintegration of *Gemeinschaft*-like relations leads simply to an atomized, disconnected non-community.

To the extent that a sense of community still persists in the university within the student body, such persistence occurs in spite of rather than due to contemporary institutional arrangements. It was already pointed out by Michael Rustin in 1994 that the focus on 'greater flexibility' in higher education, expressed in techniques such as modularization and credit transfer schemes, 'theoretically allow students, now redefined as autonomous interest-maximizing consumers, to compile programmes at the locations and in the time slots they prefer, rather than by compelling them to conform to the spatial and temporal organization convenient to the university.'[60] Moreover, the spatial proximity that traditional forms of substantialist community depend upon has been overturned by 'the development of "distance-learning techniques promises to facilitate the physical dislocation of higher education from the university's own territory, and make it possible for students to study whenever and wherever they want.'[61] Such developments do not make community—whether substantialist or non-substantialist—impossible, but they certainly transform the manner in which any type of community can be created and sustained.

Having discussed the issue of student life and its impact upon community, it is time for us to turn to another sphere of university life, one which is often ignored in discussions about higher education. This is the sphere inhabited by staff members who are not academics, such as cleaners, catering staff, library staff, security personnel, and so on.

Non-Academic Staff and Community

Almost completely absent in the standard histories of the university is the role of non-academic staff. The references to those who worked in the university but who did not partake in its intellectual activities, or indeed those who lived in the towns alongside the scholars, are few and far between in both Hastings Rashdall's magisterial three-volume *The Universities of Europe in the Middle Ages* as well as the formidable four-volume *A History of the University in Europe* edited by Hilde de Ridder-Symoens and Walter Rüegg, which stretches from the medieval period to the present. Not only that, the references that do appear are largely of no consequence to the narrative, such as Rashdall's quip that the prelates who designed the university colleges did not expect 'those who accepted [their liberality] to live like labourers.'[62]

What has become clear in many recent higher education struggles is the intimate connections between the respective forms of precarity endured by non-academic staff, students, and academics. As a result, some of the most notable campaigns on British university campuses in the past decade have involved or even centred upon the conditions of labour for non-academic staff. Of these, the anti-privatization campaign at Sussex University in 2012–13 stands out. Aside from widely deployed tactics such as the prolonged occupation of buildings, which has been utilized to differing degrees of success since the 'sit-ins' in the middle of the twentieth century, the campaigners carried out numerous temporary occupations that disrupted cafes, the conference centre, and other university services, and hosted a national demonstration on 25 March 2013 in which thousands of students from across the country descended upon the campus in Falmer, on the outskirts of Brighton.[63] Even more innovative was the creation of the 'Pop-Up Union,' which was 'a temporary, low-dues, trade union with the sole purpose of organizing industrial action to defeat outsourcing,' formed as a response to the reluctance of officials from the established unions to call for strike action.[64] Although it proved to be a temporary rather than a permanent formation, the Pop-Up Union became the second-largest union on campus for a time, assisted by the fact that it was an industrial rather than a trade or craft union, with membership open to all workers in the university.[65] In fact, the Pop-Up Union's membership swiftly exceeded that of all three official unions combined in the areas of work that were due to be outsourced.[66] Although the planned strike action was derailed by a successful technical challenge by the university authorities on legal grounds, the Pop-Up Union in its short lifespan managed to pioneer a novel organizational form and win concessions from the administration, even if the wider campaign was defeated.[67]

The historian and activist Richard Braude has pointed out that the roots of many of the recent industrial disputes involving manual labourers in white-collar workplaces, of which cleaners have formed a majority, can be traced to the novel development of a separate workforce of cleaning staff in the new clerical offices that were built as a result of 'the increasing globalization of industry [that] caused capitalists to rely more and more on vast communication networks, to facilitate everything from stock transfers to mail order services.'[68]

Cleaning had been merely one of the jobs carried out by the general labour force in factories, but given the sedentary nature of office work, it proved more cost-effective to hire cleaners as a distinct section of labour.[69] In Braude's words: 'Thus the offices became divided into two kinds of work: computing, and cleaning. An amalgamation of the great machines that have come to dominate so much of 21st century life; and beside them, a form of work that still falls outside of computerization.'[70]

In the university, the division between manual labour and intellectual labour was established long before it came to exist in many other places of work. The former was, of course, not seen as being anything other than incidental to the *raison d'être* of the institution and therefore invisible in its discourse, even if it was very visible in its everyday practical reality.[71] George Caffentzis remarks concerning the rise of white-collar labour in the late 1960s and early 1970s:

> The very image of the worker seems to disintegrate before this recomposition of capital. The burly, 'blue collared' line worker seems to blur in the oil crisis, diffracted into the female service worker and the abstracted computer programmer. ... And it all feels so different! Your wages go up, but they evaporate before you spend them; you confront your boss but he cries that 'he has bills to pay'; and even more deeply, you don't see your exploitation any more. On the line, you could literally observe the crystallization of your labor-power into the commodity, you could see your life vanishing down the line, and you could feel the materialization of your alienation. ... In the 'energy/information' sector, you seem to be engulfed by the immense fixed capital surrounding you. It feels as if you were not exploited at all, but a servant of the machine, even 'privileged' to be part of the 'brains of the system.'[72]

It is rather startling to think that students and academics throughout history have no doubt experienced the feeling of privilege that arises from their sense of being, in Caffentzis's words, 'part of the "brains of the system",' with learned treatises or at least registers of various sorts to record their existence within the university system, while a great host of manual labourers who held up the infrastructure of the institution have simply done their work faithfully for an unspecified number of years before passing into nameless oblivion. Hundreds of years before Hardt and Negri's thesis of the centrality of immaterial labour in *Empire* was to be published and critiqued for its sidelining of the (still-)material labour that sustains the world system, their gesture was actualized within the general perception of the workings of the *universitas* and *studium generale*.

In a sense, the problematic of otherness within the institutional space of the university is faced most acutely in the interactions between non-academic staff, on the one hand, and students as well as academics, on the other. Whereas the student may see in her professor an image of what she may someday become or at least emulate in her pursuit of knowledge, and the academic may see in her student a reflection of the proto-academic she once was, the non-academic staff member occupies a space that historically was not within the sphere of self-recognition or empathy.[73] Nevertheless, with the phenomenon of increasing precariatization in the Global North, this boundary appears to be breaking down, as this statement by a student participant in the aforementioned anti-privatization campaign at Sussex University demonstrates:

> The privatization of services at Sussex has created a two-tiered staff body. Catering workers who were at Sussex pre-privatization still have sick pay, holiday pay and a pension scheme for the meantime, while newer workers employed by outsourcing giant Chartwells have no such benefits and are on zero hour contracts. This casualization of work actively decreases job security: try to use your labour as a bargaining tool and your boss may decide they have no shifts for you next week. *If these jobs aren't already filled by students, these are precisely the kinds of jobs—and conditions—students can expect to be taking on after university.* Zero hours. Little pay. No benefits. It is in the interest of every students [sic] to campaign on issues like the living wage, sick pay and holiday pay. Now.[74]

The reduced prospects facing the British university student at the beginning of the twenty-first century are evinced in an August 2015 report by the Chartered Institute of Personnel and Development (CIPD), which pointed out that in 2010, 58.8% of UK graduates were in non-graduate jobs, a figure only exceeded in Greece and Estonia.[75] Although this could be explained as an effect of the economic crisis—and, indeed, figures in the second quarter of 2015 show a marked improvement of 66.4% of graduates in graduate jobs—it can be argued that the fact that 33.6% of graduates were in non-graduate jobs during a period where unemployment had decreased to pre-crisis levels demonstrates a deterioration in the relative social position of graduates. The strange but perhaps redemptive side effect of this is the greater solidarity that is felt between the student and the non-academic staff member, and between the academic and non-academic staff member as well. This increased sense of solidarity is potentially productive of perceived commonality that may lead to *Gemeinschaft*-esque ties between these groups of university denizens who have historically had little in common despite working and living in overlapping worlds.

The rise of precariatization, in other words, has created a common 'property' between them.

If we relate this development to the phenomenon discussed in the previous section of the rise of *Gesellschaft*-tending relations within the student community, we find a strange coincidence of forces pulling in both the directions of substantialist and non-substantialist communities. We have already discussed the loosening of ties within the student bodies of universities. The decline of union membership since the 1980s is another instance of the diminishing of a historical form of substantialist community.[76] However, in the rise of precarity among both non-academic staff and students, a possible new conduit for a limited substantialist community has been formed between swathes of non-academic staff and students through the sharing of the *proprium* of precarious conditions of work and life. Such a potential formation would be far from comprehensive, as even if students and graduates are becoming subject to increasing levels of precariatization, there is still a sizable proportion of students—the 66.4% in the second quarter of 2015, to use just one figure—who are still enjoying the benefits of their graduate qualifications, and who thus do not possess the common property of an ongoing experience of precarity that would give them potential membership of any 'community of the precarious.'

Academic Staff and Community

On the subject of academics and community, we may begin by observing that the form of approaching otherness favoured by Karatani, that is, society or *Gesellschaft*, fits a little too easily with the tendency in academia towards individualism and withdrawal. Indeed, it is instructive to note that in *Transcritique*, Karatani quotes with approval a passage from Descartes's *Discourse on Method* where the French philosopher speaks about his anonymous scholarly life in Amsterdam.[77] In fact, in an earlier piece, Karatani describes the role of the city for Descartes as that of a communicative space.[78] In the passage itself, Descartes states his pleasure of living in a place

> where amid a teeming, active, great people that shows more interest in its own affairs than curiosity for those of others, [he has] been able to live as solitary and as retiring a life as [he] would in the most remote of deserts, while lacking none of the comforts found in the most populous cities.[79]

More tellingly, in a letter on 5 May 1631 to his friend, Jean-Louis Guez de Balzac, he writes that 'in Amsterdam he paid no more attention to the people he met than he would to the trees on his friend's estate and the animals that browsed there.'[80] Nothing could be further from an endorsement of substantialist community and *Gemeinschaft*.

This pseudo-monastic existence within the confines of a bustling city, by his own account, did much good for Descartes's intellectual activity. Here we have to not lose sight of the fact that academic labour, especially in the humanities, tends towards individualism—and thus operates fairly well within conditions where *Gesellschaft* predominates—not primarily as a matter of principle but simply by the mechanics of the work involved, which except in certain unique cases of intense collaboration tends to produce writing that issues from the pen of a single person or, at most, two or three people.[81] Returning to Descartes, we have to recall that he was not an academic philosopher and scientist in the modern fashion; that is, he did not teach or carry out his research within the context of a university, but rather was what we would today call an independent scholar, constantly on the move as required by the vicissitudes of his controversial career and ability to find patrons who would support his work.[82] This (semi-)nomadic existence, while matching a not insignificant part of the lives of the majority of academics today who work under conditions of precarity, could not have been more different from the position of tenured or at least permanently employed professors in our present, especially when we consider the relative fame (and infamy) Descartes achieved during his lifetime in academic circles.

Hence, the precariatization within the contemporary university may be seen as a return of academic labour to an earlier historical mode, even though only in part and with certain modulations. Gary L. Herstein has pointed out the rise of independent scholars in recent years resembles the situation during the early modern era in Europe, where many critical thinkers were forced to operate outside the boundaries of traditional universities due to the conformity that was required by the latter.[83] The control of these academic institutions was intertwined with the most powerful bodies of the time, namely the state and institutional church. Indeed, the medieval writer Jordan of Osnabrück put forward the idea that the 'three mysterious powers ... by whose co-operation the life and health of Christendom are sustained' were *Sacerdotium*, *Imperium*, and *Studium*.[84] If the monolithic strength of these institutions had been divided and weakened by the early modern period as a consequence of the Protestant Reformation and its political aftershocks, their successors continued to wield great influence within their respective jurisdictional territories. For example as a result of teaching Descartes's physics,

Henricus Regius, a professor of medicine at the University of Utrecht was condemned by the rector of the university, the Calvinist theologian Gisbertus Voetius, as a 'French liar's monkey.'[85] Among the results of the rather convoluted controversy was the decree of university's academic senate on 25 March 1642 that Regius was to restrict his teaching to medicine and 'traditional authors' and an enforced truce, at the height of the debate, which was executed through a prohibition of the Utrecht magistrates forbidding 'very rigorously printers and booksellers in this city and within its jurisdiction to print or to have printed, to sell or to have sold, any small booklets or writings for or against Descartes, under penalties to be decided.'[86]

At this mention of Descartes's followers and detractors, it should be noted that although Descartes was not in his later life an absolute hermit, Desmond Clarke, a biographer and scholar of his work, writes that in Holland he was 'very much out of touch with his native country and with his family,' and only 'visited infrequently by a few close friends and supporters with whom he shared the secret of his address.'[87] Clarke judges that he 'had become a reclusive, cantankerous, and oversensitive loner.'[88] It is impossible to conceive of his situation as one evincing a radical opening up to the other in the spirit of non-substantialist community. He operated, in truth, as a solitary monad regardless of whether he was living in the busy *Gesellschaft* of Amsterdam, or in a village such as Egmond aan der Hoef, only occasionally coming into contact with a small and select group of people.[89]

Our situation in the British university today appears quite different and yet is in some ways rather similar to the independent scholars of Descartes's day, and this is indeed mirrored in most other parts of the world. The precarity and lack of academic freedom faced by independent scholars in early modern Europe seems to resonate with our higher education present. Indeed, more sustained attention to the *longue durée* of the university, which is sadly beyond the scope of this book, may yet confirm the rather likely hypothesis that the period of academic security and comfort that was enjoyed during the first three decades of the post-war years in Britain was part of a longer period of exception rather than the rule.[90] Nevertheless, the silver lining in this rather ominous cloud is the fact that if precarity has been the norm within the academy and wider society, then it is possible for us to draw lessons from the sourcebook of history for deactivating the individualizing tendencies of contemporary academic conditions by using them in a different way, as well as perhaps even building forms of community and solidarity.

In a 1993 lecture, the American educationist Alexander W. Astin discussed the system of recruiting and rewarding academic personnel within the modern research university, pointing out that although countless books and articles had been written about the ill effects of privileging research at the expense of teaching, very little had been said about the impact of the publish-or-perish regime upon the building of a sense of academic community.[91] He went on to explain:

> Scholarship is, of course, a highly competitive and individualistic activity, where the most productive and visible scholars are accorded significant professional status, pay, and recognition by their universities. While it is true that some scholarly products have multiple authors (which would signify a cooperative or joint effort), such publications generally get less credit in the personnel review process than do single-authored pieces. In other words, even *within* the field of scholarship, the reward system encourages individualism and discourages community in the pursuit of knowledge.[92]

We have here a simple and yet penetrating insight about both the academic enterprise as it has been throughout its history as well as its present configuration. It is certainly true that scholarship has by and large always been, as Astin rightly puts it, 'highly competitive and individualistic.' For evidence of this, one only needs to recall legendary instances of intellectual competition, such as the extended debate between Franciscan and Dominican friar-theologians in the thirteenth and fourteenth century on the Trinity and other matters,[93] or the duel between Newton and Leibniz on the invention of calculus,[94] to say nothing of the acrimonious (if not always significant) feuds between and within the disciplines and academic tribes that we see today. However, it is also important to note that contemporary academics work within the confines of, to requote Astin again, a 'reward system' that, in a much more extreme fashion than previous ages, 'encourages individualism and discourages community in the pursuit of knowledge.'

The radical journalist and Marxist Bob Fitch was fond of saying that 'vulgar Marxism explains 90% of what goes on in the world.'[95] It is debatable whether Fitch got the figure correct, but it is certainly the case that the roots of the present intensification of publish-and-perish need not be found in some hidden metaphysical or even ideological register, but merely in the day-to-day management of universities and their relations to our capitalist-dominant social formation. Modern universities thrive—or, for some less notable ones, survive—on grants, donations, student fees, returns on investment, and what are called 'third stream activities,' such as consultancy work for and projects with private corporations, public sector agencies, and so on. All of these funding streams are directly affected by the reputation of the institution and, as Astin has argued, 'the only function in the job description of the university faculty member that can contribute directly to the resource base and the prestige of the university is scientific and scholarly achievement.'[96]

Within the British university, the gradual withdrawal of state funding, first through the cuts from the mid-1970s—with the 1981 cuts in particular being severely felt—and then with the introduction of fees that replaced government grants via the relevant funding bodies, when twinned with the growth in the number and size of universities, has led to more hands tussling for a goodly share of the funding pie. It should not be surprising, therefore, that the pressure to publish research has increased exponentially. To begin on the anecdotal front, this crescendo has even led a notable academic figure such as the physicist Peter Higgs, of Higgs boson particle fame, to opine that had he begun his academic life in an environment such as the present, he would not have been able to carry out the pioneering work that he did, or perhaps even obtain a job, because by today's standards he would not have been considered 'productive' enough.[97]

On a more empirical front, there have been numerous studies on the intensification of the demand for academics to focus on research and, most centrally, to generate measurable output from such research. One of the most interesting is perhaps Roger Burrows's work on what he calls the 'contemporary "metricization" of the academy' and its 'affective consequences.'[98] Taking as his starting point Nicholas Gane's argument that neoliberalization in the non-privatized sector often takes the form of 'simulated' markets where 'real' markets cannot be enacted, Burrows posits that we have in the university reached

> a point where metric assemblages begin to emerge that are of such 'complexity' that they take us to a point 'beyond the audit culture'; towards a different hegemonic project where systems of 'quantified control' begin to possess their own specificity beyond mere auditing procedures; where there develops an ability not just to mimic, but to *enact* competitive market processes.[99]

From an analysis of developments in the genre of campus fiction, he suggests that there was 'a moment of the metrics' sometime between the 1996 Research Assessment Exercise (RAE) and the 2001 RAE, a 'point at which academics could no longer avoid the consequences of the developing systems of measure to which they were becoming increasingly subject.'[100] After detailing the various modulations of the ongoing metricization—including research assessments, measures of teaching quality, and self-assessment of one's division of labour in terms of time spent on various immaterial activities—Burrows ends with an examination of league tables, and remarks:

> In many ways these 'league tables' epitomize many of the themes discussed here: they are the result of a whole range of other metrics generated at different levels of individual and organizational life that all become folded and nested into a common scale; they attempt to collapse heterogeneous concrete activities into supposedly commensurable value scales, allowing comparison and competition; they are, themselves, a source of commercial value—providing some sort of a shadow metric of the underlying abstract value of the neoliberal university; and, for the individual academic, they are also inescapable—to work in the academy today inevitably involves enacting intellectual life through such metrics with all of the affective consequences that follow from this.[101]

The 'affective consequences' that Burrows refers to have been documented in other recent publications, with the most emotive possibly being Rosalind Gill's article, 'Breaking the Silence: The Hidden Injuries of Neo-liberal Academia.'[102] Utilizing a combination of material from interviews and private conversations as well as theoretical analysis, Gill maps out the contours of contemporary academic life, peaking in the middle of the article with a statement from a younger academic's mentor in response to her complaints about an unbearable workload: 'Welcome to modern academia. We're all working these crazy hours. I'm sorry to be blunt, but you know what you have to do: if it's too hot, get out the kitchen.'[103] Gill follows this up with her own riposte:

> The 'kitchen' of academia is, it would seem, too hot for almost everyone, but this has not resulted in collective action to turn down the heat, but instead to *an overheated competitive atmosphere in which acts of kindness, generosity and solidarity often seem to continue only in spite of, rather than because of, the governance of universities.* Increasingly, requests to perform activities that would once have been considered part of the 'civic' *collegial* responsibility of being a university lecturer (such as examining PhDs, refereeing articles or reviewing grant proposals) take on a tone of pleading desperation, as journal editors or course managers find no one prepared to do the necessary work.[104]

Here we are back to Astin's assertion that a sense of community is lacking in the contemporary university due to an overemphasis on tasks and 'outputs' that require and reinforce individualism. It is clear that what emerges from this confluence of various individualizing forces—institutional pressures, affectual difficulties, and indeed the solitary context of significant segments of academic labour—is an environment that is, at its worst, positively prohibitive of, and, at its best, seriously detrimental to the formation of substantialist community within a university or even a subunit such as a university department. When the 'proper' thing to do is work alone, forgoing adequate rest and recreation, all for the sake of producing more publications, there can be very little of the commonality that is proper—i.e. common property—required for a real (or even illusory if we are to follow Nancy et al.) sense of academic *Gemeinschaft* to develop. In other words, academics in general are being pushed to operate in a solitary, *Gesellschaft*-oriented fashion akin to how Descartes lived in his later years in exile, regardless of whether they wish to or not.[105]

The (Al)lure of Non-Substantialist Community

The following question then arises: If substantialist community is, in practice, largely closed off to us, given the present conditions of British academic labour, is it not a good idea to abandon the ideal of substantialist community and pursue instead the formation of non-substantialist communities within and beyond the institutional sphere of the university? Such a view would align itself with, for example the para-academic medievalist Eileen A. Joy, who, quoting Bill Readings (see chapter two), writes in favour of 'creat[ing] a collective that could cultivate and sustain such continual unsettlement, ungrounding, and abandonments, and which would be willing to dwell in a "university in ruins" as a mode of "try[ing] to do what we can, while leaving space for what we cannot envisage to emerge."'[106]

Joy's proposal may appear rather appealing, especially to those of us within a certain academic milieu. The British Critical Legal Conference, for example is often considered by its participants to be an example of an inoperative community, being as it is 'a broad church that exists for 3 days once a year and goes into abeyance once it is over,' with 'no officers or posts, chairpersons and secretaries, committees or delegates.'[107] More adventurously, the BABEL Working Group, which Joy co-founded, describes itself as 'non-hierarchical scholarly collective and para-institutional desiring-assemblage.' It aims 'to develop new co-disciplinary, nomadic, and convivial confraternities between the humanities, sciences, social sciences, and the fine arts (both within and beyond the academy) in order to formulate and practice new critical humanisms.'[108] Importantly, the activities of BABEL are far more extensive than most self-organized academic collectives, and include not just the usual journal but also Punctum Books, an independent open access publishing house, Punctum Records, an open access music label, and Studium, described on its Facebook page as a 'co-disciplinary space for critical and creative inquiry' in East Austin, Texas.

However wonderful these instantiations of community that aspire towards the transgressive and horizontally organized are, there is a sense in which it is not possible to see them as supplying the whole answer to our present woes. Joy defines the task of an inoperative community as '*thinking* community beyond its bad histories and beyond any futurizing ideologies that seek specific (utopian) ends.'[109] Such a critique of utopia—embodied only in part due to its focus on 'thinking'—is always necessary, but it is arguably the case that these communities fail to meet the challenge raised by Costas Douzinas himself in his 2005 article, 'Oubliez Critique.' If what he calls the 'global biopolitical turn' has rendered '(the dominant types of) critique' in the preceding period, such as deconstruction and the ethical turn, worthy of being 'forgotten' in favour of 'acts of resistance,'[110] then surely the model of inoperative community accompanying the rise of these dominant types of critique in Britain is one which has to itself be called into question. After all, it should be remembered that the British Critical Legal Conference began in 1985; that is, while the non-substantialist critique was emerging and gaining strength.

The most significant weakness of non-substantialist community is that in its principled opposition to substantialist community, which it rightly critiques as promising more than the latter can ever achieve, it ends up setting the bar too low. Nancy himself, in a dialogue with Esposito first published in Italian in 2001, states that 'with the definition of an "inoperative community" I wanted precisely to speak of a community that does not put into effect any community.'[111] In order to avoid what he considers 'the terrible germs that we know so well and that today can be used again for the flags of diverse ethnic and ethno-religious identities,' which he identifies in 'the communitarian and/or communal premise,' Nancy and his co-philosophers of non-substantialist community provide us with a concept that has great theoretical worth but little practical utility. At the point at which their work leaves us at an impasse, some renewed creativity is necessary. Two decades down the road, having passed through a romance with substantialist community and a period of disillusionment leading to a dalliance with non-substantialist community as its opposite, could we be in a place and time where a third form of community, that is neither a synthesis of the earlier two nor a stable third position, may emerge?

Prolegomena to an Associationist University

To begin our sketch towards a third form of community that can overcome the limitations of substantialist and non-substantialist forms within the sphere of the university, we shall turn to investigating the fate of a concept of Karatani's that played an important role in his work during his earlier period but which has almost silently modulated into other forms in his more recent work. This concept is that of the inter-crossing or communicative space (in Japanese, *kōtsū kūkan*). Karatani initially forged this idea, which he sometimes refers to as 'space of intercourse' by relating it to the early Marxian idea of *Verkehrsraum*, in the fires of his own singular context but using the theoretical tools of deconstruction. Given this combination of his aversion to Japanese interiority and the deconstructive dynamic, it is unsurprising that the concept shares with non-substantialist community a preference towards *Gesellschaft* over the often insular and even xenophobic tendencies of *Gemeinschaft*. Nevertheless, in the 1990s Karatani's thought underwent an important shift, to the point that he stated in a 2000 paper that books from his earlier period such as *Architecture as Metaphor* no longer 'reflected [his] thinking.'[112]

What did this shift entail? One way of explaining it is that in the wake of the demise of really existing communism, Karatani realized that his previous strategic advocacy of the global market as a deconstructive force that could erode 'the autonomy and closure of national communities' such as that of Japan, even if justified under the former state of global affairs, was no longer correct.[113] As a result, his earlier idea of an intercrossing space, which had political and practical elements to it, was converted into the almost entirely methodological idea of the transcendental topos where transcritique occurs. At the same time that this happened, Karatani began to articulate a new basis for counteractions within the social formations we find ourselves in the twenty-first century. To grasp this shift, we have to turn to his most central concept since the turn of the millenium, namely the *mode of exchange* or—for some such as Kanishka a better translation due to its proximity to the original and broader Marxian concept of *Verkehr*—the *mode of intercourse*.[114]

Beginning with the essays that formed the basis for *Transcritique* and onwards, Karatani began to argue that the various social formations and societies throughout human history have been influenced by four modes of exchange, each of which is 'grounded in its own distinct set of principles,' but which combine to constitute the particular matrix of a particular society, with one dominant mode forming the fulcrum.[115] Mode A is based on reciprocity and originates in tribal communities based on relations of gift and counter-gift.[116] Mode B is based on plunder and redistribution, and first comes onto the scene with the emergence of the state and empires.[117] Mode C is based on commodity exchange, which although existing for a long time emerges in its strongest form with the rise of capitalism.[118] Finally, Mode D or X is a Freudian 'return of the repressed' in which Mode U, the archaic communism of the nomadic band—which upon settlement is replaced by the semi-lookalike Mode A—re-emerges as a critique of the other three modes.[119] Unlike Modes A, B, and C, Mode D has never become a dominant mode, and indeed has only intermittently stepped onto the stage in the form of universal religions and their accompanying communistic political theories.[120]

It is possible to correlate parts of Karatani's fourfold system of modes of exchange with the distinction between *Gemeinschaft* and *Gesellschaft*. To return to Tönnies himself, it has been pointed out that his formulation of the two was in fact loosely inspired by Marx, with *Gemeinschaft* corresponding to primitive communism and *Gesellschaft* to modern capitalism.[121] Hence, we can see that Mode A is related to the former pair and Mode C to the latter. What about Mode B? It is historically linked to neither the substantive reciprocity of organicist community commonly found in tribes or nations, nor the dynamic of procedural reciprocity present in impersonal commodity exchange, but rather what Karatani calls the 'principle of empire.' This principle allows for ethnic and religious (and sometimes even economic and political) heterogeneity beneath an overarching *imperial* political structure, and remains the (often repressed) foundation of the modern state, and indeed state-centric policies such as the welfare state.[122]

To use the language of modes of exchange, Karatani's strong distaste for Mode A led him in the 1970s and 1980s to a tactical advocacy of certain forms of Mode C. Even in *Architecture as Metaphor*, which is an updated version produced in the early 1990s—that is, after his post-Soviet 'turn'—of material he wrote in this earlier period, we find a characterization of the marketplace as an example of an inter-crossing space between communities that do not share a single set of rules; such a 'social space' or society being the way to escape insularity.[123] Having said that, even at that point he recognized that the global economy constitutes 'one single gigantic community' with 'a certain regularity (system of rules).'[124] By the time *Transcritique* was first published in 2001, he was clearly distancing himself from any perceived positive appraisal of *Gesellschaft*, saying that 'it was when the trade with outside worlds was internalized within *Gemeinschaft* that *Gesellschaft* was formed.'[125] This is simply another way of saying that Mode C is intrinsically tied up with Mode A in what he calls the 'Borromean knot' of Capital-Nation-State, the social formation within which we presently live. Karatani summarizes our difficult predicament as follows: 'It is impossible to overthrow one of [the three elements] alone. If we try to overcome capitalism by means of either the state or nation, we will end up reinforcing the state or nation; Stalinism is the former case while Nazism is the latter.'[126] In other words, any attempt to undermine the knot by assaulting one of the three 'rings' only leads to the others taking over and stabilizing the system.

When we shift our gaze from our wider social formation to the sphere of the British university, it is not difficult to see the resonances between the modes of exchange and the various 'questions' of the university we are faced with. The instrumentalist question has much in common with Mode C or commodity exchange. The idealist question tends to lead towards state-centric or Mode B-style solutions. Karatani has pointed out that the expression of Mode B within our present social formation dominated by Mode C—which he terms world economy—takes the form of the sovereign state, and one of the most effective ways of safeguarding its authority is through the enactment of social democratic policies.[127] Finally, the various theories of community we have examined in this chapter mirror the dynamics of Mode A or reciprocity in their focus on a bond of solidarity leading to reciprocal exchanges of labour between denizens of the university, for instance, in the mechanisms of peer review. If we transpose Karatani's insight of the ultimate barrenness of adopting an inward-facing, communal outlook within our wider historical conjuncture, then a turn toward a simple revival of *Gemeinschaft* as a solution to the woes we presently face in UK higher education begins to look far less attractive.[128]

The only way out of this bind, for Karatani, is Mode D, which he has also termed 'associationism' or X. It can be argued that it is at the point where Karatani realizes his formulation of inter-crossing spaces correlates too closely with the deconstructive dynamic of capitalism,[129] which he later terms Mode C, that he is forced to develop the more unique alternative of associationism. What then is it? The associative Mode D is, to extend what has already been said, the return of repressed mode of exchange U, for example, in the form of universal religions at the stages where modes of exchange B and C are dominant.[130] What it really entails is 'the restoration of nomadic society.'[131]

It is perhaps crucial to note that Karatani's nomadic society is far from any form of contemporary ultra-liberalism, captured in images such as that of 'the beautiful nomad' in a recent advertisement for Pullmans hotels, which Giles Fraser describes as follows:

> The music pulsates. A young man is going for a run in Shanghai, off to some high-powered meeting, then returning to his hotel. The narrator sounds sexy and enticing. 'No frontiers, no borders, no limits. You are the beautiful nomads. And our world is your playground.'[132]

This advertisement—and, by extension, the wider 'global' or 'digital nomad' movement surrounding it—is in fact an expression of and propaganda piece for Mode C in the twenty-first century, and is completely antithetical to Mode D.[133] The latter remains to be fully fleshed out in practical terms, given that it is an ongoing project for Karatani, the discreet working title of which is 'a study of D' (*D no kenkyū*).[134] However, there are hints and sketches in the work that we have available to us. Most notably, he has argued that mode of exchange D has generally emerged in our historical actuality 'in the form of universal religions.'[135] It can be found, to take one example from his survey of the many world religions, 'in its classic form in the teachings of Jesus.'[136] Its recurring components are, first, criticism of the priestly class and state-colluding hierarchy (Mode B); second, a critique of family and community (Mode A); and, finally, resistance towards the 'inequalities of wealth and class society' as a result of 'the money economy and private property' (Mode C).[137] He goes on to explain:

> Jesus's teachings can be summed up in two points: 'Love the Lord your God with all your heart' and 'love your neighbor as yourself' (Mark 12:30, 12:31). The love that Jesus speaks of is not simply a matter of the heart. It means in reality a gift without reciprocation. Jesus's sect was, as Frederick Engels and Karl Kautsky stressed, communistic. ... All universal religions in their early stages display this tendency, which shows that they are in fact the return of the repressed, mode of exchange A. In this way, universal religion appears in the form of something that intends a reciprocal mutual community (association) that resists merchant capitalism, its community, and the state.[138]

However, the radical core of these universal religions—that is, their going beyond the limitations of the other three modes—is lost when they degenerate into either, on the one hand, state religions by merging with the state-centric Mode B (plunder-redistribution), or, on the other, communal religions by merging with the inward-looking Mode A (reciprocity).[139] One could reasonably extrapolate this analysis to argue that universal religions can also be co-opted by Mode C (commodity exchange) and turned into trendy consumer 'products' that one can try, buy, and even subsequently discard for the next new thing. As Tobias Jones has argued, Cardinal Basil Hume's assertion that 'shopping is the new religion' should today be inverted, given that in some spheres in our present, 'religion is the new shopping.'[140]

In order to illuminate this degeneration of Mode D more clearly, we can turn to the work of, perhaps surprisingly, Ivan Illich. It has already been mentioned that Illich is often seen as a champion of the traditional or 'vernacular' ways of embodied *Gemeinschaft,* inveighing like a prophet against the forces of abstract, isolating, and impersonal *Gesellschaft.* I submit that this reading of him as an apologist for Mode A is easy to construct from his earlier work and occasional interventions after he receded, as David Cayley narrates, from the popular limelight after the poor reception of *Gender* (1983), his last book for a major trade publisher.[141] Even in the text from which the quote this chapter opens with was taken, Illich seems to rather unproblematically take the side of rootedness, virtue, local culture and—perhaps most alarmingly for those of us who continue to be laden down and horrified by the history of communal conflict—*soil*.[142] Esposito passionately expresses this standpoint in his 2001 dialogue with Nancy, where he says: 'We need to be ever on the lookout for *every substantialist lapse* of the idea and the practice of community.'[143]

In parts of his final work, and perhaps most clearly in *The Rivers North of the Future*—a posthumous text consisting of conversations with David Cayley partially edited into the first-person perspective—a more nuanced view emerges. The central figures of this book are two characters from a Gospel parable, that is, the Jew wounded by robbers on a dangerous road and the Good Samaritan who stops to care for and remove him from further harm. Jews and Samaritans of that era considered each other strangers—some might even say enemies—to whom no obligation to love or even assist existed. Illich believes that this story illustrates the incredible potentials and dangers of the primitive Christian message. In his words:

The Incarnation [and Jesus's teaching] makes possible a surprising and entirely new flowering of love and knowledge. ... A new dimension of love has opened, but this opening is highly ambiguous because of the way it explodes certain universal assumptions about the conditions under which love [is] possible. Before I was limited by the people into which I was born and the family in which I was raised. Now I can choose whom I will love and where I will love. And this deeply threatens the traditional basis for ethics, which was always an *ethnos*, an historically given 'we' which precedes any pronunciation of the word 'I.'[144]

If Illich's language of love seems at first to be too fluffy, it is worth noting that Karatani himself states in a 2014 interview that 'mode D,' which may be mistaken for Mode A, 'also has this power of gifting in abundance, but only in the higher form. You may call it the *power of love*, if you like. Perpetual peace or the world republic will be based upon this real power, which is far stronger than other powers.'[145] When this aspect of Mode D is taken seriously, the gulf between it and the non-substantialist community advocated by, for instance, Esposito, becomes clear. Esposito states that the *munus* or gift that is the origin of *communitas* has an element of duty or obligation.[146] In response to the potential objection that there must be 'something spontaneous and therefore eminently voluntary in the notion of gift,' he invokes Marcel Mauss's work on the gift, whereby the latter thinker stresses the aspect of reciprocity of gift and counter-gift.[147] Karatani, on the other hand, places the Maussian gift solidly within the scope of Mode A, where the form of reciprocity involved takes place within a framework of obligation.[148] Hence, despite the valiant attempt of Esposito et al. to escape from substantialist community, the very grounding of a non-substantialist alternative in Maussian reciprocity ironically leads them back to the framework that Karatani terms Mode A, and thus a form of substantialism.

The new ethic of virtue flowing from Illich's reading of Jesus's parable is not only a negation of Mode A reciprocity, based as it is on a shared *ethnos* and thus a certain set of social rules upholding traditional-communal virtue, but also the principle of abstract and hierarchical command upon which Mode B is based. There is no categorical imperative involved, for the Samaritan's rescue of the injured other is done 'in response to a call and not a category, in this case the call of the beaten-up Jew in the ditch,' and so 'cannot be reduced to a norm.'[149] Finally, given that call to which one responds has a *telos* in a '*some body*,'[150] the instrumentalist or consequentialist Mode C relation based on impersonal exchange is denied as well.

Illich goes on to argue that the hospitality of the Samaritan—which is very close to what we, inspired by Karatani, are calling Mode D—is something presented to the believing listener as a singular person and must be taken up on that horizontal and decentralized level. This non-obligatory, gift-giving form of human intercourse, however, was rapidly institutionalized in the era following the recognition of the church under Constantine, leading to the creation of, for example, houses of hospitality funded by the organized Christian community for the homeless.[151] This, Illich holds, was a corruption of the original call that Jesus issued, as the Greek Church Father John Chrysostom recognized when he argued that 'by assigning the duty to behave in this way to an institution ... Christians would lose the habit of reserving a bed and having a piece of bread ready in every home, and their households would cease to be Christian homes.'[152] In Karatani's language, this is a clear instance of a co-option of Mode D under the structures of Mode B, resulting in universal religion turning into state religion.

Indeed, it is this susceptibility of Mode D to be co-opted by the other modes that renders it a 'regulative idea' which, first and foremost, 'function[s] as an index for us to gradually approach, despite its not being fully realizable.'[153] This striving towards the horizon of Mode D is connected with a practical method we can adopt. Within the dance of instrumentalism-idealism-community, we can but endeavour to create and/or liberate '*space[s] for transcritique*,' that is, to bring the '*transcendental topos*' into the realm of embodiment.[154]

Such spaces would be nuclei where expressions of Mode D could potentially emerge, forming what Charles Taylor calls a new 'skein of relations' to which we could perhaps give the name of an 'associationist university.'[155] The word 'potentially' is crucial here, for as Karatani himself argues, Mode D is not something that can be engineered or brought about by will, but appears to arise spontaneously when the conditions are right. Here he contrasts its dynamics, once again with Mode A, stating for example that in the case of universal religion, it 'arose in the form of an unconscious, compulsory "return of the repressed," as opposed to Mode A, which if invoked in a modern social formation, is generally enacted through 'a conscious, nostalgic restoration of the past.'[156] Therefore, it is right for us to keep associationism as a regulative idea or horizon, but we must be careful not to slip into turning it into a new constitutive idea.

Nonetheless, the notion of transcritical spaces may seem attractive yet vague. A question rings out from the aether: 'What must we do for such spaces to be actualized?' For many it may seem like Karatani's writings on the elusive Mode D posit an end without any feasible means to get there. For instance, his concrete proposals for our wider political-social-economic spheres in *The Structure of World History*, such as radically reforming the United Nations via a 'simultaneous world revolution' involving nations surrendering their sovereignty to engage in war,[157] have been criticized as outlandish and naïve.[158]

Thus we find ourselves in a paradoxical situation. Having abandoned the constitutive approach to ideas, we are left with a regulative idea as a rather distant horizon, which although providing a general direction for action, does not come with clear instructions as on a tin on what we should do in the present. Through the vision of an associationist university, we are, as it were, lifted to a lofty glimpse of what doing higher education differently may be like, and yet when we return to our practical circumstances, we realize we are still enmeshed in the workings of instrumentalism-community-idealism. Moreover, we are often not entangled as an insect in a hated web, but have our own preferences and leanings among the threads that bind us. For some of us, if pressed to express a preference for one of these imperfect actualities, community seems more attractive; for others, idealism or instrumentalism may appear better.

In the following chapter we shall carry out an investigation into how a singular person is to navigate the choppy seas in which she generally feels drawn towards one or more of the well-established ports of instrumentalism, idealism, and community, even if she may also concurrently experience a certain pull towards that elusive radical calling, which is the vision of an associationist university.

4

Singularity, Particularity, and Structural History: On Personal and Collective Vocations in a Plural University

> Sociality is inseparable from singularity.
> — Kojin Karatani[1]

> The apple tree never asks the beech how he shall grow, nor the lion, the horse, how he shall take his prey.
> — William Blake[2]

> Accordingly, I use heart, head and hand All day,
> I build, scheme, study, and make friends.
> — Robert Browning[3]

In 1926, when he was twenty years old and at 'a time where virtually every young intellectual in Japan was embracing either Marxism or modernism,' the Japanese writer Sakaguchi Ango began a course of studies on Indian philosophy at Toyo University, with the aim of becoming a Buddhist monk.[4] He was later to abandon this religious vocation, but during this period published a journal with fellow students of Buddhism. One issue contains a section discussing Japanese temple life and its future, and in Ango's brief contribution, which is very far from the commonplace pieties one might expect from a young aspiring monk, he downplays the virtues of asceticism and states that 'a life that, as it were, follows the earthly passions also contains the power of the moral code and knowledge.'[5]

In two related essays of Karatani's—one of which has been translated into English multiple times—he quotes the entire short text by Ango. In all of these translations, one elusive sentence of Ango's has produced highly divergent renditions in English. For example, in a 2010 translation by James Dorsey of the first essay, titled 'The Irrational Will to Reason,' the line is translated thus: 'Life is to be led according to the individual's convictions and, in short, anything goes *so long as we* do not give up on love and the ties that bind us.'[6] Seiji M. Lippit, in a 2012 translation of 'Buddhism and Fascism,' the second essay, renders the sentence as follows: 'Life is something that should follow each person's principles and can essentially take any form, *but I* cannot abandon the bonds of sexual desire.'[7]

Both translations agree on the first half of the sentence, in which Ango makes a universal statement tending towards pluralism: each person is to lead her life according to her principles. In the second half of the sentence we find what for the English reader must seem to be a peculiar discrepancy. In Dorsey's translation, Ango makes another universal statement: regardless of our different convictions, *we* must not surrender love and close ties. In Lippit's version, Ango switches to the first person and confesses that despite the diversity of personal beliefs, *he* cannot surrender the bonds involved in love and desire. This strange disparity is the result of an interesting aspect of the Japanese language, where subjects and other words in a sentence can be omitted if the writer or speaker believes they can be inferred from the context. In the case of Ango's sentence, the latter half of the compound sentence lacks a subject, and so it is possible for the reader to interpret that he is either continuing his universal train of thought, as Dorsey does, or, conversely, transitioning to a more personal note, as Lippit appears to believe was his intention.

This ambiguity as to the subject in Ango's statement about giving up the ties involved in passion and desire, captures in a unique form the wider uncertainty that is involved in any statement of personal conviction. When someone says, for example, that 'clearly humans are social beings,' the utterance's outward appearance as applying to all cases often obscures the fact that such clarity is only present for the speaker and those who agree with her view. On the other hand, when someone says, 'I am a social being,' the apparent humility of this personal declaration hides that it often, in fact, desires to receive the affirmation of those to whom it is addressed. This, as we shall see below, is characteristic of what Karatani has called the circuit of singularity-universality, where practically every singular expression made contains a tacit universal address within it. Recognizing this allows us to see that even if we were to opt for Lippit's translation, Ango is hardly making a statement with relevance only to himself.

Hence, in this chapter we shall explore the workings of this circuit and the other that Karatani has identified within theory and philosophy, namely that of individuality-particularity-generality. As Karatani writes:

> I stress the distinction between universality and generality. These two words are almost always confused, and the same is true of their opposing concepts: singularity and particularity. Gilles Deleuze drew a lucid distinction between universality and generality in *Difference and Repetition* (1968) while touching upon Kierkegaardian repetition: 'Generality, as generality of the particular, thus stands opposed to repetition as universality of the singular.' His point is that while the connection between particularity and generality requires a mediation or a movement, that between singularity and universality is direct and unmediated. Which is to say, sensu stricto, that while generality and individuality are mediated by particularity, the latter pair can never be mediated. ... [W]hile for Hegel individuality is connected to universality (in his case, universality equals generality for this precise reason) by way of particularity (qua the nation-state), for Kant there is no such mediation. What exists in between the terms is only incessant ethical determination (or, for Deleuze, repetition). This latter way of being individual is precisely the way of being singular. Only the singular man can be universal—this is Kierkegaardian terminology, but it is implicit already in Kant.[8]

The aim of this enquiry is to tease out what is at stake in the relations between persons and collectives. Why should we turn to these questions? In the preceding chapter, it was argued that the Manichean view of the British university as being characterized by a titanic clash between instrumentalism and idealism is both misleading and disempowering, in that it limits our range of vision and action within the state that we find ourselves in. Where such a dualistic reading fails, could our triadic conception provide an alternative way forward? In order to answer this question, the chapter then proceeded to examine the third term in our conceptual triad, namely community. By the end of the chapter, we were able to see how both substantialist and non--substantialist community, for all their respective virtues, ultimately fall short of what appears to be needed in our present conjuncture. Moreover, our sketch of a third alternative, that of an associationist university, displayed some potential, but its status as a regulative idea or horizon means that it cannot provide us with a practical agenda. It is with this apparent failure of community to rise up to the challenge that we begin the present chapter, for if neither instrumentalism, nor idealism, nor a vision of community can save us, then what can?

At this point it is necessary for us to turn to a *speculative* mode of thought that—as Karatani asserts in a creative reading of Kant's wager in his First Critique that some of the planets visible to us are inhabited—is useful to grasp in both the modern sense of a *spec* or bet as well as the similar Latin word *spes* or hope.[9] In the section titled 'On Having Opinions, Knowing, and Believing' in the First Critique's Doctrine of Method, Kant argues that there are three stages of being persuaded. The first is 'having an opinion,' which is 'taking something to be true with the consciousness that it is subjectively as well as objectively insufficient'; the second is 'believing,' which is holding something to be true despite it being only 'subjectively' and not 'objectively' sufficient; the third is 'knowing,' which is 'taking something to be true [that] is both subjectively and objectively sufficient.'[10] Subjective sufficiency may be termed 'conviction,' while objective sufficiency may be referred to as 'certainty.'[11] For Kant, the test of someone's belief—that is, being persuaded at the second level—is the extent to which she is willing to place a bet on it. Thus, a strong belief is one where its possessor 'would wager many advantages in life' on it being correct.[12] The hopeful gamble that will be carried out here—that is, on the level of belief and conviction—is to bet *against* there being a silver bullet, one-size-fits-all solution such as '*such-and-such* community is always the answer,' and instead place 'many advantages in life' on the side of there being singular and dynamic resolutions for singular persons, collectives, and situations, which are themselves ever-shifting.

Such a bet can only be put to the test in the context of singularities, a level of discussion we have not undertaken in great length. However, we should recall that in the introduction to this book, the personal experience which led to the genesis of this project was briefly laid out. I related how my involvement in the Save Middlesex Philosophy campaign led me to question how the present situation of British higher education came to be. In the chapters that followed this singular story faded quickly into the background even as we directed our attention to the structural history of the post-war British university.

Having moved swiftly from the singular to the structural, which can be also deemed the social, in this chapter we shall descend from the altitude that afforded us an overarching view from above, and return instead to the domain and perspective of the singular actor—whether personal or collective—from which we quietly began.[13] This move should not be misinterpreted as an inward-facing turn, or an abandonment of the wider *universitas*, for, as we shall see, there is a keen sense in which universality is tightly bound up with singularity. In order to clarify these dynamics, the first section of this chapter explores the connections and contradictions between the seemingly similar but nevertheless distinct concepts of singularity, individuality, particularity, universality, and generality. We then turn in the second and third sections to examining, respectively, the notions of vocation and gifts, using as a conceptual resource the writings of St Paul on the related and indeed foundational Greek terms of *klesis* and *charismata*, as a way of grappling with the plurality of singularities and particularities.

On the Singular Person and the Specific Context

Having so far traversed seventy years of British higher education history at a rapid pace, a journey undertaken at the levels of structure and macrohistory, it can be difficult to ascertain where to begin a discussion on intervening in the university sphere in order to have an impact upon its present manifestation and future direction. The task is truly immense, given the size and complexity of the institution as well as its entanglement in a web of other forces in contemporary society. In the preceding chapters, we have encountered a university intimately connected to not only the giant waves of post-war British history, with all the national and transnational factors which are involved, but also local conditions in the sphere of higher education. Faced with this gargantuan constellation, we can but ask how we could possibly proceed.

There are a number of potential approaches that we have to eliminate before we can reach a satisfactory option. Firstly and most straightforwardly, unlike Alexandre Kojève, we cannot attempt to find a way out of the immensity of what we are concerned with by addressing ourselves solely to a single 'man of action' (or 'tyrant') whom we recognize, seeking to become his personal 'Hegelian' philosopher or consciousness, as Hager Weslati suggests the French philosopher attempted in his lost 'letter' to Stalin.[14] Such an appeal to individual power—that is, a specific recommendation to/for a specific person—is not only illusory and impossible, but also elitist and anti-democratic. In other words, it is objectionable on both practical and theoretical grounds, the latter being relevant due to the underlying political orientations of this book. However, it would be equally misguided for us to venture to formulate a blanket strategy that could be deployed by all persons in all circumstances, given the plethora of contexts and situations that exist. Such an endeavour, which would amount to a general recommendation to/for a general audience, would either descend into banal slogans—such as 'work towards a non-repressive university'—and/or fail to connect with or even take account of local or personal conditions. In the first instance it would be of limited practical use, and in the second it might lead to counterproductive attempts to superimpose a broad-brush sketch upon situations of greater complexity.

We shall adopt a third option: namely that of formulating an approach that can be adopted by *singular* persons, but which contains an engagement with both a striving towards *universality* as well as the very real difficulties of *particular* contexts. This requires us to engage with both the circuits of individuality-particularity-generality and singularity-universality that Karatani distilled from the philosophical canon, rather than dismissing one and privileging the other. This latter move is one that he himself performs in his explicit advocacy for the singularity-universality circuit.[15] We shall resist it in the interests of being resolutely transcritical, a manouevre which Karatani himself appears to have taken in his more recent work. The practice of transcritique may sometimes appear on the surface as a form of prevarication, but it is in truth founded on a simple acknowledgement that the actual conditions of existence rarely allow us to affirm any one side of an antinomy in an unproblematic fashion. Nevertheless, we should also recognize that this transcritical approach is simply one of many approaches and techniques for enquiry. Indeed, the persistence of certain persons within stubbornly partisan and non-transcritical modes yields insights and perspectives that practitioners of transcritique are able to draw from. As we shall see further below, this fecundity of single-mindedness is what William James had in mind when he argued that 'the one thing that has *counted* so far in philosophy is that a man should see things, see them straight in his own peculiar way, and be dissatisfied with any opposite way of seeing them.'[16] However, *pace* James, the ability to see things in more than one way should not be dismissed as a mere 'mixture of opposite ingredients,'[17] for it too has a role to play in the whirl of consciousness, a dance we experience through a historically shaped prism that refracts the mixed content of personal and collective existence into categories such as thought, affect, and action.

Singularities Seeking Universality in a World of Particularities

To begin with a perhaps seemingly obscure and/or audacious question: What would it really mean to address the fruits of our ruminations to singularities in a way that can also be termed universal? Is this extended gesture merely a variation of the famous Lord Kitchener and Uncle Sam recruitment posters which, to briefly adopt Althusser's formulation, incessantly address the 'I' who comes into being upon being interpellated by the hailing word 'you'?[18] The short answer is no, for although the person who answers positively to this interpellation may like to think his response is one of a kind, the overall context of war through the ages, which reduces unique persons to being mere parts of the figures of those raised, trained, dispatched, and killed, creates a situation whereby, in the eyes of the powers that be, it matters little whether it is Person A or Person B who responds to the call, for the end result sought is simply having two additional boots on the ground—the specific person whose feet are in those boots is secondary at best.[19]

What we find here is not what Karatani terms the circuit of singularity-universality but rather that of individuality-particularity--generality. In the present example, the person who responds to the poster is entering a space where he is not considered an irreplaceable singularity but rather a substitutable individual within a scheme of generality. That is to say, individuals are interchangeable and replaceable like parts of a machine, while singularities are not. To be blunt, if this volunteer soldier dies, his specific task within the larger war plans will have to be carried out by another, and conversely, if he survives certain operations, he may be moved to take on the task of another who has died. It should be noted that one can be both a singularity and an individual at the same time, for the lover of a fallen serviceman mourns for the one who was to her/him a singularity, even as he is simply replaced by another individual or removed from the equation in the world of warcraft.

In *Transcritique*, Karatani traces another important point of contrast between the two circuits. Whereas generality 'can be abstracted from experience,' universality 'cannot be attained *if not for a certain leap*.'[20] The circuit that leads from the individual to the general is empirical in that what is generally held to be true or correct is an adding up and harmonization of discrete individual cases, such as in the case of the hosts of a party who conduct themselves and arrange things in a way that please their guests as a whole, but who cannot claim universality for their choices.[21] In contrast to this, the pathway from singularity to universality involves a presumptuous, even unreasonable *demand* that what is quite clearly a subjective judgement is given the assent of all others.[22] The sphere of aesthetics provides us with the most familiar instances of this paradoxical dynamic, for when a person declares that King Crimson is the greatest band in the history of progressive rock, although she knows that she is making a subjective judgement of taste, her assertion implicitly hopes to attain universal agreement from all who are concerned with the matter. Steven Shaviro in his reading of Kant and Karatani points out that what separates personal preferences such as one's favourite ice cream flavour from judgements of taste is that in the case of the latter there is a certain reaching for the universal that goes 'beyond the statement that things are this way "for me".'[23]

The upshot of this is that we are not proposing or even seeking to sketch a master plan that only requires individuals to occupy the roles we may designate. Much less are we trying to map out a single path or revolutionary road that all must traverse. Indeed, the singularity of each person can be said to matter because of—to introduce here a word that is not always invoked in this context—*vocation*. We shall discuss this concept in greater detail in the following section, but for now it suffices to say that we shall take as our starting point the theological concept of vocation as developed in the Western Judeo-Christian tradition, tracing its evolution in medieval Catholicism and the Reformation as well as under the pressure of modern and contemporary critiques, in order to work towards an integration of the singular and the universal. The reason for this turn to Christian metaphysics is to supplement Karatani's understanding of singularity and sociality, which although well developed overall, does not provide the rather specialized tool needed to examine the interconnectedness and potential complementarity of the different perspectives in the university triad. As shall become clear, the understanding of vocation to be explored is one that provides us primarily with a procedural rather than a substantive approach to the difficult questions we face, in other words, a *how* but not a *what*.

Returning to our discussion of the two circuits, we may ask, what is the role of the particular in the circuit of individuality-particularity-generality? After all, the term is used by certain thinkers as a synonym for—or at least to occupy the place of—individuality. According to Karatani's reading of Hegel and the German Romantics, it in fact serves to mediate between individuality and generality, hence the order in the circuit.[24] In his words:

> 'Nation' has always been considered the middle term (particularity) between individuality and humanity. ... For the Romantics, the idea of nation came to be privileged because of a grounding logic according to which particularity synthesizes, even originates, individuality and universality. Within this logic, it is only particularity that assumes the concrete. ... The individual becomes an individual person primarily within one's own national language (and nation). The universality of the human being—a human in general—is abstract and empty when the particularity is absent.[25]

Perhaps Karatani moves too quickly from speaking of particularity as a middle term in general to criticizing the nation-state as the assumed space and context of mediation. While it is true that many of the thinkers he cites, from de Maistre to Wilhelm Humboldt, considered the nation as the pathway to their conception of humanity[26]—which, it is important to emphasize, Karatani considers as a form of generality rather than universality due to its inward-facing orientation—there are other forms of particularity that exist, as we shall see below, including some that have an at least pseudo-universal dimension.

Karatani's sharp critique of particularity stems from his aversion towards the nation(-state) as a mediator, but there are in fact at least two main ways in which mediation and relationality take place. The philosopher Peter Hallward has pointed this out in his careful distinction between what he calls the 'specified' and the 'specific.' The specified, in Hallward's framework, is akin to the individuality-particularity-generality circuit that Karatani is suspicious of—albeit with an ambit wider than simply the nation—for it treats persons 'as individuated by certain intrinsic, invariant and thus characteristic properties, innate or acquired, racial or sexual, national or cultural, physical or spiritual' and so 'reduces the universal to the status of the general or normal.'[27] Like Karatani he cites the German Romantics and other Counter-Enlightenment figures such as de Maistre as examples of this form of thought.[28] Crucially, Hallward underlines the fact that, as the use of the past participle indicates, the specified is the *result* of an application of 'recognized classifications,' and it matters little whether what is specified is construed narrowly, such as with a nativist or culturalist particularity, or more broadly, as with some forms of seemingly humanist and universalist visions, for in his biting words, 'mere appreciation of the fact that "everyone is different and special in their own way" belongs to such sophisticated institutions as Sesame Street and McDonald's as much as to some recent postcolonial theories.'[29]

Against the essentialism—whether monist or pluralist, parochial, or globalist—of the specified, various thinkers have put forward philosophies of the specific, which must nevertheless be distinguished from the singular. The key difference can be explained as follows. The singular, as we have seen, simply disregards the question of mediation in its leap into the universal—it is, in Hallward's words, 'beyond relationality.'[30] The specific, in contrast, chooses to persist in the realm of mediation with its surroundings and others, but in contrast to the fixity of the specified, it 'presupposes an empty, transcendental universal as the necessary medium of its open-ended relational field.'[31] Relationality is not sidestepped, but radicalized by the assertion of a dynamic subjectivism.

Furthermore, we should be aware of the limitations and blind spots of the circuit of singularity-universality. In his seminal essay, 'An Answer to the Question: What is Enlightenment?', Kant argued that the public exercise of one's reason required one to extricate oneself from one's specific responsibilities and entanglements within a particular community in order to enter the space of cosmopolitan society (*Weltbürgergesellschaft*).[32] While he certainly did not deny the necessity of engagement within one's more situated spheres of commitment—in his terms, the private exercise of one's reason—it is undeniable that he considered it an inferior, less enlightened form. Such exertions of one's reason were necessary, perhaps, for making a living and discharging one's civic duties,[33] but it was ultimately one's activity within the cosmopolitan public that was of primary significance.

Of course, Kant could hardly have argued otherwise given his commitment to the Enlightenment and its conception of reason. We have already mentioned Counter-Enlightenment thinkers such as de Maistre who were focused on the national *polis* rather than the *kosmo-polis*. Whereas many thinkers in Kant's lineage (including Karatani) view particularistic sentiments, culture, and ideas as reactionary or at least damagingly parochial, those who oppose or at least call into question the rationalism of the Enlightenment often bewail the destruction of community in the interests of what Kant calls 'the society of the citizens of the world.'[34] In the first case, what appears to be demanded is a form of 'reverse-*kenosis*.' St Paul in his Epistle to the Philippians says that 'Christ Jesus, who, though he was in the form of God, did not count equality with God a thing to be grasped, but emptied himself [*ekenōsen*], taking the form of a servant, being born in the likeness of men' (Phil. 2:5–7, RSV). According to theorists of kenotic theology, this *kenosis*, or 'self-emptying' was necessary in order that the eternal and creating Word, the Second Person of the Trinity, could 'descend' and take the form of a human being, Jesus of Nazareth.[35] When Kant and his followers speak of becoming cosmopolitan, however, what appears to be required is also a form of self-emptying, but of one's particular characteristics in order to 'rise' to the level of discourse and societal life in the *kosmos*.[36]

Granted, for Karatani being cosmopolitan appears to be an additional rather than a completely alternative way of living. He writes that Kant 'never denied that everyone always belongs to a certain community. He simply urged that individuals behave as cosmopolitans in thinking and action.'³⁷ Therefore, 'in the concrete, [being enlightened] means becoming a member not (*only*) of a national community but (*also*) of a cosmopolitan society.'³⁸ Yet the parentheses he uses in this last quote indicate a degree of reticence to concede this point, and it is unsurprising that he writes subsequently in *The Structure of World History*: 'True fraternity and free association are only possible once individuals cut ties with their communities (in Kant's language, cosmopolitans).'³⁹ That is to say, for him membership and participation within a national community is an unavoidable practical necessity, but as far as possible it should be tempered and trumped by a cosmopolitan orientation, which would be an expression of transcending A and moving towards the X in the universalist Mode D.

Given that we are tracing Karatani's line of argument, we have once again crossed over into speaking as if the nation(-state) is the only, or at least the most centrally, relevant aspect of our particularities. There are, of course, many other particular alliances and entanglements involved. In the sphere of the university, these include disciplinary boundaries, institutional affiliations, as well as inter- and intra-disciplinary cliques (which often are organized according to theoretical/practical interests and/or political tendencies).

Even in the restricted space of national and other inwardly-facing communities, it should be noted that Karatani's perspective appears to have broadened in the decade or so between the writing of *Transcritique* and *The Structure of World History*. Whereas in *Transcritique* he simply opposes the individuality-particularity-generality circuit to the singularity-universality circuit, considering them to be at odds with each other even where they coexist, in the later text he appears to have moved towards a more transcritical position. Speaking in the context of universal religions such as Judaism and Christianity, he states that they 'do not become universal by negating the particular. Rather, they become universal through an incessant awareness of the contradiction between universality and particularity.'⁴⁰ In other words, if we do not wish to collapse in one or the other direction what is in many respects a productive antinomy, we cannot but endure the unsettling nature of dwelling within such contradictions.

This discomfort is not to be lamented, for it is within this space of tension between particularity and universality that responses to the history of the post-war British university that are truly singular may be forged. Through the operation of transcritique—that is, bracketing—these responses will also be able to access the other circuit and thus engage with their respective particular contexts in a resolutely specific manner. Kant was able to resolve the third antinomy between nature and freedom by paradoxically affirming the truth of both through essentially a bracketing operation. By bracketing the determining operations of natural causality, it is possible to establish practical freedom; conversely, by bracketing the assumption of free will, it is possible to observe the motions of causality.[41] Likewise, so long as we are prepared to oscillate from one circuit to the other, we do not necessarily have to choose between singularity-universality and individuality-particularity-generality, although it should be added that it is best to engage with the latter circuit under the aegis of the specific and not the specified.

Having said all this, how do we deal with the obvious fact of the multifarious and conflicting responses to the set of circumstances we find ourselves in? If we wish to move away from the easiest 'solution' of finding like-minded others to combine one's efforts or identifying contrary-minded others to oppose, we will have to acknowledge the *necessary plurality* in *vocations*. This is where the aphorism from Blake quoted at the beginning of this chapter may help us find a way forward. In a famous section in *The Marriage of Heaven and Hell* titled, 'Proverbs of Hell,' the radical poet and artist wrote, 'The apple tree never asks the beech how he shall grow, nor the lion, the horse, how he shall take his prey.'[42] This simple recognition of multiplicity, which consists in accepting that we are not all identical beings and therefore cannot be expected to adhere to identical forms of life, may seem banal,[43] but we shall use it as a starting point for discussing vocation, the subject of the next section of this chapter. Nevertheless, we must meet the challenge, already alluded to in the aforementioned quote from Hallward, that any such talk not fall into the truly banal mass media message that 'everyone is different and special in their own way,' but seriously grapple with the specific and the singular, for our aim is to formulate an adequate way of dealing with the conflicting demands of the conceptual triad in the university.

Vocation

The term vocation is one that often elicits rather strong reactions, at least in part due to its complicated history. In some spheres of academic and political thought, any positive resort to language or concepts that have a religious—especially Christian—provenance is still deemed slightly suspect, if not completely anathema. Nevertheless, the legacies of twentieth-century thinkers such as Carl Schmitt and Walter Benjamin who engaged with theological thought, as well as the recent popularity and prominence of continental thinkers who have followed in their steps, including Alain Badiou, Slavoj Žižek and—in the most extensive fashion—Giorgio Agamben, have altered the scene to a significant degree. Hence, it has become possible for declarations such as that of legal theorist Anton Schütz (from which an extended quote is necessary):

> The line between 'religion' and 'outside religion,' between the 'spiritual' and the 'temporal/secular,' has collapsed as such. And it is its disappearance and the resulting indissociability of the two sides which opens up, for the first time, the possibility of viewing the Western experience in toto *as one immense* (although empirically finite) *unitary event*, a 'singularity.' Not only is there a relation linking Lenin and Saint Paul, but without the Pauline 'un-coupling from law' no Western Science, no Enlightenment anti-institutionalism, no socialist revolution, no post-modern human rights philosophy, can as much as be conceived, no social-peace-pampering Western-type 'civil society' as much as be dreamt of. The task consists in retracing the history of Christianity-*cum*-postchristianity as a West-*internal longue durée*, in drawing the general map of the Western adventure, in inscribing Humanism, Enlightenment philosophy, socialism, etc., within this one overarching Western event.[44]

In other words, the project of extracting from this 'Western experience' a secularized essence that can be synthesized with one's favoured revolutionary or reformist views (that is, the exercise that fuelled experiments such as the French republican calendar,[45] as well as other attempts to clear from the messy slate of Western history any influences from religion and, to risk some vain repetition, Christianity in particular) has to be rejected as an ahistorical and ultimately counter-productive cause. Even if one is a thorough believer in secularism, a participant in the postcolonial or decolonial movements, or even an anti-Constantinian Christian, any investigation that is either premised upon or engages seriously with Western thought has to pass through Christendom and its contested legacy rather than attempt to leap over it.

Therefore, if we wish to grapple with the relations between universality, singularity, and particularity—that is to say, the problematic stated in the previous section—there is much that can be gained from engaging with Judeo-Christian ideas on vocation, in that this textual and lived tradition has for millenia wrestled with the tensions between, in the Christian case, universalist visions and singular lives, as well as, in the Jewish context, the roles played by particular communal vocations and the singular person in the fashioning of a world-affirming approach to life. At this point of setting off, if we wanted to summarize the overarching argument of this section, we could say that the concept of vocation allows a person to hold on firmly and act boldly according to her views, principles, and deepest stirrings, and yet avoid the danger of considering them to be superior to or more true than all others and in all cases.

The Invention of Vocation

We begin our enquiry into vocation by examining its lexical and conceptual history. Etymologically, the Latin word *vocatio* simply means a calling, and in Ancient Rome it had been used in various senses, including a legal summons or even an invitation to dinner.[46] However, the use of the word by Jerome in the Vulgate to translate the Greek *klesis*, which itself had similar meanings to *vocatio* in the legal and non-religious social realm,[47] in the New Testament epistles led to its meaning acquiring a distinctly Christian context and content, which with the rise of Christendom indelibly marked its history from then on.

Of course, the religious concept of vocation predates textual sources that utilize the respective Latin or Greek terms like the Vulgate or indeed the New Testament, for the idea of calling has a much older provenance. Even within the biblical canon,[48] Walter Brueggemann has argued that the creation narrative in the Hebrew Book of Genesis, wherein God assigns to the human being the task of 'tilling' and 'keeping' the Garden of Eden (Gen. 1:15, RSV), implies that 'from the beginning, the human creature is called [and] given a vocation.'[49] As for a vocation given to a singular person, the paramount example in the Hebrew Scriptures is that of Abraham, but both the Old and New Testaments are replete with stories of those who received special tasks, almost without exception as a result of divine revelation. In fact in the Septuagint, the Greek translation of the Hebrew Scriptures, words from the same family as *klesis* are used in narratives involving 'Adamic naming,' where a person or place is given a name that corresponds with a deep truth of its reality, as in the mythical naming of the animals by Adam in the second chapter of Genesis.[50] Therefore, Adamic names are considered 'perfect linguistic representations of nonlinguistic realities.'[51] It should be noted that these underlying realities are not necessarily eternal or even preexisting, for there are numerous instances in the Hebrew Scriptures where a new name is given to fit a new identity or ontological reality, such as when Abram, the 'exalted father,'[52] becomes Abraham, the 'father of many nations' (Gen. 17:5, KJV). Thus we see that *klesis* need not be understood as a static, essentialist notion, but can in fact be framed as a dynamic concept with much affinity to philosophies of becoming.

Still, we have to be careful not to indiscriminately read into the textual canon a modern conception of vocation that involves, to put it simply, choosing between multiple options for one's central (pre)occupation. Such a task generally arises wherever and whenever a significant degree of social mobility exists. In the various times and places in history and the present where social stratification is rigid, the possibility of living a life that veers away from the path that appears to be set out for one from birth—whether due to class, caste, or any other social constraint—is highly unlikely. In such situations, the question of vocation in terms of 'work' appears to have a rather restricted range of answers, the most common one being to simply follow the family occupation or trade, or, in the case of women in certain strata and societies, becoming a wife and mother. However, it would be equally mistaken to assume that the possibility of choosing one's primary (pre)occupations is an entirely modern phenomenon, for the historical record does provide instances of this even in relatively socially immobile settings, most dramatically perhaps in the decision to abandon the life of 'regular' work for that of philosophical contemplation, such as that of Socrates, the son of a stonemason.[53] Indeed, the primary barrier to social mobility in traditional societies such as that of Ancient Greece is one less tied to occupation but rather to status or estate, for although a slave, a foreign resident and a citizen may all exert their strength and skill in the same workshop, a social chasm separates the latter from his less privileged workmates.[54]

Here we have one of those areas of life where the premodern situation is closer to our 'postmodern' present than the modern one. It can be argued that the modern understanding which originated in the Protestant Reformation whereby one's everyday occupation or work is the primary locus of one's vocation distracts us from more infrastructural questions. For if we extrapolate from the image from antiquity of fellow craftsmen who, although they cooperate in their activities, are nevertheless very distinct from each other due to their different legal statuses, we may say that the issue of vocation today is less a question of what the primary activities that one engages in are but rather one's way of being and becoming. Such an understanding of vocation is indelibly tied to *how* one lives, of which practical tasks—that is to say, the *what*—are but one consideration. Two young academics may share an office, and outwardly appear to be of one occupation, yet it is possible that one has a state of being and becoming that is aligned to what we may call her vocation, while the other does not.

What then is this idea of vocation that concentrates upon the *how*? Before we can answer this question adequately, we will first have to conduct a brief genealogy of the development of the notion of *klesis*, observing both its use in the early texts as well as its most important permutations in the ensuing centuries. Through this investigation we shall see that the idea of vocation focusing upon *form* superimposed upon a minimalist yet essential *content* is not only closer to the original use of *klesis* when compared to its subsequent manifestations, but is also much more radical in its nature and consequences.

A Very Brief History of Vocation in the Christian Context

As we have already seen, the Latin word *vocatio* first acquired the sense of a religious calling or vocation when Jerome used it to translate the Greek term *klesis* as it was used in the New Testament letters, for instance in the First Epistle of St Paul to the Corinthians, where the apostle writes, 'For ye see your *calling*, brethren, how that not many wise men after the flesh, not many mighty, not many noble, are called' (1 Cor. 1:26, KJV, italics added). Or, again, in his Epistle to the Philippians, 'Brethren ... this one thing I do, forgetting those things which are behind, and reaching forth unto those things which are before, I press toward the mark for the prize of the high *calling* of God in Christ Jesus' (Phil. 3:13–14, KJV, italics added). From these examples we can see that Paul is not speaking of calling in the modern workaday sense of an occupation—nor even an occupation one feels a special affinity with—but rather 'the general Christian "calling" to belong to Christ.'[55]

To some contemporary eyes and ears, this may seem a narrow or even insignificant matter, but it is important that we not forget the marginality of the Christian faith when Paul was writing. Far from the conformist default of Christendom or the personal and/or private choice of the modern and postmodern age, to become a Christian in the first century CE was to join a strange sect that sprang out from Judaism in the eastern backwaters of the Roman Empire. Moreover, the exclusivity of the claims of the Christian faith within its theological framework, which led to its adherents refusing to engage in the official imperial religious rites, made embracing it a dangerous choice, for it was not just a matter of refusal or exodus but rather a counter-narrative that challenged the discourse of the Empire by appropriating its key concepts and seemingly subverting them.[56]

This choice to respond to this calling to the Christian faith was not a wholly individualistic one, for one's response made one a member of the church or Christian community, whose original word in Greek, *ekklesia* or assembly, itself shares the same etymological filiation as *klesis*.[57] The heroism of early Christianity, however, almost came to an end with Constantine's embrace of the faith and its rise to become the religion of the Empire. With the inversion of Christianity from structurally disadvantaged sect into state religion, the radical idea of *klesis* had to evolve or risk complete dissipation. Hence, it mutated from being simply the call to be a Christian to that of an 'authentic' Christian life, which in its earliest manifestations generally took the form of a flight from the city in order to live a life of a solitary or cenobitic (i.e. communal) ascetic in the desert. Nevertheless, to use the terms that we discussed in the previous section of this chapter, in both these cases the core of the vocation was, strictly speaking, particular and not singular, in that they each involved a general exhortation inviting whoever may respond to a general and not a universal calling. The demands placed on the respondent were generic and not singular. For the message was 'become a Christian' or 'become a consecrated religious,' and for this task the singular qualities of the hearer were insignificant, or even irrelevant, which leads us back to the interpellating posters depicting Lord Kitchener and Uncle Sam.

Thus, from the early monastic athletes—who gained the name Desert Mothers and Fathers—onwards until the Protestant Reformation, the word *vocatio* came to refer solely to the special vocation of becoming a priest or consecrated religious.[58] It is easy to critique this development as being a hierarchical turn that created an ecclesiastical elite—and, indeed, in many ways it was—but it is also worth noting that it also preserved the notion that *vocatio* was something other than simply the instrumental demands of whatever practical social and economic structure was in place. Granted, the social structures and ideologies of Antiquity and the medieval era, where productive work was seen as inferior to a life of contemplation, helped to produce this elitist conception.[59] However, to return to Schütz's argument, which highlights the continuity of secular post-Christian developments with the Christian period that preceded and still conditions it, it can still be argued that the figure of the ascetic under religious vows is the precursor to subsequent countercultural roles such as the rebel, the revolutionary, and the activist. Indeed, numerous figures in historical insurrections, revolutions, and protest movements have been either clerics and/or monastics or former clerics and/or former monastics, from the late medieval Lollard priest John Ball and radical reformer Thomas Müntzer to, more recently, Sr Anne Montgomery RSCJ and Fr Daniel Berrigan SJ of the antiwar Plowshares Movement.[60] Of course, the two exemplary examples of this phenomenon from the United States in the twentieth century were Rev. Dr Martin Luther King Jr and Malcolm X. With such persons we find a rebellion against the conformist and conforming elements of the consecrated religious vocation, which converts and subverts the particular-general medieval notion of such a vocation into singular yet not necessarily solitary expressions. It is as if having responded to the religious equivalent of a Lord Kitchener poster—and there are many instances of such literature in churches—such persons then decide that a precarious path between 'loyal' rebellion and heterodox resistance is one they really are to walk upon.

The next major modulation of vocation in Western Christendom took place during and as part of the Protestant Reformation. In 'An Open Letter to The Christian Nobility,' written in 1520, the German reformer Martin Luther attacked the Catholic doctrine that divided the world into a 'spiritual estate' comprised of 'pope, bishops, priests and monks' and a 'temporal estate' made up of 'princes, lords, artisans, and farmers.'[61] This conception, which elevated clerics to a special status, Luther rejects in his characteristically truculent manner as 'a fine bit of lying and hypocrisy.'[62] It is important to note that Luther maintains a distinction between the sphere of secular government, which he terms the worldly kingdom of 'law,' and that of spiritual striving, which he terms the heavenly kingdom of 'grace,'[63] but he expands the boundaries of the latter to include all Christians, and not just the 'spiritual professionals.'[64] The theological path towards this 'democratization' is mapped through a reading of selected New Testament epistles, which allows him to challenge the very foundation of the specifically Catholic division of spiritual and temporal, namely the distinction between clerical and laypersons.

Traditional Catholic theology held that the priesthood was a special ontological status conferred by the sacrament of priestly ordination by a bishop. Luther, on the other hand, puts forward a notion that has become known as the 'priesthood of all believers.' He justified this conception by citing both St Peter and St Paul. In the First Epistle of Peter, the author, addressing his audience of Christians who were 'scattered throughout Pontus, Galatia, Cappadocia, Asia, and Bithynia,' writes: 'Ye are a chosen generation, a royal priesthood, an holy nation' (1 Pet. 1:1–2, 2:9, KJV). If all Christians are already priests, then the role of dispensing the sacraments and preaching is not premised upon a unique ontological status, but is rather an office undertaken by the office holder within the boundaries of church order.[65] Luther cites Paul's Letter to the Romans, where it is said that 'for as we have many members in one body, and all members have not the same office: So we, being many, are one body in Christ, and every one members one of another' (Rom. 12:4–5, KJV).

At first glance, this levelling of the priesthood to simply one role in the body of believers at the same time appears to elevate all forms of human activity—including non-economic labour, e.g. being a spouse, parent, or child—to the status of vocations, a position that is taken by various commentators such as William E. Placher.[66] After all, in a Christmas sermon written around 1521, Luther argues that 'all works are the same to a Christian, no matter what they are.'[67] Nevertheless, it may be more accurate to say that Luther's broadening of the concept of vocation, like some instances of democratization in the political realm, is primarily a levelling down rather than a levelling up.[68] A particularly telling expression of Luther's theology of vocation can be found in his translation of a key passage in Paul's First Letter to the Corinthians (7:20) in which the word *klesis*—or, to be exact, its equivalent form *klesei*—is translated as *Beruf*, that is, 'job' or 'occupation,' rather than *Berufung* or *Ruf*, that is, 'calling.'[69] The King James Version maintained the straightforward and widely accepted concept of *klesis*: 'Let every man abide in the same *calling* wherein he was called' (1 Cor. 7:20, KJV). Luther, on the other hand, translated the passage as follows: '*Ein jeglicher bleibe in dem Beruf, darin er berufen ist*' (L1545). It is no exaggeration to say that Luther's choice of word, *Beruf*, in this passage has had significant consequences for the history of the concept of vocation ever since.

Luther's intention, in translating what had been understood as *vocatio* into *Beruf*, was 'to demonstrate and prove that not only the monk has a vocation, but every Christian in the world and in secular employment as well.'[70] The effect of this daring translation was to subsume the concept of vocation under a socially conservative rubric, for together with Luther's attempt to horizontalize the previously hegemonic idea of vocation came his teaching that Christians should not seek to change their 'external position[s],' just as the shepherds who worshipped the infant Jesus returned to their flocks and did not attempt to retire to a 'higher' monastic life.[71] Thus, Luther's democratization of vocation is formal rather than substantive, as the upshot of his treatment of all varieties of *Beruf* as of equal standing before God, when twinned with the idea that one's place in the world is no accident but rather appointed by God, is to legitimize the actual hierarchies that exist. The peasant is to remain a peasant, the artisan an artisan, and so on. This attitude of indifference and resignation to what one is 'given' is ironically a central part of the internal life of the religious orders that Luther opposed. As the *Principles* of the Anglican Society of the Sacred Mission counsels the member potentially disaffected by an uncongenial assignment: 'If you have given your whole life to God why should you prefer to lose it in this way rather than in that?'[72]

Hence, New Testament scholar S. Scott Bartchy has argued that *Ruf* is the German word that corresponds best to *klesis*. Although *Berufung*, a word that carries the meaning of vocation or calling, is preferable to the technical/vocational term *Beruf*, and certainly better than alternative terms even more tied to social class such as *Stand* (status) or *Platz* (place) that have been used in translations since the Luther Bible, he nevertheless cites German feminist theologian Luise Schottroff's scepticism that *Berufung* is 'a clear advance' over *Beruf*.[73] This is probably so because although the difference between *Ruf* and *Berufung* is subtle, the former's advantage is that it is associated with a call from an external source, as in the traditional *Ruf* to take up a professorship in a German university.[74] In other words, with *Ruf* the (proto-)liberal element of autonomous choice is downplayed, as one does not initiate the vocational 'move' but rather responds to a call from *outside* oneself. Still, it can be argued that this response is itself only possible if it is in accord with something that is *inside* oneself. To use, analogically, the example of the *Ruf* to become a professor at a particular university, if one has absolutely no inclination towards the position, then the call will almost certainly go unheeded. In other words, a connection must be made between the within and the beyond for there to be an instance of a fulfilled *klesis* or vocation.

As Weber famously pointed out, Luther's radical reworking of the concept of vocation in his translation of the Bible spilled over into other Protestant societies, with the clearest example in the English-speaking world being that of the Calvinist Puritans.[75] Puritan divines such as William Perkins formulated a twofold conception of vocation, dividing it into the 'general calling' of Christian life, 'common to all who live in the Church of God,' and 'particular' or 'personal callings' that correspond to specific forms of labour or offices.[76] The closeness of his terminology to our discussion in the previous section is significant, although there are certain finer distinctions that should be made. First of all, Perkins is generally considered to be among the Calvinists who hold to an understanding of the Christian *klesis* that is, in the terms we have been using, particular rather than general (and certainly not universal). It is a central doctrine of Calvinism that God has chosen an 'elect' to be saved from eternal damnation, and by extension excluded many others from salvation. This is what is commonly known as 'predestination.' However, the particularity of this calling is further strengthened by those who hold to what has come to be known as 'limited atonement.' These Calvinists, whose patrimony some trace back to Theodore Beza, the sixteenth-century French theologian and disciple of Calvin, hold to the idea that Christ's atonement on the cross was 'limited,' and by this it is meant that Christ died not for the sins of the whole world but rather only for the elect.[77] Perkins, like other theologians of his time, spoke of 'redemption' and 'satisfaction' rather than 'atonement,' the latter being a term that came into use later,[78] but his denial that Christ died for those outside the elect nevertheless gives him a place among this group. In his own words, 'the price is payd in the counsell of God, and as touching the event *only for those which are elected and predestinated.*'[79]

Secondly, Perkins's understanding of a 'personal calling' is what we would call an individual and not a singular calling. In his view, one is called to fill particular roles or 'offices' in society, and he names and categorizes them under two headings. The first are 'of the essence and foundation of any society,' and include that of a master or a servant, a husband or a wife, a parent and a child; the second are 'only for the good, happy and quiet estate of a society,' such as that of a merchant, a husbandman, a physician, a lawyer, and so on.[80] All of these roles are pregiven, and require only persons to be inserted into them, thus following the pattern of the individual-general relation we discussed earlier.

The upshot of this is that we can see how the classical Protestant understanding of vocation, from Luther through to the Puritan Calvinists and up until the present day, is based on the individual-particular-general circuit rather than the singular-universal one. This being the case, it is perhaps no wonder that such thinking could not resist, and indeed went hand in hand with, the rise of alienated labour under capitalism, as studies from Weber and R. H. Tawney onwards on the intimate relationship between religion and the economy in the countries where the capitalist mode of production arose have shown. For if one's vocation is simply filling in a role that has to be played in a given socio-historical situation, this role is not only infused with religious significance, as Weber pointed out,[81] but also eradicates the singularity of the person. For if the person is not singular but merely individual, even if, as Perkins acknowledged, 'every calling must be fitted to the man,'[82] the fit is akin to, it can be said without excessive exaggeration, a specific nut being sought for a specific bolt, thus resulting in a rather mechanical view of society with people as interchangeable parts.[83]

The aforementioned transformation of labour under capitalism brought about another gradual shift in the Christian understanding of vocation. To begin, it should be noted that in the Catholic regions of Europe, the intellectual and spiritual legacy of the Counter-Reformation was such that the medieval understanding of vocation as restricted to special religious callings was maintained, and would not change significantly until after the church-shaking event of the Second Vatican Council in 1962–5.[84] It was this divergence that Weber pointed towards in *The Protestant Ethic and the Spirit of Capitalism* when he noted that the conception of vocation as *Beruf* or practical sphere of work was in fact absent in the languages of the Catholic peoples of Europe.[85] This can be attributed to the rejection of the Lutheran innovation in understanding vocation we discussed earlier. Hence, we find that in Pope Leo XIII's famous 1891 encyclical, *Rerum Novarum*, which inaugurated the body of theology known as Catholic Social Teaching, he deals with the question of work not in terms of vocation but rather primarily as a means of earning a living, supporting a family and bettering one's condition by acquiring private property.[86]

With the advent and intensification of capitalist hegemony across the Western world, voices began to be heard from even Protestant quarters that called into question the equivalence of vocation and work brought about by Luther, the Puritans, and other Reformers. Often this took the form of a critique of capitalism or, at least, the principle of competition that it is generally founded upon, as in the work of Baptist minister and social gospel pioneer Walter Rauschenbusch most notably in *Christianity and the Social Crisis* (1907), his powerful broadside against not only the inequality and injustices of the time but also the apolitical and asocial forms of piety that explicitly or tacitly legitimized them. He pointed out that the 'right to work' had become a slogan deployed by employers to hire strike-breakers,[87] and that the principle of cooperation based on the Christian idea of human relations of love was increasingly difficult to practise in a capitalist culture, with the 'higher principle' of service to others greatly obscured unless one was in a line of work such as medicine, teaching,w or art.[88] For all that, Rauschenbusch still believed that a person's daily work could be filled with divine purpose if society could be reconstructed on the basis of service to humanity, which he linked to the Gospel idea of the Kingdom of God.[89]

Subsequently, the entire project to sanctify everyday labour came under attack from dissident voices such as the French Protestant theologian, social theorist, and Christian anarchist Jacques Ellul. Ellul writes in a 1980 essay (which appeared in English in 1985): 'I scarcely know a biblical text which presents work as valuable, good, or virtuous. ... In the Bible work is a necessity, a constraint, a punishment, except in a few, unusual texts.'[90] In another piece published in English in 1972, he insists that 'nothing in the Bible allows us to identify *work* with *calling*. ... [Work] is an imperative of survival, and the Bible remains realistic enough not to superimpose upon this necessity a superfluous spiritual decoration.'[91] Here we find that Ellul rejects the Protestant *Beruf*, but also refuses to return to the traditionalist Catholic *vocatio*, thus opening a way for him and others to reach back to the primitive understanding of *klesis* as the 'mere' calling to follow Christ.

Versions of Academic Klesis

Having examined the invention and development of the concept of *klesis* within the Christian context in the preceding section, the question naturally arising is simply this: If the *klesis* of the New Testament, understood in its primitive and most meaningful sense, is to belong to and follow after Christ, what is the *klesis* of the university? What are we who dwell within it *called* to do? In order to answer this seemingly simple and yet rather controversial question, we shall consider the rather interesting taxonomy of academics formulated by Stanley Fish in a 2012 series of lectures, published as *Versions of Academic Freedom: From Professionalism to Revolution*.[92] Fish categorizes academics according to their various views on the contentious subject of academic freedom, but it can be argued that his analysis is relevant to not just this particular aspect of higher education, but in fact the university's calling as a whole. An examination and extension of Fish's arguments will reveal that the broad periods in which the conception of vocation developed within the Christian West, as discussed above, have in fact more specific analogues within the sphere of higher education. However, we will see that we cannot easily leap into an understanding of a primitive *klesis* for the university as is possible in the Christian context, given the canonical textual resources available to the latter that we unfortunately do not have in the same manner. It is also important to note that, in employing Fish's taxonomy, we must avoid the trap of reducing the entirety of higher education to simply the work of academics, who form but one of its parts. Hence, with each of Fish's classifications, we have to be careful to not forget the perspectives of the other major human segments of the university community, namely non-academic staff and students.

Fish identifies five 'schools' that differ in their assessment of the boundaries and responsibilities of academic freedom, which he organizes in an ascending fashion from the most inward-facing and conservative to the most outward-facing and radical; or, in his own words, 'plotted on a continuum that goes from right to left.'[93] For the purposes of our argument, we can divide the five into two main categories, for at the core of Fish's classifications is one simple question: Does academia exist for a good or an end that lies outside its practical activities—whether in part or *in toto*—or is its *raison d'être* contained simply in its primary internal activities, that is, those directly involving or indirectly linked to learning, teaching, and research?

For four of Fish's five schools, the answer to this question is that there is indeed a *telos* or at least a justification that is added on to the 'bare' work of the university. The differences between them arise from varying opinions as to what exactly this additional justification is, and how it transforms how one understands the basic activities carried out in the higher education sphere. It is clear, however, that Fish sees in them a trajectory of increasing radicalism in the expansion—which in some cases is paradoxically accompanied by a certain narrowing—of the purposes of the academic institution, a radicalism that he disapproves of.

Let us begin with the first school in which Fish places himself, and half-jokingly but rather unpersuasively suggests that he may be the only member of.[94] He calls it the 'It's just a job' school, and its perspective on higher education, which he describes as 'deflationary,' considers academia to be 'a service that offers knowledge and skills to students who wish to receive them' and not 'a vocation or holy calling.'[95] It is important to note that Fish's antipathy to the word vocation arises from his disagreement with the 1915 Declaration of Principles on Academic Freedom and Academic Tenure promulgated by the American Association of University Professors (AAUP), which he claims is founded upon a distinction between what is considered a 'job' and what is considered a 'vocation.' In his words:

> A job is defined by an agreement (often contractual) between a worker and a boss: you will do X and I will pay you Y; and if you fail to perform

as stipulated, I will discipline or even dismiss you. Those called to a vocation are not merely workers; they are professionals; that is, they profess something larger than the task immediately at hand—a religious faith, a commitment to the rule of law, a dedication to healing, a zeal for truth—and in order to become credentialed professors, as opposed to being amateurs, they must undergo a rigorous and lengthy period of training. Being a professional is less a matter of specific performances ... than of a continual, indeed, lifelong responsiveness to an ideal or a spirit.[96]

Rejecting the concept of 'vocation' which the AAUP Declaration and its intellectual successors are founded upon,[97] Fish and other adherents to the 'It's just a job' school believe that they are not in their academic labours 'exercising First Amendment rights or forming citizens or inculcating moral values or training soldiers to fight for social justice'; instead, 'their obligations and aspirations are defined by the distinctive task—the advancement of knowledge—they are trained and paid to perform, defined, that is, by contract and by the course catalog rather than by a vision of democracy or world peace.'[98] Given that the AAUP's invocation of the concept of vocation or calling is clearly rooted in the Protestant innovation in the idea of *klesis*, the desacralization of the work of the academic that Fish's first school advocates can be seen as a break with the sanctification of everyday labour embodied in the Lutheran notion of vocation as *Beruf*. However, this school goes beyond the critique of Luther's *Beruf* we examined earlier, namely the one made by Christian critics such as Ellul, because in this case there is not even a baseline *klesis*, such as the calling to a Christian life, that can be returned to. The gesture here is towards disenchantment and secularity pure and simple: there is no such thing as an academic *klesis*; there is not even Luther's *Beruf*, but only the pre-Reformation understanding of the German word and its corresponding analogues in other languages. Therefore for Fish, academic teaching, research, and other related labours are all merely instances of work, and nothing grander. This is not to say that he thinks academic work is of not great value, but rather that its value lies solely in itself. We might call this autotelic approach, borrowing from the famous aesthetic slogan that first came to prominence in the nineteenth century, 'academia for academia's sake.'

The second school arises directly out of the 1915 AAUP declaration quoted above, and Fish terms it the 'For the common good' school. Here we find a conception of vocation similar to Luther's *Beruf*, although the sacred dimension of calling has here been largely secularized. Rather than performing one's work for the glory of God, it is rather to democracy and the community that one renders one's service.[99] Alongside the extension of human knowledge and the education of students, the university's task is to provide expert advice 'for various branches of public service' that will contribute 'toward the right solution of ... social problems.'[100] The university in a democratic society bears the responsibility 'to help make public opinion more self-critical and more circumspect, to check the more hasty and unconsidered impulses of popular feeling, to train the democracy to the habit of looking before and after.'[101]

A third school, Fish says, comes into being as 'a logical extension' of the second. This is the 'Academic exceptionalism or uncommon beings' school.[102] If academics are meant to be 'a counterweight to the force of common popular opinion, they must themselves be *un*common, not only intellectually but morally; they must be in the words of the 1915 Declaration, "men of high gift and character."'[103] The underlying principle of this school is eerily reminiscent of the elitist idea of vocation that was hegemonic in pre-Reformation Christendom and that continued in the Catholic world from the Counter-Reformation until the Second Vatican Council. Here we find that academics are the equivalent of nuns, monks, priests, and apostolic religious in the realm of higher education; that is, they are the spiritual athletes of the university, bearers of a unique calling, which carries not just special responsibilities but also special rights, for in their role of correcting 'the errors of popular opinion, they escape popular judgment and are not to be held accountable to the same laws and restrictions that constrain ordinary citizens.'[104]

For Fish, the next step away from seeing academic labours as simply a job whose value lies wholly in itself is taken by the fourth school, the 'Academic freedom as critique' school. He cites Judith Butler's work on the concept and practice of critique as being exemplary of this approach, whereby 'academic freedom is understood ... as a protection for dissent'; furthermore, 'the scope of dissent must extend to the very distinction and boundaries the academy presently enforces.'[105] In this vision, the boundaries between academic labours and political imperatives become blurred, for the drawing of definite lines 'has the effect of freezing the status quo and of allowing distinctions originally rooted in politics to present themselves as apolitical and natural.'[106]

Finally, we have the most daring school, namely the 'Academic freedom as revolution' school.[107] Its academic members equate the duties of teaching to that of a citizen, with the latter generally construed in a leftist political fashion, leading to radical pedagogist Henry A. Giroux's pronouncement that university teachers have a responsibility to

> fight for an inclusive and radical democracy by recognizing that education in the broadest sense is not just about understanding, however critical, but also about providing the conditions for assuming the responsibilities we have as citizens to expose human misery and to eliminate the conditions that produce it.[108]

Interestingly, this approach erases, in a sense, the uniqueness of the academic: she is merely carrying out the general tasks of preparing the way for and fomenting revolution in the specific realm of her daily work. Here we find a conception of vocation, then, which at first seems, in terms of structure, remarkably close to the primitive Christian understanding of *klesis*, for the calling to work for social justice and to challenge an unjust world is common to all who choose to embrace it, in response to it reaching their ears. However, this is *not* a *klesis* specific to the university, but rather one that leads to a *doxa* and *praxis* of activists, revolutionaries, and their fellow travellers. In this sense, it lies halfway between Luther's *Beruf* and traditionalist Catholic *vocatio*, as it paradoxically involves both the baptism of worldly activities in the light of higher aims, as well as the sense that one is carrying out a special task.[109]

In light of the discussion above, it can be argued that Fish sees the fairly moderate perspective of the 'For the common good' school as the beginning of a slippery slope. By admitting that there are 'higher values' or aims that transcend the 'severe professionalism of the 'It's just a job' school,'[110] one takes the first tentative step onto the top of the slope, and, from where Fish stands, it becomes difficult either to avoid sliding all the way to asserting that the value of academia lies in its service to the revolution, or to validly criticize those who happily do so, even if one has latched on to an intermediate point down the hill.

Fish's one-dimensional continuum, in which the latter four of his five schools represent incremental shifts away from the simple and pure 'It's just a job' perspective, is far too simplistic. It is possible to map out Fish's framework more accurately as well as bring it into a conversation with the various other theoretical threads we have explored so far in this book, an encounter already begun in the last few pages.

Figure 3 represents the discussion so far and what is to come.[111] The diagram allows us to see convergences and divergences that may not always be as visible while engaging purely in the linguistic mode. For

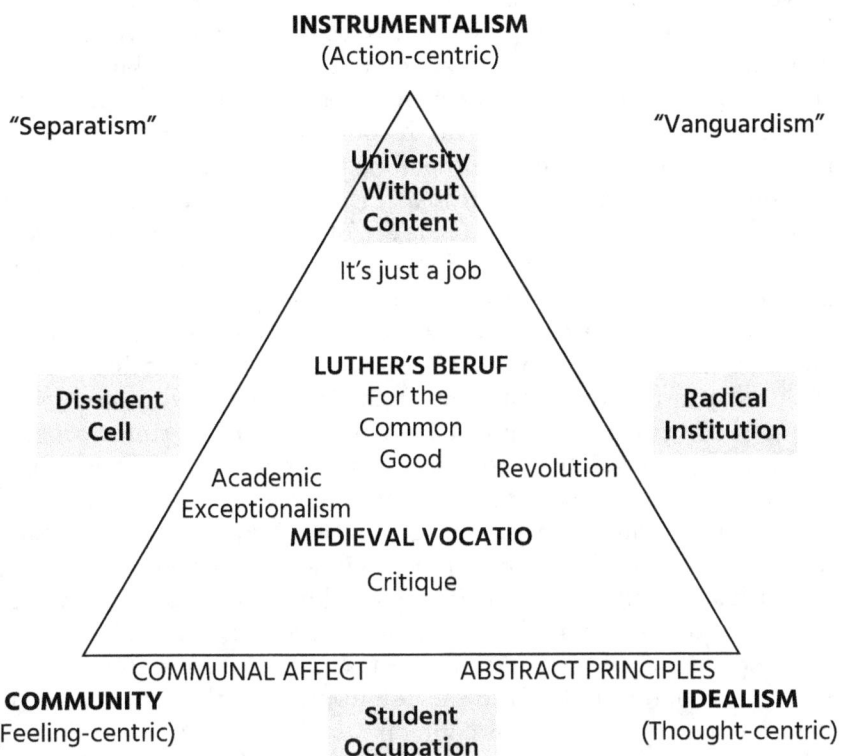

Figure 3

example, it becomes easier to see that Fish's desire to resist external validation or vindication for the activities of the university can be turned against right-wing tendencies as well as the left-wing ones he trains his fire upon.[112] Hence, his framing of his five schools as being 'plotted on a continuum that goes from right to left' is misleading.[113] To begin with, his denigration of the 'Academic freedom as revolution' school as subsuming academic activities completely under a foreign rubric applies as well to the economistic instrumentalism we analyzed in chapter two, because in both cases the university does not have its own justifying content—that is, it does not exist and operate for itself—but is judged according to its furtherance of extrinsic goals. The key difference is that whereas academic radicals of the revolutionary sort hold in a febrile tension their idealistic commitments and their instrumentalist aims, economistic instrumentalism formally ignores the matter of principles, and so even though its practitioners are often not themselves devoid of abstract ideas, the primary source of justification(s) for their decisions and policies lies squarely at the top of the triangle.

We can also enquire into certain curious affinities in the diagram. For a start, how can it be that economistic instrumentalism, which is the hegemonic manifestation of the 'university without its own content' discussed in chapter two, is located in the same corner of the triangle as Fish's 'It's just a job' school, given that Fish is against justifying academic labour through any *telos* apart from the work itself? What in fact unites them is their commitment to what we may call a 'pure'—that is, pre-Lutheran and post-Lutheran—conception of *Beruf*, in which academic labour is neither special nor sacred. Ironically, Fish's disavowal of any external validation of academic work does not lead to a *telos*-free zone, for his minimalist withdrawal from the sphere of wider aims naturally leads to the colonization of that very sphere by the dominant framework of contemporary life in the university and beyond, namely economistic calculation. After all, academic activities conducted according to the principle of 'academia for academia's sake' do not, even in the tallest ivory tower and under the most rarefied of conditions, operate in a vacuum. As David Harvey observes in the analogous case of 'art for art's sake,' it is often swallowed up by the very dynamics of commodification that it is opposed to in theory.[114]

The respective locations of the four non-autotelic schools in our diagram is also instructive, as it complicates Fish's conception of the five schools as a sequence that can be depicted on a single line that runs from right to left. The 'For the common good' school is indeed often the first move away from the 'It's just a job' mentality, but once one reaches the centre of the triangle, to shift one's perspective towards any of the final three schools takes one in different directions.

Academic exceptionalism, with its assertion that the task of the university is a unique one with its own distinct premises and perhaps even deserving of *sui generis* privileges within wider society, takes one down-and-leftwards in the direction of the university-in-itself and its emphasis on community, and also, as we have already observed, very close to medieval *vocatio*. It is particularly concerned with its own internal consistency and counter-hegemonic position, which entails a more 'separatist' approach, which is expressed most closely by the image of the dissident cell.

The revolutionary school, on the other hand, is premised more upon abstract ideals and principles such as social justice and emancipation than community per se. But there is a strong instrumentalist streak in its operations as well, and so it involves a movement primarily to the right side of the triangle. On the vertical axis it lies in between Luther's *Beruf* and medieval *vocatio*, as we discussed earlier, and it sees its operations as being that of a 'vanguard' within the university and society. Its purpose is to exert power over and harness existing institutions towards wider societal transformation, rather than to create spaces of exception via a strategy of exodus, and therefore can be represented by the image of the *radical institution*.

Finally, adherents to the school of critique are the most critical of any form of instrumentalism, and thus joining this party entails a move downwards and far away from the top end of the triangle. Its idea of calling involves some elements of medieval *vocatio*, but is also perhaps the closest among the five schools to the New Testament conception of *klesis*, with its critique of narrow professionalism and a general orientation towards an entire way or form of life. On the horizontal axis, it straddles precariously the middle point between community and abstract principles, separatism, and vanguardism. The countercultural aspects of critique lead to and presuppose a strong sense of community, but it is also a school involving strongly held ideals. Perhaps the image that symbolizes it best is the student occupation.

Having synthesized Fish's useful taxonomy with the theoretical framework constructed over the course of this book, we are now in position where we may return to the question with which we began this subsection, namely: What is the *klesis* of the university? There is sadly no single answer, for one's response to this question depends on what one's conception of calling is, which is in turn linked to one's relation to each of the three poles of the conceptual triad of the university. All these complicated dynamics can be represented by where one is located on the diagram in *figure 3*. Nonetheless, it is important to emphasize that the mapping of the ideal types in Fish's taxonomy onto the diagram are not meant to be static, unshifting points, but rather something closer to a 'home base' from which singular and collective actors begin their work and return to. For instance, there will be those aligned to the school of critique who choose at certain times to engage in more instrumentalist struggles.[115] This neither invalidates the heuristic value of the diagram nor necessarily indicates a rupture in the dominant position of such actors, but in many cases simply signals a tactical and often temporary shift.

This situation of stark plurality both in understanding the idea of *klesis* or calling within the university as well as how such an idea is expressed in thought, affect, and practice may seem rather overwhelming in its unruliness. How then are we to deal with these conflicting forces? One way of doing so is to dip once again into the Pauline toolbox and bring into the discussion the concept that is the necessary partner of *klesis*, namely *charismata*, that is, the various *charisma* or gifts that accompany the calling. For it is through delving into the dynamics of convergent, divergent, and even patently irreconcilable expressions of and attempts to live out the academic *klesis* that we may interrogate what at first appears to be the meta-antinomy running across and dividing the pluralistic university, namely that of partiality and integration.

Partiality and Integration in a Web of Pluralism and Exclusivism

There are two opposing yet complementary ways in which denizens of the university may manifest their respective callings. The first is the path of *partiality*, which involves holding firmly to the specific perspective and approach one feels most passionate about, and not allowing oneself to be distracted or swayed by opposing viewpoints. Despite a few decades of postmodern and post-structuralist currents in academic discourse, it can be said that this is still the default mode in which most within the university operate. The second path is that of *integration*, which involves careful listening and observation of the various strands of *doxa* and *praxis* in the university, and then developing a synthesis of sorts, allowing one to create a valuable if seemingly motley blend of these elements.[116] In terms of the diagram above, we can understand the partial approach as finding one's spot in the triangle and rooting oneself there, while the integrative approach involves hovering within a particular area and staking out what is often a new point between existing positions. Hovering over these two approaches is the possibility of a *pluralist attitude*, in which one may adopt either a partial or integrative strategy, yet acknowledge that one's viewpoint does not explain the whole of the field, and indeed value the multiplicity of expressions. The opposite of this is, of course, an *exclusivist attitude*, which considers one's specific position to be the complete truth or, at the least, very close to it. It can be said that pluralists recognize that their personal and collective stances are located somewhere on the triangle—or to use a common phrase, are but part of a bigger picture. Conversely, exclusivists generally refuse to acknowledge that anything like the diagram exists, for it does not fit with their vision, which sees things in one-dimensional terms of black and white. Even if they do accept that they can be placed on a particular taxonomic diagram, they hold to the view there is in fact a correct spot on it where one should be.

Exclusivism is fairly straightforward to practise and to preach. By contrast, a large part of the challenge of adopting and maintaining a pluralist attitude is the fact that the format of academic discourse favours its exclusivist 'rival.' It is true that Julia Kristeva argues, building upon the work of Mikhail Bakhtin, that a text contains underlying capacities for 'intertextuality' due to its relationship with prior, synchronic, and future texts. In her own words, a text 'relat[es] communicative speech, which aims to inform directly, to different kinds of anterior or synchronic utterances.'[117] However, the conventional academic text, considered on its own, is at the same time a monologic, centripetal medium due to the requirement that it put forward a unified, non-contradictory main argument. This aspect of academic texts is clearest when we compare them with the explicitly dialogical, centrifugal approach that Bakhtin identifies in the novel, although these elements are also present in other genres, such as the Platonic dialogue.[118]

The fact that no piece of writing is in truth formed outside of exchanges with others living, deceased, and to come nonetheless does not puncture one of the official pretensions of academic writing, in which the formal acknowledgements offered still stand apart from the author. And yet Bakhtin's argument that 'the culture of essential and inescapable solitude' conceals that 'the very being of man (both external and internal) is the deepest communion' is only one surface of a multi-sided phenomenon.[119] To move momentarily from Bakhtin to some of those who can be said to extend his work, it is accurate to say that reports of the death of the author have been greatly exaggerated, for an exaggeration necessarily presupposes an actual truth that has been blown out of proportion. The received wisdom of post-structuralist textual indeterminacy has not put to an end the attribution of thoughts expressed in words to those from whom those words have come. Even if the writer is a shell filled entirely with elements from outside, the existence of the shell cannot be done away with. Hence Bakhtin's assertion that 'a person has no internal sovereign territory, he is wholly and always on the boundary' misses the fact that this boundary, if semi-porous for the most part, not infrequently closes upon itself, if only to open up again.[120]

There initially appears to be a meta-antinomy between partiality and integration, which is connected to but far from identical with the leaning towards either exclusivism and pluralism that lies in the background. A closer consideration of this dynamic reveals that partiality and integration are not diametrically opposed but are rather the two extremes of a continuum, for it is perfectly possible to strongly favour a particular approach while accepting approaches that are more integrative as equally valid alternatives, and vice versa. The real antinomy is, in fact, the opposition between the exclusivist attitude and the pluralist attitude, for adherents to one almost always consider those on the other side to be completely mistaken. What if it were possible to understand both these positions as mutually supportive when viewed from a second-order perspective?

Adopting a frame of reference that is both wider and deeper, it can be argued that both exclusivists and pluralists have something to contribute to the university as a totality. The passion of the former for their specific particularity or synthesis allows them to act and speak with great decisiveness and conviction. This ties in with William James's characterization of a great philosopher, already quoted above, as she who sees things 'straight in [her] own peculiar way, and [is] dissatisfied with any opposite way of seeing them.'[121] To demand that such persons give up their singleness of mind, heart, and hand would be to deprive us of their valuable contributions, attained through the deployment of—and even surrender to—the powerful internal forces that drive them.

However, unflinching conviction is not the only virtue that is needed in a sphere such as the university. The pluralist view may be caricatured by its detractors as overcautious, indecisive or wishy-washy, but it too has an important part to play. Especially in situations that have become extremely polarized, the impulse impelling some to recognize the partial truths among the various actors locked into agonistic stand-offs can be remarkably helpful. To use an everyday metaphor, in a highly oppositional situation in which one perspective is emerging as hegemonic, the exclusivist attitude is like the pedal in a motorized vehicle that allows it to accelerate in a particular direction, while the pluralist attitude often acts as the brake pedal, which allows for a more considered survey of one's surroundings and turning, if required, to the left, to the right, or even around. In fact, in certain circumstances such braking is necessary to prevent a horrendous accident. In a different situation—for instance, one that is less polarized and more conciliatory—these roles may be reversed, and pluralism may be the throttle while exclusivism may act as the brake pedal. Regardless of which roles are taken up by the two attitudes in the situation concerned, it is clear that the university, to link it by analogy to an automobile, needs both pedals in order to be driven well.

If both exclusivist and pluralist attitudes have valuable contributions to make to the university's overall vocation, then the question on the level of a singular person or group of persons is this: How does one choose between them? Indeed, is choice even the right concept to deploy, given that, strictly speaking, one does not generally *decide upon* a vocation but is rather, quite often, seized by it? Following on from this, if taking an exclusivist or pluralist stance is a 'decision' or acquiescence that only forms the backdrop to one's expression of the academic vocation, how does one reconcile the manifold partial or integrative expressions of these two stances, of which the five schools Fish identified are but a few ideal types? The answer to these two questions lies in the concept that we will now delve into, namely that of *charismata* or gifts.

Charismata: The Counterpart that Provides Form to Klesis

When it comes to debates about the purpose and essence of the university and those who labour within it, the temptation is to attempt to convince every other actor that one's specific notion and expression of the academic *klesis* is the right one. Given that we have explored the various conflicting understandings of what having a vocation within the university even means—from 'pure' or secular *Beruf*, at one end, to New Testament *klesis*, at the other—such an endeavour is quite futile, for it is nearly impossible to agree upon a certain substantive content when one does not even agree upon the form in which that content is to be contained within.

It must be emphasized that what is being advocated here is not a weakening of one's particular positions, beliefs, or practices in favour of a bland middle-of-the-road liberalism that only admits into the terrain of dispute and decision a constricted band of theory-affect-practice considered 'reasonable.' Neither is it necessary for *all* of us to abandon our objections to particular ideas, affects, and practices of those on the other sides of the divide. Indeed, as already stated above, it is important for there to be *some* of us who resolutely refuse to entertain the possibility that conflicting perspectives have significant (or even any) validity. Such absolute convictions often assist the rigorous development of those positions. However, it is equally important that there are *others* who are willing to stand in the unstable middle ground and, when faced with matters of great contestation, attempt to broker workable compromises between rival groups, or at least carry the pluralist flag. For it is also crucial to note that compromise is simply one of the many possible resolutions to a certain conflict. But perhaps one way of summing up the heart of the matter is this: it is essential for at least certain persons in the university to recognize the distinctive charisms of its various actors. It should be noted that this is not a special task for an administrator or manager, as if it were possible to hover over the various participants in the university with an attitude of studied indifference in order to maintain the distinctive charisms. Rather, such a recognition can come to any singular person, although a predisposition towards pluralism often encourages its emergence and development.

The term 'charism' is a religious one, and comes from the Greek word *kharisma* or *charisma*, which means a 'gift of grace.'[122] In the Pauline tradition, this concept is tied to that of *klesis*, for while the latter is universal, the former—in its plural form, that is, *charismata*—provides both singular and particular renderings of that universal vocation among the various persons who embrace it. It can be said that *charismata* have both singular and particular aspects, for often life in human society requires that persons combine their efforts and energies in collective endeavours, which then results in the creation or affirmation of a particular charism that structures the common life of an organization or even a group of friends such as the Bloomsbury Group or the Clapham Sect. Such particular charisms are rarely identical to the singular charism that a person experiences as developing during the course of her life, but one clear exception can be seen in the case of a notable figure who founds an organization according to a particular vision that overlaps significantly with her singular one.[123]

Paul addresses the relation between *klesis* and *charismata* most significantly in a text we have already referenced above, namely his First

Letter to the Corinthians. To begin with, he recognizes that he himself has a specific constellation of gifts that make up his singular *charisma*, and his passion for this charism can easily lead to him wishing that all possessed it. Nonetheless, he is aware that his singular charism is not that of everyone else. Thus he states in a passage discussing celibacy and marriage, 'For I would that all men were even as I myself. But every man hath his proper gift [*charisma*] of God, one after this manner, and another after that' (1 Cor. 7:7, KJV). Paul tempers his obvious enthusiasm for celibacy, which came from his personal experience of the freedom that it gave him to carry out his missionary endeavours, by acknowledging that the merits of such a way of life do not negate those of other ways, such as marriage. This move of Paul's is a remarkable gesture towards a pluralist stance, even if within a rather particular frame, namely that of the Christian faith.

He goes on to write that 'as God hath distributed [*emerisen*] to every man, as the Lord hath called [*keklēken*] every one, so let him walk' (1 Cor. 7:17, KJV). In an unpublished note by Bartchy,[124] he argues that we should understand *emerisen* and *keklēken* not as synonyms used by Paul to merely underscore a point, but rather as two distinct terms corresponding to, respectively, *charismata* and *klesis*. Citing Wolfgang Schrage's German commentary on the letter, he also asserts that *charismata* is bound up with one's external situation—that is, the distinct location and set of circumstances that one finds oneself in—while *klesis* pertains to the essential call. It is important for us to stress that one's distinct location in the world, whether understood as being purely contingent or imbued with some greater sense of meaning or purpose, is always the practical starting point for any form of life. Even in an age that elevates personal choice as one of the highest ideals, any person who has lived for a certain number of years will recognize that there are many things in life that are beyond the autonomous determination of a single person. It is by recognizing this fact of overarching heteronomy that we may be able to accept that our talents and defects, our capacities and limitations, our resources and poverty, and so on, are all in some way *charismata* or gifts. Given the choice, we may have not chosen some of these things for ourselves, yet, whether we like them or not, they are the raw materials with which our lives must be fashioned.

If it can be said that *charismata* provides forms for the living out of *klesis*, it is equally the case that *klesis* provides an underlying structure for the exercise of *charismata*. It is, of course, a truism that a gift can always be misused, because if something is truly handed over to the use of a person, that person has the power to utilize it for whatever she decides upon. Here is where the concept of *klesis* returns to perform its role, for the actions of a person who takes on a certain calling—that is, the exercise of her gifts—can always be measured by their congruence with the basic content of the essential vocation in question. Thus *charismata*, far from displacing or superseding *klesis*, in fact enters into a mutually supportive relationship with it.

'That's all very well and good,' one might say, 'but what does all this hullabaloo about *klesis* and *charismata* have to do beyond the sphere of Christianity, especially since we have deconstructed the secular conception of vocation?' What the word *charismata* signifies outside its ecclesiastical setting and the framework of Christian theology is, like the existence of multiplicity we discussed above, a banality. It is widely recognized that some of us are or have become better at certain things than other things, although it is also recognized that there is generally ample room for persons to venture into activities that they do not—on the surface and according to the usual criteria—seem to be 'fitted' to. We may call the first instance 'ability' and the second 'potential,' and they connect with Manuel Delanda's idea that it is not simply presently manifested *properties* that are real, but also latent *tendencies* and *capacities*.[125] The strength of the concept of *charismata*, however, lies in the fact that it, when paired with *klesis*, holds together the antinomical poles of pluralism and exclusivism, as alternatives to mere fragmentation and/or totalitarianism.[126]

Indeed, the best way of valuing the various interpretations and expressions of the academic vocation (see *figure 3*), is to (re)conceive them not as conflicting versions of *klesis* but rather as strangely complementary versions of *charismata*. To each of us has been distributed [*emerisen*] a singular *charisma*, which is far from static but constantly evolving and developing. It is by embodying this *charisma* that a person or group is able to engage in the overarching and underlying *klesis* of the university. Faced with a divisive ecclesial community in Corinth, Paul chose the metaphor of a body to illustrate the value of plurality:

> For the body is not one member, but many. If the foot shall say, Because I am not the hand, I am not of the body; is it therefore not of the body? And if the ear shall say, Because I am not the eye, I am not of the body; is it therefore not of the body? If the whole body were an eye, where were the hearing? If the whole were hearing, where were the smelling? ... And the eye cannot say unto the hand, I have no need of thee: nor again the head to the feet, I have no need of you. Nay, much more those members of the body, which seem to be more feeble, are necessary. (1 Cor. 12:14–17, 21–22, KJV)

Perhaps the greatest barrier towards such an understanding of the varied expressions of vocation in the university is the fact that many of us, if scratched hard enough, reveal (semi-)exclusivist tendencies below any surface pluralism. The metaphor of the body simply does not work if one considers another actor to be part of not the wider body one is a member of but rather another body. Here the spatial aspects of the triangle in *figure 3* are instructive, as often one may not be entirely sectarian in one's conceptualization of who is part of the same body as oneself, but will nevertheless delimit this body to a certain section of the triangle instead of embracing it in its entirety. This is a less dogmatic and more strategic form of exclusivism, because it believes that collaboration with those outside one's specific area can take place on the basis of certain congruent aims, but it remains exclusivist because clear boundaries are maintained. Thus it is conceivable that the proponents of the school of 'critique' may make common cause with those in the school of 'revolution,' the 'academic exceptionalism' school, or even those in the 'for the common good' school, but refuse to have anything to do with the 'it's just a job' school.

We must now return to the difficult question around which we have skirted: Can we formulate a 'baseline *klesis*' for the university, in the manner of the simple Christian pledge to follow Christ discussed in the preceding section? Even despite the manifest disagreements between the various ideal types of the university vocation, as well as the structural contingency of the alliances and divergences between these types we have just discussed, it is possible to say that if we retrace the variegated academic vocations to 'ground zero,' we will find an agreement upon Fish's description of the most basic mission of the university, namely to educate and advance knowledge. From this starting point, many denizens of higher education have set off in contrasting directions, which has led to inevitable differences on what educating and advancing knowledge means and involves, and what should be added unto these basic activities. Yet at the level of bare academic praxis there still exists this common ground. In the end, this is not something to be scoffed at, but rather valued as a possible basis for mutual recognition, if not appreciation between the various contesting sides. This is so despite the fact that the task of education within a social formation dominated by capitalist exchange is inextricably bound up with the production of the labour-power commodity, that is, willing workers with the right qualifications and skills.[127]

At this point it is necessary for me to pause the relatively impersonal form of argumentation being pursued and make a personal declaration and admission. In the previous chapters, I have followed a trajectory that can be said to be ultimately partial rather than disinterested. The critique of instrumentalism and idealism in the post-war university in chapters two and three, as well as the elucidation of the university-in-itself in chapter four, are latently grounded on the methodological presupposition that although bracketing all other viewpoints in order to focus the reader's attention on one particular perspective is possible in part, and indeed necessary, it is impossible to completely escape one's subjective position in the world and to engage in absolutely 'objective' reflection. With the partial exception of this chapter, largely hidden behind this book is an overarching view coloured by my own inclinations towards a 'feeling-centred' approach, that is, towards the bottom left corner of the triangle, with the closest of the five schools being, perhaps unsurprisingly, that of 'critique.' Therefore, transposing the alleged words of Martin Luther at the Diet of Worms into what we are here considering, I am left with no choice but to admit, 'Here I stand; I can do no other.'[128] For I am of course not completely exempt from the statement in chapter four that 'convinced proponents of one of the three perspectives ... carry their home terrain within them wherever they go and thus instinctively reframe everything they encounter in its terms.'

On the issue of exclusivism versus pluralism, my tendencies lean towards the latter, and so I am less of a 'convinced proponent of one of the three perspectives' than someone who recognizes his instinctive leanings and who wishes to moderate them through productive oscillation. Although I can attempt to minimize the influence of my partiality in the last instance, and briefly enter, for example, the world at the top of the triangle—where extreme instrumentalism reigns and everything is just a job—in order to grasp its underlying logic, it is nonetheless a difficult operation for me, one that I cannot presume to execute with complete precision or success. Having already critiqued the aspects of instrumentalism I find to be damaging, the follow-up question of whether there is anything to be redeemed from the wider sphere in which it arose, namely action-centricism, needs to be addressed. However, given my residual partiality, the best that I can do is to firstly assume, as a matter of methodology, that there is a contribution to be made from that section of the diagram, and then do all I can to discern what it may be. For what I am unable to fully present (much less represent), I can still posit in principle. That is to say, even though I may be personally disinclined towards a strongly instrumentalist perspective, and may struggle to articulate its merits, I am still convinced that the broader action-centric perspective that has brought about this instrumentalist approach has its place within the larger whole.

It is at this point that the dangers of an unreflective form of pluralism become apparent. It is all well and good to wish to include the action-centric perspective from which the rapacious instrumentalism documented in chapter two arose, but if this is done at the expense of critically assessing the impact of such an approach, then what we end up with is a form of insipid relativism, i.e. the sort of 'equivocating' that, as we have seen, Karatani rightly excoriates.[129] The underlying search for truth that drives exclusivism will be completely surrendered to an inclusivity-obsessed approach masquerading behind a mask of pluralism. Thus we would be unable to identify the misuses of *charismata* that we have already gestured towards above, because in the name of transcritical oscillation we will have suspended the equally pertinent task of measuring a particular expression of any of the three overarching perspectives according to the *klesis* of the university. True pluralism—that is, a careful grappling with plurality—does not say, 'anything goes,' but rather, 'despite our differences, let's work together for a common good.'

This leads us to a difficult question: How are we to identify when a particular *charisma* is being abused or expressed in a negative form? One way has already been mentioned, namely to examine whether the expression is in line with the core *klesis* of the university, which we have defined as to educate and advance knowledge. This is a *substantive* method of assessment. There is another, more *procedural* method, which takes as its focus the manner in which the *charisma* is being manifested. Although we have said that it is sometimes acceptable and even helpful for an exclusivist approach to be taken, when this is done in a way that not only denigrates all other perspectives but also seeks to marginalize or even destroy them, we have a strong indication that the *klesis* of the university is being lost to an out-of-control abuse of *charismata*. Indeed, the hegemonic instrumentalism presently regnant in much of the university qualifies as an instance of abuse from both substantive and procedural standpoints, for not only does it subordinate the baseline *klesis* of the university to non-educational externalist aims grounded on narrow economism, it also fails to recognize whatsoever the value of thought-centric and feeling-centric views and practices. Hence, it is not only a dominant framework, but can also be considered as an at least incipiently totalitarian one.

Furthermore, the incapacity of any of us to encompass the totality within a single frame of vision is simply a symptom of subjectivity and finitude. For to return once again to a previous argument, this time from chapter two, we cannot but accept Žižek's assertion that 'the trap to be avoided here, of course, is the naïve idea that one should keep in view the social totality.'[130] Adorno's captures this most succinctly when he writes that 'the whole is the false.'[131] This insight has also been expressed in terms more down-to-earth, and indeed more applied, by G.K. Chesterton, who in a piece entitled 'History Versus the Historians' argued as follows:

> No good modern historians are impartial. All modern historians are divided into two classes—those who tell half the truth, like Macaulay and Froude, and those who tell none of the truth, like Hallam and the Impartials. The angry historians see one side of the question. The calm historians see nothing at all, not even the question itself.[132]

Having said all this, in the conclusion of this book I will attempt to explore the practical contours of what it means to take a side and to 'tell half the truth,' or perhaps even less than half. On the level of analysis I am bounded by my own subjective limitations—here I take humble leave of the project of Kantian objectivity—yet on the level of meta-analysis, it is, I submit, possible to enquire into how analysis is by and large done. In other words, what is to be carried out is an investigation into *process* rather than *substance*. The central argument that I have put forward is that vocational expression is a form of truth-telling, and thus a singular and personal affair, but which on the intermediate level of particularity, intersects with certain categories explored in the preceding chapters and represented in the triangular diagram in *figure 3*; what we might inelegantly call the University Triangle. For from this confluence we have been able to sketch what is close to a taxonomy of life within the university, linked to the concept of vocation as conditioned by both *klesis* and *charismata*. The concept of *charismata* helps us to explore the varied responses to the question of 'how is it to be done?' where the divergent extrapolations of *klesis* beyond the baseline of education and research mean that the old Leninist question 'what is to be done?' is unable to be answered in a straightforward manner.[133]

Conclusion: Toward a Past-Future University

In the last section of chapter one, we explored the triadic discursive-practical structure of the university in terms of both the constitution of each element of the triad as well as, in outline, the relations between them. It was argued that each question arises through the bracketing or temporary suspension of the other two questions. This operation can be said to be the underlying cause of the inability of those who primarily employ one of the three perspectives to comprehend the standpoints of those who generally opt for either of the other two. Indeed, for some, the perspective they favour contracts their field of vision so acutely that they cannot conceive of any other valid view. This does not, of course, mean that they simply deny the existence of other perspectives, or that they never oscillate into viewing the university from them, but rather that these other perspectives are seen as deficient in 'value' or 'truth.' The terrain that they choose to fight from—instrumentalism, idealism, or community—easily becomes the only terrain that they admit as permissible for engagement.

However, this territorial analogy is imperfect in that it may mislead the reader into thinking that convinced proponents of one of the three perspectives refuse to venture from their home terrain. It is rather the case that they carry their home terrain within them wherever they go and thus automatically reframe everything they encounter in its terms. Hence, the idealist does not deny the need for practical decisions, but approaches them in a resolutely idealist fashion, such as with Kant's categorical imperative; likewise, the instrumentalist is able to converse about principles, but derives them from utilitarian calculations and empirical observations. Nevertheless, such one-sided manoeuvres are never without contradictions and incongruences, because as Karatani points out, 'when one seeks to explain everything from one and the same positionality, one is inexorably confronted by antinomy.'[134]

It is, of course, beyond the scope of this book to enquire deeply into how or why any person or group comes to prefer—or, indeed, have an orientation towards—one (or, at most, two) of the three perspectives in the triad. To carry out such an investigation adequately would require delving into spheres such as psychology and sociology that, while not unrelated to this present study, are nonetheless sufficiently distinct from it that any treatment of them would distract more than it would enlighten. After all, it is unnecessary to establish a link between a person's individual propensities towards specific modes of thought, feeling, and action and the substantive views that she puts forward. It is sufficient to identify the wider pattern of her engagement through an examination of the arguments made. Hence, the questions of how and why are bracketed even as we focus on what exactly this dynamic entails and what we could do in light of such understanding.[135]

Although the initial analogous triad upon which the conceptual triad of the British university has been elaborated in this book has been drawn from the philosophy of Kant, it is important to emphasize that Karatani himself identifies its recurrence in various theoretical triads since Kant, most prominently in Lacan's triptych of the Symbolic, the Imaginary and the Real, but also—albeit with less elaboration—in Marx and Nietzsche.[136] In his words: 'The fact that Kant's triadic concept is replaceable with different triads indicates that it forms a kind of structure that can be grasped transcendentally.'[137]

In the section titled 'The Architectonic of Pure Reason' in his First Critique, Kant argues that it is necessary to practise architectonics, or 'the art of constructing a system,' because 'without systematic unity, our knowledge cannot become science; it will be an aggregate, and not a system.'[138] Although in the preceding chapters my discussion of this triad has been grounded primarily upon Karatani's reading of Kant's architectonic, it should be recognized that Kant himself was not free from his own individual perspective, which can be categorized as an instance of thought-centric thought, as distinct from action-centric or feeling-centric thought. This partiality makes his conceptual triad or architectonic less 'universal,' scientific, or pure than he and his followers, past and present, might have believed.

In prosaic, everyday terms, each element in the conceptual triad is necessary because all of us have an approach to the three dimensions of life that it describes: firstly, how we interact with the outer world, that is, our day-to-day *doing*; secondly, how we engage with ideas as well as employ them to understand the world, that is, our mechanisms of *thinking*; and thirdly, how we deal with the unruly dimensions of life that escape both practical action and conceptual cognition, which is captured by terms such as affect, emotion, prehension, or simply *feeling*.

Here it is possible to identify a link, albeit not an entirely straightforward one, to the three Neoplatonic 'transcendentals' deriving from Antiquity but formally established during the Renaissance, namely, goodness, truth, and beauty.[139] These three transcendentals connect directly to Kant's three *Critiques*, which examined each in turn, beginning with truth, then goodness, and finally beauty. In an exchange in 2013 with Korean literary critic, Kim Uchang, Karatani carries out a concise genealogy of the three transcendentals as they have developed in competition with each other through the centuries, forming what he termed 'intellectual, ethical and sensible approaches.'[140] He points out that at different points in time and space, one (or sometimes two) of these three approaches have been regarded with greater favour. The sensible approach which approaches the world through beauty has generally been considered 'inferior,' but there have been times and places where it has become ascendent, such as Japan in the Heian period and with the Romanticism that emerged in the West in the wake of Kant.[141] In the Occident, Romanticism was followed by realism in literature, marking the return of truth and the intellectual approach to a central position, before Socialism, which was a secular form of morality, came onto the scene to indicate a new rise of the ethical approach.[142] The dynamics of these complex shifts between intellectual, ethical, and sensible stances constitute, in effect, the history of relations between humans and other beings and objects in the world, as well as within human societies.

At this point it is important to note the fuzziness of divisions between the approaches, particularly the intellectual and the ethical, especially when connecting them with the categories of thinking and acting. In Kant's system, for example, practical action is governed by the faculty of reason, and thus one's *acting* has to proceed through rational principles. On the other hand, the search for truth takes place for Kant within the domain of phenomena or sensible nature, and so one's *thinking* is far from divorced from the world. In other words, each approach presupposes and is sustained by the other. Just as a point of contrast, in a different system that privileges direct experience, the guiding thread of acting would not be reason but perhaps an embodied life force, and so under such a paradigm, ethics would be linked to something akin to libido.

Likewise, if one were to consider the sphere of the post-war British university one can see that the patent antagonism between instrumentalism and idealism masks their mutual contamination. For there is a sense in which a hidden residue of instrumentalism lies at the heart of the most vigorous forms of idealism, and vice versa. What this means is that there is, strictly speaking, no such thing as a 'pure' form of either perspective, but that each is penetrated by the other, resulting in the silent subsistence of undercover elements at the core of that which may appear at first to be unadulterated. That is to say, bracketing is an artificial operation involving ordering, rather than a simple 'accessing' of cleanly delineated spheres that are, as it were, already 'there.'

The semi-porousness of the borders between the domains does not override the fact that particular philosophies tend to privilege one of them. For instance, a thought-centric system such as Kant's subsumes the other two domains of action and feeling under the rubric of thinking. Although Karatani does not himself make this point—and it is uncertain that he would agree with it, given his own secondary thinking-centred sympathies that aligns partially with Kant's—he nonetheless recognizes that Kant's critique reshaped what was meant by scientific thought, morality, and the arts.[143] In his words, 'before and after Kant the categorization of scientific thoughts, moralities and the arts was totally altered.'[144]

It can, for instance, be seen that Kant's ethical prescriptions for acting in the world—in his own words, his practical *reason*—are based not upon a consideration of concrete reality, which for Kant is only accessible to humans in the mediated form of phenomena, given that things-in-themselves are obscured from human perception, but rather upon the pure principles derived through the faculty of reason, which deals not with the sensible or *nature* but rather the suprasensible (or supersensible).[145] The question, 'How are we to act?' receives the response, 'In accordance to the maxims which your exercise of reason has led you to legislate for yourself, and if you wish to be moral—that is, truly free from your tempestuous desires—according to only the maxims which you are able to will to be universal laws.'

Here it should also be noted that Kant's thought-centric architectonic has a strongly pseudo-juridical flavour, as is obvious from the distinctly legal terminology that he constantly employs.[146] The cognitive faculties of reason, understanding, and judgment are *law-givers* for the faculties of the soul, namely desire, knowledge, and feeling.[147] Each faculty in the first triad has its corresponding *jurisdiction* in the second triad.[148] Kant's injunction to follow the exercise of reason in one's moral conduct extends also to his political theory. In the words of the postcolonial theorist and anthropologist Talal Asad: 'It was Kant who replaced the model of the "republic of letters" with another model: the "court of reason."'[149] Against the focus of the republic of letters upon the egalitarian mental jousting between ideas and their progenitors, Kant's court of reason posited the possibility and indeed superiority of rational critique—that is to say, the elevation of a philosophical science over literary rhetoric.[150] It could even be said, borrowing a distinction that Cornel West invokes in contrasting Plato and American pragmatism, that this results in the return of 'objective' *epistēmē* to triumph over 'subjective' *doxa*.[151]

Indeed, the rational law-giver is the centre of Kantian political life. As Asad puts it, 'in Kant's political philosophy it is *law*, not critique, that ends the chaos of metaphysics and holds the corrosive effects of skepticism in check. And its concern is no longer with mundane life but with epistemology,' that is, political action is not grounded upon immediate experience but rather with the true.[152]

Having examined Kant's *modus operandi* in relation to ethics, it is important for me to briefly examine Kant's thought-centric approach to the question of aesthetics, so the effects of his particular perspective in this sphere might be seen.[153] It has been shown that Kant's architectonic necessitates a turn away in the sphere of practical action from empirical experience to the categorical imperative—the maxim that can be willed as a universal law—as the bearer of objective morality. In the aesthetic component of his triadic system is a similar concern for the universal as the guarantor of an exercise of human rationality so that aesthetic judgement may be designated as a higher human faculty, that is, together with understanding and reason and above that of sensibility. In his 'Analytic of the Beautiful,' it is clear Kant appreciates that empirical agreement by everyone upon matters of taste—that is, *general* agreement—is impossible. Nevertheless, he posits that an instance of proper exercise of taste is *universal*, in that it demands the assent of all to its judgement. In his own words:

> The judgement of taste itself does not *postulate* the agreement of everyone (for it is only competent for a logically universal judgement to do this, in that it is able to bring forward reasons); it only *imputes* this agreement to everyone, as an instance of the rule in respect of which it looks for confirmation, not from concepts, but from the concurrence of others. The universal voice is, therefore, only an idea—resting upon grounds the investigation of which is here postponed.[154]

As Karatani points out with regard to the original German, '*postulieren* [i.e. to postulate] means to assume as self-evident, while *ansinnen* [i.e. to impute] means to make an (unreasonable) request or demand.'[155] Or as Michael Wayne puts it: 'We accord the aesthetic judgment a certain universal validity *as if* it were a logical objective judgment, when in fact it is merely a subjective one, but one which [nonetheless] escapes private and individualistic subjectivity.'[156] This elegant (if somewhat questionable) operation ensures that within the Kantian system, judgements of taste are lifted to an idealistic, 'rational' and universal plane, despite their manifest difference from what other theoretical systems may consider as rationality.

In summary, it can be said that in order to fully benefit from Kant's architectonic, it is important to recognize its limits and limitations, particularly its bias towards reason or thinking, which leads to the recasting of both the spheres of acting and feeling within a rational mould. Nevertheless, the great strength of Kant's system is its underlying drive towards comprehensiveness and internal coherence. Although it is ultimately (and indeed inevitably) unable to cut itself off completely from its thought-centricism, its valiant persistence according to the 'will to architecture'—a term used by Karatani to denote 'the will to construct an edifice of knowledge on a solid foundation' that he considers the 'foundation of Western thought'—makes it one of the deepest explorations of the conceptual triad within the Occidental canon.[157]

Finally, it must be noted that to point out Kant's overemphasis on reason is not to abandon reason itself *in toto*. Karatani is right to argue that 'as Kant has shown, the critique of reason, or the critique of its grounding that is caused by the constitutive use of reason, cannot be made but by reason.'[158] Here some insight may be gained from the work of the cultural historian Morris Berman, whose book *Wandering God* criticizes what he calls the 'dominant tradition' in the West, a tradition that privileges logic and form over process, matter, and paradox.[159] However, discussing the evolution of Wittgenstein's philosophy, which Berman perceives as moving from a logic-centred system with some concessions to process in the early years to one embracing paradox, he argues that, even in Wittgenstein's later work, the philosopher 'never completely left the [dominant tradition] because it is this form of intellectual transcendence that makes any rational discourse and analysis ... possible,' including Berman's own book.[160] Hence, what was begun in chapter four and followed through until this point can be regarded as a contribution to the Kantian exploration of 'the boundaries or limits of human subjective faculties,'[161] not ignoring the more severe critiques of rationalism arising from traditions such as Romanticism, postmodernism, and post-structuralism, but weighing them up in light of the present moment and specific context.

A sceptic, especially one who is wary of highly theoretical investigations may ask at this point: Does all of this really help us understand the university? Has all the sound and fury of this book's historical-philosophical explorations truly led us to a greater grasp of how we are to intervene practically in our current conjuncture? In response to these queries, I would like to pose a different question: Do the contents of this book have a contribution to make to the study of not just the British university in the post-war period, but indeed the totality of human experience? This may seem to be a grandiose question, and so I pose it with a degree of reserve but also with sincerity.

Although I have been chiefly concerned with the case of higher education in Britain after the Second World War, the arguments put forward with regard to the triadic structure of life in the university can, I believe, be generalized and deployed in almost any other sphere of human existence. I have been led to this conviction not by my own design but seemingly, as it were, by accident. I began this research project to understand the British university in which I found myself in that moment, but I ended up with a consciousness of the wider sweep of the history of higher education in the British Isles. I started out with no pretensions toward comprehending anything remotely like a totality—not even that of the university—and indeed travelled along such a methodological path for a while with the aid of Foucault and other prophets of postmodern fragmentation. Along the way, I found inspiration in Karatani's fresh and daring formulations.

There is much in Foucault's method and thought that I believe is of its time and place (as well as, although he would vehemently deny it, personality), but I am still haunted by his statement in a 1982 interview that

> the main interest in life and work is to become someone else that you were not in the beginning. If you knew when you began a book what you would say at the end, do you think that you would have the courage to write it? What is true for writing and for a love relationship is true also for life. The game is worthwhile insofar as we don't know what will be the end.[162]

Foucault's likening of writing to love is particularly intriguing, for even if one is an adherent to the traditional formulation of 'till death do us part,' the wedded couple never knows exactly how, when, and to whom first death will come. Likewise, in the task of writing, the end of the undertaking is guaranteed, but its circumstances are shrouded in great mystery, even when we sense we are close to its arrival.

When starting this research, I had—rather overambitiously—intended it to be a manifesto of sorts, to contribute to the development of a very different sort of higher education than the one I saw as crumbling into a soulless oblivion. As time passed, I began to realize that my investigations were leading in the direction of a text that would be far from the last word on the situation at hand, and even further from being a spark for an activist movement of sorts. Instead, I have come to believe that what this book offers is a structural framework for diagnosing the situation that the university is presently in, in order that we who are concerned for its well-being might begin to discern a way out of the dangers looming on the horizon.

Though some of my extrapolations and applications may be contested, I am confident that the conceptual triad, in and beyond Kant and Karatani, is a tool that can lead to great insights and openings for fruitful interventions. Some of these interventions may seem completely novel, but historical consciousness may lead us to comprehend the words of the Catholic self-taught radical intellectual Peter Maurin, who argued that a movement that 'aims to create a new society within the shell of the old with the philosophy of the new' has to realize that this philosophy may not be 'a new philosophy but a very old philosophy, a philosophy so old that it looks like new.'[163] If Karatani is right, the re-emergence of a 'very old philosophy' would be none other than the return of the repressed 'Mode U,' the communism of the nomadic band before fixed settlement that has only transiently reared its head in the ages since in the form of the 'Mode D' of universal religions and similar radical movements. To properly examine this question in the sphere of the university would require another very different book. It is my great hope that it will be written by someone someday. If what I have written helps to lay a foundation for such a study, then I will have achieved the aim I did *not* start with, but only discovered along the way.

Appendix A

On the Reception of Karatani's Writings in the Anglophone World

The initial discovery of Karatani's work in the English-speaking world focused on his literary and cultural criticism, which although distinctively grounded in theory and history, nevertheless took as its 'main subject' works of literature and aspects of Japanese culture. It was thus unsurprising that his first monograph to be translated into English was *The Origins of Modern Japanese Literature*, with translation work beginning in the late 1980s and the book appearing in print in 1993.[1] Subsequently, his involvement in the ten-year series of 'Any' conferences on architecture from 1991 to 2000 introduced him to scholars and practitioners in the field and those working more generally with issues of space. Karatani participated in six of the ten conferences, together with thinkers such as Jacques Derrida, Saskia Sassen, and David Harvey as well as architects such as Rem Koolhas, Arata Isozaki, and Peter Eisenman.[2] This contributed directly to the translation and publication of *Architecture as Metaphor: Language, Number, Money* in 1995.[3]

The appearance of *Transcritique: On Kant and Marx* in 2003 expanded the breadth of Karatani's readership.[4] This astonishing work of philosophy, politics, and political economy has become the most widely known of his books, not least of all through Slavoj Žižek's appropriation of his conceptualization of the Kantian parallax in his book *The Parallax View*.[5] Thus, *Transcritique*, broadly speaking, marks a turn in the reception of Karatani's work from being concentrated in the circles of literary and cultural studies to spilling over into various disciplines involving politics and philosophy. The fact that the publication of *Transcritique* in Japan followed shortly after Karatani's foray into the politics of social movements as one of the co-founders and primary theoreticians of the New Associationist Movement (NAM) certainly contributed to this turn as well.[6] The subsequent publications in English of *History and Repetition* in 2012, *The Structure of World History* in 2014, as well as *Nation and Aesthetics* and *Isonomia and the*

Origins of Philosophy in 2017, alongside a number of journal articles in a similar vein have contributed to the continuation of this trend.[7]

Karatani himself has described a break between his work in the 1970s and 1980s (which is, it should be noted, the period in which he wrote *The Origins of Modern Japanese Literature* and *Architecture as Metaphor*, although they appeared in English in the 1990s) and that of the 1990s and 2000s.[8] Still, to borrow a distinction made by Eduardo Mendieta in his consideration of developments in the oeuvres of Foucault and Habermas, it is argued that Karatani's shift was not one of 'general orientation' but merely rather 'how that orientation, or philosophical attitude, [has been] directed to a set of problems.'[9] In other words, the central threads of his work have been more or less consistent, even as they have been deployed in different ways depending on the context. Jonathan E. Abel also makes a similar case for reading Karatani in a spirit of continuity rather than rupture in his preface to the English translation of *Nation and Aesthetics*.[10]

From *Transcritique* onwards, it can be said that the foremost concept in Karatani's work has been that of the 'mode of exchange,' which he develops in order to analyze contexts from our political present (as he does in the final chapter of *Transcritique*) to those as maddeningly ambitious as the whole sweep of recorded human history (as he attempts in *The Structure of World History*). From this concept comes, for example, his diagnosis of the hegemonic trinity of Capital-Nation-State, formed from the modern amalgamation of three forms of exchange that he refers to as reciprocity (Mode A), plunder-redistribution (Mode B) and commodity exchange (Mode C), with Mode C being the dominant partner. Alongside this diagnosis also comes a suggested 'cure' to the problems that we face under the system of Capital-Nation-State, namely the possibilities of going beyond it through a fourth mode of exchange, the elusive Mode D, which he sometimes terms association or simply X.

Hence, in the view of commentators such as Yamoi Pham, the most fertile areas of Karatani's work for those who wish to apply his ideas appears to be 'his unique approach to world history' through the prism of the modes of exchange, which can be extended through 'further empirical studies' and developing 'a more concrete vision of Mode D by exercising our sociological imagination.'[11] Although I am in agreement with Pham with regard to the significant potential of such directions of research, I have chosen to focus, as I explain in this book's introduction, on his historical-philosophical methodology of transcendental retrospection as well as his work on the Kantian conceptual triad.

With regard to the former, it is instructive to note that Karatani's approach to history and theory bears not a few traces of the idiosyncratic iconoclasm with regard to disciplinary boundaries for which he is well known. His method, I venture to suggest, arises from his—perhaps deliberate—location at the margins of the disciplines that he finds himself categorized under. Although he first came to distinction as a literary critic, his work, as Sabu Kohso has observed, did not focus on the conventional 'judg[ing] the value of oeuvres in a specific genre' but rather 'engag[ed] "transcendentally" in the mechanisms of discursive historicity, penetrating a multitude of domains.'[12] In his introduction to *Architecture as Metaphor*, Arata Isozaki listed some of the 'domains' traversed by Karatani in the book as including 'philosophy, logic, political economy, cultural anthropology, sociology and urban studies.'[13] But perhaps one of the best statements of his (at least partial) disciplinary 'homelessness' can be found in his final paper to the series of Any conferences, where he stated, rather poignantly:

> These conferences have long been considered a place of interaction between architects and philosophers. However, I do not really see myself as a philosopher, and I have no interest in discussing architecture theoretically. With a couple of exceptions, I have attended all the Any meetings over the past ten years, but who then have I been at these conferences? In effect, I have been a thing-in-itself as other. That is to say, I have not shared the same language with most of the other participants, nor did I try to do so. I refused. As a consequence, I was rejected. At Any, I have been a thing-in-itself but not a phenomenon. Indeed, many people were even unaware of my presence. Perhaps the organizers hoped that I would fulfill just such a function. But for me, this is not a pleasant position to be in. And so, in many ways, it comes as a relief to me that this role is finally over.[14]

Ever a unique contributor to any academic or political endeavour, even if not always fully appreciated by those who encounter his work, Karatani continues to be one of Japan's most novel theoreticians on the international scene. It is hoped that this book provides proof that his ideas and method are applicable to spheres far from the specific topics that he has concerned himself.

Appendix B

Foucault's Genealogy and Karatani's Transcendental Retrospection Compared

In this appendix we shall compare the historical-philosophical methodology developed by Michel Foucault, famously known as genealogy, with the partially resonant yet distinct approach of Kojin Karatani, which he has termed 'transcendental retrospection.' The argument that will be advanced is that Karatani's method is preferable for an investigation such as the one conducted in this book. While it may seem odd to devote space to a methodological approach deemed inadequate for one's purposes, given the relative fame—or notoriety—of Foucault's genealogical method, it is nonetheless worthwhile for us to use it as a foil to introduce Karatani's method of transcendental retrospection. Indeed, despite some areas of overlap and affinity, the former provides a revealing contrast to the latter procedure that many in the English-speaking world are unfamiliar with.

Attempting to sketch in some detail the concept of genealogy as it was enunciated and practised by Michel Foucault is not a straightforward task. In his most detailed discussion of his approach to it—namely in the essay 'Nietzsche, Genealogy, History'—Foucault speaks of genealogy in a way not too dissimilar to how Buddhist scriptures traditionally speak of the concept of nirvana, that is to say, in Wendy Brown's words, by elaborating not what it is but rather 'what it defines itself against.'[1]

In the article, Foucault distinguishes genealogy from conventions of progressive historiography and metaphysics by taking a route Brown sees as characteristic of genealogical practice itself in its 'embattled "emergence" [that] must fight for place, and more specifically, must displace other conventions of history in order to prevail.'[2] This method of constant opposition to progressive historiography and metaphysics—in a style reminiscent of the fictional method of 'calculatus eliminatus'[3]—leads to the recognition that both are 'implicated in the other,' and hence genealogy enables the development of a 'philosophically self-conscious historiography' and a 'historically self-conscious philosophy.'[4] Put simply, genealogy sets out to help one realize the mutual entanglement of both history and philosophy, and open up the way to fresh, ignored, or barely trod paths.

Karatani's writings are premised on a similar assumption that the history of a particular object of study is illuminated most brightly using the tools which philosophical and theoretical reflection provides us with. Although he first came to prominence in Japan as a literary critic rather than a historian or philosopher per se, Karatani's work has always been characterized by a keen attention to historical and philosophical elements. For example his celebrated monograph, *Origins of Modern Japanese Literature*, which was first published in book form in 1980, consists of a series of essays examining the formation of a constellation of interconnected concepts—including interiority, sickness, the child, and the confessional mindset—which he argues did not exist in the Japanese psyche before the third decade of the Meiji era (1868–1912) but were crucial in the emergence of what is considered modern Japanese literature.[5]

Despite his broad academic interests, Karatani was still considered during the first half of his career as engaging in 'criticism' (*hihyo*) rather than philosophy or critique (*hihan*).[6] However, sometime in the 1990s, in part due to a choice to shift away from analyzing works of literature and instead deal more directly with philosophy and society, Karatani began to be described as a 'philosopher.' In his preface to the English translation of Karatani's *Nation and Aesthetics*, Jonathan E. Abel quotes a 2004 interview with Sekii Mitsuo in which Karatani says: 'When I was called a philosopher abroad at first it made me extremely uncomfortable; I even argued against it for a while, but from that point I began to think, well, if people call me that, maybe it's alright.'[7] Abel comments on this, opining that Karatani's 'eventual coming to terms with the title may well reflect an acceptance that he was finally being labeled in a way that was more accurate to the work he had been seeing himself as doing for a long time.'[8]

This ambiguity in how to best characterize Karatani's work and the correct label to assign to him is another thing that he shares with Foucault, whose distinctly heterodox historical-philosophical writings led to debates as to whether he should be considered a historian, a philosopher, or something else entirely.[9] These noticeable affinities between these two thinkers should not lead us to neglect the more subtle differences between their respective methods and theoretical inclinations. As we shall see, Karatani's methodology, which he has called 'transcendental retrospection,' is itself a unique species of critical history-cum-philosophy, even if it shares with Foucault's genealogy some genetic kinship in the figures of Kant and Nietzsche.

The Starting Point and the Purpose

Wendy Brown states in *Politics Out of History* that the 'starting point [and] object' of Foucauldian genealogy is the present.[10] This is supported by numerous statements Foucault made throughout the history of his work, outlined by Clare O'Farrell.[11] As early as 1967 he stated that 'I seek to diagnose, to carry out a diagnosis of the present. To say what we are today and what it means, today, to say what we do say.'[12] A decade later in *Discipline and Punish* he declared he was 'writing the history of the present.'[13] And as late as 1983 he said in an interview: 'The question I start off with is: What are we and what are we today? What is this instant that is ours? Therefore, if you like, it is a history that starts off from this present day actuality.'[14]

However, the relationship between the past and the present in a genealogical study is a complex, perhaps almost counter-intuitive one. The 'duty' of genealogy, writes Foucault, is 'not to demonstrate that the past actively exists in the present, that it continues secretly to animate the present.'[15] And this is because, for Foucault, there is no 'predetermined form to all [the present's] vicissitudes' and hence it is impossible to 'pretend to go back in time to restore an unbroken continuity that operates beyond the dispersion of forgotten things.'[16]

So, it seems clear that, for Foucault, the present cannot be analyzed by tracing an uninterrupted line from the past that leads into where we are today. In other words, the present cannot be subordinated to the past, and is not overshadowed, much less dominated, by it. However, he counsels us to avoid making the reverse assumption, that is, to unduly privilege the present and view the past through the lens of our time. After all, in *Discipline and Punish*, he distinguishes 'writing a history of the present' from 'writing a history of the past in terms of the present.'[17] In a 2008 article, Karatani also points out how the latter mistake is all too easily made, and approves of an argument he attributes to Marx, i.e. that 'concepts of historical "origins" are shaped by a projection of the present onto the ancient.'[18] According to Karatani:

> Marx stressed that commodity exchange began between communities. This was an explicit criticism of Adam Smith, who assumed that commodity exchange began between individuals. Marx asserted that such a view was a projection of the modern capitalist economy onto

APPENDIX B   165

previous social formations, a projection that blinds us to the historicity of the capitalist economy.[19]

It can be said that the starting point for genealogy is a feeling of severe discomfort, even horrendous disgust at a present state of affairs. Andre Glucksmann has offered an interpretation of the ethic of Foucault's work as centred around a notion of 'the intolerable.'[20] The choice faced by someone wishing to take this path, he writes, is not between the two Weberian ethical poles of responsibility and conviction, but rather 'between, on the one hand, a morality of extreme urgency which analyzes the cases of what is intolerable and, on the other, a kind of edifying, fine-thinking thought or morality aiming to resolve all problems at once and for the eternity of ages.'[21]

It can be argued that Karatani's writings have also been initiated by a keen attention to the urgent pressures that he identified in the particular extended moments in which these research projects were conceived. For example, he has repeatedly attributed his turn in the 1990s to studying Kant and adopting a more affirmative philosophical-political stance to the collapse of the Communist Bloc that began with the fall of the Berlin Wall. In *Transcritique* he writes:

> Up until the climate change of 1989, I also despised all ideas of possible futures. I believed that the struggle against capitalism and the state would be possible without ideas of a future, and that we should only sustain the struggle endlessly in response to each contradiction arising from a real situation. The collapse of the socialist bloc in 1989 compelled me to change my stance. ... I realized that my critical stance had been paradoxically relying on [the] being [of Marxist states and communist parties]. I came to feel that I had to state something positive. It was at this conjuncture that I began to confront Kant.[22]

It was his reading of what was called for in the moment then-present that was the starting point of his 'transcritical' reading of Marx and Kant. In responding to what he calls an 'urgent need,' Karatani then embarked on an even more ambitious research endeavour, the most succulent fruit of which is *The Structure of World History*, an analysis of the entire sweep of human history through the lens of what he calls the four 'modes of exchange.'[23]

O'Farrell has argued that any Foucauldian attempt to write a 'history of the present' is 'not simply a diagnosis, [but] also an intervention.'[24] Such an intervention gazes into the past, but its focus is to open up avenues in the present in which change becomes possible. Nevertheless, as wonderful as such an interventional procedure sounds for the scholar-activist, what Karatani's transcendental retrospection allows us to see better is that diagnostic operations cannot be avoided, for without them one will crash into seemingly invisible, but real 'walls' that lie in the world. These are not gnostic elements of the past that secretly steer the present, an obsessive understanding Foucault rightly warns us about. They are rather structural patterns which, once formed or constructed, have a tendency to persist, and which can be identified through careful enquiry. However, the labour of diagnosis is merely the beginning, because without a complementary orientation towards possible interventions, the former risks becoming mere archival or analytical work.

On Origins

Before we can proceed, we have to be clear about what it is that a historical study such as the one carried out in this book is aiming for. Are we, for instance, attempting to locate and eludicate the 'origins' of our present malaise? Genealogy is commonly linked to the idea of the rejection of origins, or to be more precise, the rejection of the exaltation of the origin as the site where the multilayered mire of history becomes as clear as the source of a stream. Nietzsche and Foucault obviously do not deny the fact that an institution (e.g. one linked to morality) or a practice (e.g. incarceration) came from somewhere. What they clearly distance themselves from is the search for an *origin* as the key to understanding such an institution or practice. As Foucault writes, quoting Nietzsche's words in *The Wanderer and His Shadow*: 'The lofty origin is no more than "a metaphysical extension which arises from the belief that things are most precious and essential at the moment of birth."'[25]

It is this idea that there is an actual point of emergence that where there lies a pure, untainted ideal with which all subsequent discussion of a practice must be coloured that is disputed. In the words of Foucault, genealogy 'rejects the meta-historical deployment of ideal significations and indefinite teleologies. It opposes itself to the search for "origins."'[26] In a lecture delivered two years later, Foucault speaks about the distinction Nietzsche draws between 'origin' (*Ursprung*) and 'invention' (*Erfindung*), saying that for Nietzsche, there is no *Ursprung*, no origin of things such as religion, poetry, or the ideal but only their *Erfindung*, their invention.[27]

Karatani makes a similar argument in relation to the apparent 'discovery' of 'landscape' in Japanese literature:

> We might say that 'landscape' was not so much *discovered* within the epistemological *inversion* concentrated in *genbun itchi* as it was invented. In this book I used the term 'discovery of landscape' to connote the inversion whereby something which had never existed before came to be seen as self-evident, as an existence which in fact preceded the inversion.'[28]

In other words, for Karatani, the notion of 'discovery' confuses the history of a particular thing and is likely to result in a faulty genealogy. Therefore, Karatani's use of the word 'origin' should not be taken to mean an embrace of the obsession with origins that Foucault critiques, but rather a problematization of the term. Brett de Bary notes in her introduction to his *Origins of Modern Japanese Literature* that '[Karatani] wrote in the afterword to the first edition of his book, each of the words of its title, "the words 'Japanese,' 'modern,' 'literature,' and especially 'origins,' should in fact be bracketed."'[29]

This insight may admittedly seem rather banal when applied to the subject matter at hand—'of course the post-war British university was invented,' one might say. 'Of course it does not have a non-material origin. There is no doubt about this fact in the first place, unlike with, say, a particular religious tradition, with its complicated, mythically-and-metaphysically-bound history.' The point, however, is not so much to argue for a material invention over a metaphysical origin, but to recognize that—to repeat what has been stated above—there is no 'unbroken continuity that operates beyond the dispersion of forgotten things.'[30] To return to Bologna in 1088, or to the motto *universitas magistorum et scholarium,* is a quest that will teach us very little if we are hunting for a pure line of descent.[31]

The University: A Universal?

What is this university?' 'The university' is a 'universal'—that is, an entity that is said to be present in various particular things; in this case, all the discrete universities in the world or in a particular region, such as the 'British university.' Other examples of universals include 'the state,' 'the people,' and 'capitalism.' In his 1978–9 lecture series at the Collège de France entitled *The Birth of Biopolitics*, Foucault proposes a bold methodological starting point for his lectures: 'Let's suppose that universals do not exist.'[32] A person wishing to follow Foucault's radical gesture would have to take the university not as a 'thing' existent in its own right, but rather as an 'effect' that is constituted or composed of 'phenomena of coagulation, support, reciprocal reinforcement, cohesion, and integration.'[33] Viewed in this manner, it can also be apprehended as a 'social relationship,' as the German anarchist theorist Gustav Landauer argued with regard to another composed effect commonly deemed an institution—that is, the state.[34] Foucault himself describes the 'state effect' as the result of 'a thousand diverse processes';[35] in other words, it is the cumulative, dynamic and ongoing outcome of a multitude of relations, rather than an organized and organizing force in itself.

Foucault's dismissive attitude towards the state as an object of enquiry and critique can be linked to his critical dialogue with Louis Althusser with regard to the latter's writings on ideology. In his famous mature text, 'Ideology and Ideological State Apparatuses (Notes toward an Investigation),' Althusser locates ideology *not* in the traditional sphere of ideas or human consciousness—such conceptions being premised upon the ancient dichotomy of soul and body, ideal and material—but rather in what he called Ideological State Apparatuses (ISAs), which are part of the very materiality of the state. For example, he writes that 'an ideology always exists in an apparatus, and its practice, or practices. This existence is material.'[36] To be sure, Althusser in his formulation of the notion of ISAs broadened the boundaries of the state to include other (material) spheres such as 'the religious ISA (the system of the different churches), the educational ISA (the system of the different public and private "schools"), [and] the family ISA,' thus preserving the state as a central concept for critical analysis.[37]

Although Foucault is commonly—and correctly—seen as taking a view different to that of Althusser's, Warren Montag has insightfully observed that the former's formulation of the technologies of power, which he called the 'disciplines' in *Discipline and Punish*, can be seen as an extension of Althusser's attempt to get away from the ideality of ideology in order to place it upon a more materialist foundation, rather than as a diametrically opposed project.[38] The radical thrust of Foucault's work in that text, Montag says, is in

> refus[ing] to regard the histories of psychiatry, medicine, or criminology apart from their practical and institutional forms, namely, the asylum, the hospital, and the prison, the forms of the ordering and distribution of bodies in space in which these knowledges participate, the position that they, in their material incarnations, occupy in a field of conflicting social forces.[39]

In this insistence upon the preeminence of the material technologies of the body over disembodied ideals, Foucault joins with rather than departs from Althusser. Where they do part ways is in Foucault's aforementioned jettisoning of 'the state' as a productive concept, preferring instead to speak of 'the state effect.'[40] Thus, a genealogical excavation of the post-war British university, if it desires to be consistent in its methodological foundation in Foucault, would be required to abandon 'the university' as an object of critique and look instead at something akin to 'the university effect.'

Karatani, despite his earlier formation in the worlds of poststructuralism and previous reputation as a figure of twentieth-century Japanese postmodernism, has in his recent work manifestly gone far beyond Foucault's refusal to theorize the state. Indeed, he has attempted to explain the origins and continued functioning of the state in his formulation of 'mode of exchange B,' which he says is grounded upon the dynamic of 'plunder-redistribution.'[41] The present book follows Karatani's implicit gesture in declining Foucault's 'nominalist method in history,'[42] which would require its adherents to speak only of 'the university effect' or, at least, substitute the latter understanding for a more realist understanding of the university as a universal, thus retaining the term 'the university' but dramatically modifying its meaning in a nominalist fashion. Rather than dismissing 'the university' as an overly realist abstraction that distracts, this book understands its functioning through an analysis of the dynamics of the triadic structure of the post-war British university.

The Totality of the University

Perhaps the strongest point of divergence between Foucault's genealogy and Karatani's recent work is their stance on thinking or grasping the totality. In a 1978 interview with Colin Gordon and Paul Patton, Foucault stated his position baldly, '[A]ll that I do is partial, it has no vocation to totality.'[43] A classic example of his resolutely non-totalizing orientation can be found in his analysis of the discourse of 'general war' in *Society Must be Defended*, where he declares:

> It is true that this discourse about the general war, this discourse that tries to interpret the war beneath peace, is indeed an attempt to describe the battle as a whole and to reconstruct the general course of the war. But that does not make it a totalizing or neutral discourse; it is always a perspectival discourse. *It is interested in the totality only to the extent*

that it can see it in one-sided terms, distort it and see it from its own point of view.[44]

Although some of Foucault's critics, such as Jürgen Habermas, either impliedly or explicitly argued that such an embrace of partiality was an irresponsible celebration of fragmentation and relativism, it is possible for us who have the benefit of nearly thirty-five years of hindsight since the death of the maverick French thinker to value both sides of this debate. On the one hand, Foucault's attention to 'local struggles' by adopting the approach of what he called a 'specific' intellectual, rather than the more traditional 'universal' intellectual, was a courageous attempt to get away from the latter's positioning of herself as 'master of truth and justice' and obtain a more fine-grained perspective on the matters his studies enquired into.[45] Also, there is some truth in the claims of the broader post-structuralist tendency, with which Foucault's work can be associated, that 'the search for unity entails a limitation of discourse within a predefined range of possibilities, a range defined by the supposed real nature of the totality to be discovered,' which can imply 'totalitarianism[,] in that thought is directed along a single channel where differences and oppositional elements are suppressed.'[46] However, it can be contended that this twentieth-century critique of totality has led us to a theoretical dead end, where the perpetual fear of straying into totalitarian patterns of thought has constrained our political imaginations, and by extension hindered our political praxis. Karatani, having himself passed through the crucible of post-structuralist thought in his work in the 1970s and 1980s, was able to free himself from its limitations when he recognized that such a philosophical orientation had outlived its usefulness. One central way in which the aversion towards totality took form was in the disavowal of thinking about the future. As Karatani explained in the passage already quoted above, it was the demise of Soviet communism that awakened him to the renewed importance of positive proposals in politics and philosophy.

Hence, Karatani goes on to say, a few pages later in the same book: 'Beginning in the 1990s, my stance, if not my thinking itself, changed fundamentally. I came to believe that theory should not remain in the critical scrutiny of the status quo but should propose something positive to change the reality.'[47] This statement is a clear break from the attitude of 'critique' pervading many circles of the intellectual left since the 1960s, an orientation that majored in opposition but often shied away from positive proposition. Foucault is considered, even by many of his followers, to be an 'oppositional thinker' par excellence, and although it would be wrong to imply that his work is devoid of affirmative proposals, any occasions of the latter tend to be on the scale of 'micropolitics' which he favoured rather than the ambitious 'macro-politics' of intellectual traditions such as Marxism which he constantly distanced himself from.[48] It is perhaps instructive that while Karatani's was heavily involved in the formation of the New Associationist Movement (NAM) in Japan, which had aspirations to become a rallying point for national and international 'counteractions' against the forces of what he termed 'Capital-Nation-State,' Foucault's signature project was the far more micropolitical *Le Groupe d'information sur les prisons* (GIP), which took up the task of disseminating information about the French prison system to the public.

Kanishka Goonewardena has pointed out that *The Structure of World History* is notable for its 'production of a new concept of history, by way of *a new concept of totality* based on the trialectic of capital, nation and state.'[49] An examination of the current state of the world, in which opposing religious and political fundamentalisms have been clashing over the past two decades, may lead some to believe that such a return to thinking the totality is long overdue. It takes great courage for a thinker to break out of a preexisting postmodern or post-structuralist mindset. Karatani's radical act of leaving behind the detached sphere of critique and entering the far more dangerous realm of philosophical thinking which, in its endeavour to grasp the bigger picture, tends inexorably towards activism is an example of the boldness that, I believe, is required for us to face our current historical conjuncture. In this book I have tried to follow his lead.

Appendix C

The Structure of the Book

The structure of this book, visually represented by *figure 4*, involves the coming together of two triads, namely the 'university triad' and the 'epistemic triad.' The former triad is outlined in this book's introduction and then expanded upon in the chapters that follow it. The epistemic triad, however, lies beneath the surface of the book, as a hidden but crucial foundation.

The order in which the university triad is deployed is largely a result of the external constraints of the historical narrative, moving from instrumentalism to idealism, then to community. The order in which the epistemic triad is deployed, on the other hand, is related to the structure of argumentation chosen, thus the book moves from determining what is *true*, to what is *timely* and *appropriate*, and finally to what is *authentic*. What is consistent in both cases is that 'objective' or external issues are addressed before 'subjective' or internal ones. It is important to emphasize that each element in the university triad can be subjected to all three forms of enquiry in the epistemic triad. The specific combinations of infrastructural questions and superstructural perspectives occurring in each chapter of the present book—which may at first sight look like strange mix-and-matches—are the result of a chronological narrative (in the case of the university triad) meeting a structure of argument (in the case of the epistemic triad).

In chapters one and two, the underlying epistemic question addressed is, 'What is true?' This thought-centric method of enquiry is deployed to examine the two most prominent strands of discourse-practice in the university, namely instrumentalism (which is action-centric in orientation and content) in chapter one and idealism (which is thought-centric in orientation and content) in chapter two. Both these strands can be said to be 'objective,' in the sense that they deal with matters that are supposed to be external to subjectivity, although the first focuses on calculations based on a given context while the second focuses on principles deemed context-independent.

Much debate and dispute within the British university at present, both in terms of formal academic debate as well as everyday conversations and grievances, is founded upon certain assumptions about its history in the post-war period. One of the most common of these divides the history of higher education since the end of the Second World War into two periods, the first characterized by the formation of an ostensibly 'public' vision of the university, linked to the project of the post-war welfare state, and the second by a 'neoliberal' turn in its underlying philosophy, linked to the era of Margaret Thatcher and her ideological successors. This formulation, which in this book is called the 'two ruptures thesis,' is challenged through a scrutiny of relevant documents and statements from this era when connected to a wider societal frame. The veracity of the default narrative in most 'critical' circles, which charts the rise of a progressive and humanistic 'public university' followed by a fall into a neoliberal system, is contested by, firstly, assembling in chapter one an interpretation emphasizing the continuity of the instrumentalist policies of the 1980s and beyond with the immediate post-war period with which they are rarely associated. The basic argument here is that far from being a Thatcherite distortion, the 'neoliberal' university of the present has in fact its point of invention in the post-war Labour government under Clement Attlee, which justified its social democratic policies, including that of higher education, in instrumentalist terms. Thus, it was suffused with what we may identify as a form of 'action-centricism,' a perspective that focuses on pragmatic concerns, for what was deemed necessary and expedient took precedence over other factors.

This explication of post-war instrumentalism in British higher education is followed by an investigation in chapter two into the roots of the broadly idealist vision of a 'public university,' often symbolized by the 1963 report of the Committee on Higher Education, chaired by Lord Robbins—commonly known as the Robbins Report. This vision of higher education is often posited as the principled alternative to the neoliberal university, and thus it will be taken as the representative form in the post-war period of idealism, a perspective focusing on consistent principles as the central guiding force. Such idealism is a species of the genus of 'thought-centricism,' a mode of operation founded upon rationalism. It will not only be argued that the Robbins Report is far from the progressive document that it is commonly taken to be, but also that the sort of idealism the 'public university' ideology is grounded upon is untenable, founded as it is upon what Kant would call a 'constitutive' use of reason, rather than a 'regulative' one. A constitutive idea is taken to be realizable as a whole, while a regulative idea is meant to be an index to guide one's actions, but never realized in its entirety. It is demonstrated through an engagement with Kafka that the regulative idea provides a means of practising idealism in a form that avoids the snares that the public university ideology has fallen into. Overall, the central concern of these two middle chapters is the accuracy of the tale normally told of this period, and thus by dispelling some of the most widespread myths through historical and theoretical analysis, a way is cleared to a less straightjacketed view of the present state of British higher education.

After this redrawing some of the battle lines in the recent history of the British university, chapter three addresses a different epistemic question, namely 'What is timely and appropriate?' This question, which focuses on the temporal-spatial context, can be phrased more specifically as, 'What strategies or interventions are called for given the present state of play in the British university?' If we now see the clash between instrumentalism and idealism in a quite different light to that of the prevalent narratives, what is to be done? What supplements can be provided to make up for what is lacking or deficient? What current trends should one be wary of? These are some of the questions explored, in particular by examining a third element of the university triad that does not always receive adequate attention, which I term 'community.' By this I mean the aspects of higher education that coalesce around issues of human life together as well as the sensible conceived and experienced through the aesthetics involved in encounters with otherness. This element of the university triad is feeling-centric in orientation, in the sense that it is the affective dimension of life which is most involved in its workings.

In this fourth chapter, two differing and indeed competing conceptions of community and relating to otherness, the substantialist and the non-substantialist, is compared, using as an aid the concepts of *Gemeinschaft* and *Gesellschaft* as outlined by the sociologist Ferdinand Tönnies. These conceptions are then utilized to examine the role of community in recent times in three spheres of the university, namely that of students, non-academic staff, and academic staff. The present challenges in this sphere are explored before an alternative to substantialist and non-substantialist community, which would address these difficulties, is proposed. This is a vision of the university community that could provide a horizon for action, but which needs to be supported by a structure affirming the singular and potentially mutually supportive vocations that denizens of the university are to live out.

This foray into vocation leads us into a consideration in chapter four of the third element in the epistemic triad, which is captured in the question, 'What is authentic?' Here the 'objective' assessments of the post-war British university's historical contours and its present state are placed to one side, and the 'subjective' matter enquired into is how various actors in the university can intervene and participate in it in a manner congruent to their personal and collective stirrings. The nature of this investigation thus involves all three elements of the university triad, and following a general treatment of the concept of vocation, its variegated expressions in the sphere of the university are mapped out in a diagram that treats instrumentalism, idealism, and community as three poles in a triangular 'space.' It is argued that vocation involves the expression of specific gifts or *charismata*, a term adapted from the writings of St Paul.

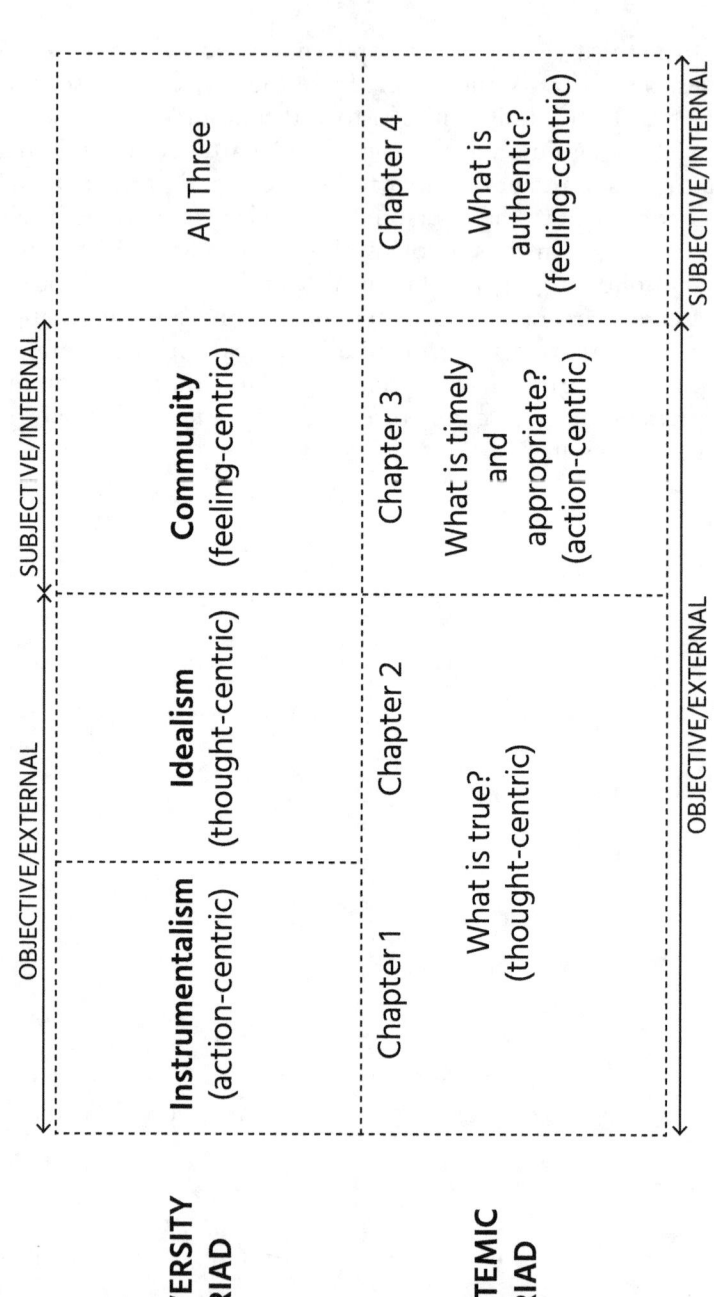

Figure 4

Notes

Introduction

1. Michel Foucault, 'Critical Theory / Intellectual History,' in *Politics, Philosophy, Culture: Interviews and Other Writings, 1977–1984* (London: Routledge, 1990), 35–36.
2. William P. Germano, *From Dissertation to Book*, 2nd ed. (Chicago, London: The University of Chicago Press, 2013), 42, italics added.
3. Save Middlesex Philosophy, 'About Our Campaign,' *Save Middlesex Philosophy* (blog), accessed 14 December 2014, http://savemdxphil.com/about/.
4. Department for Business, Innovation and Skills, 'Success in a Knowledge Economy: Teaching Excellence, Social Mobility and Student Choice' (HMSO, May 2016), 38.
5. For example, Sam Dillon, 'Troubles Grow for a University Built on Profits,' *The New York Times*, 11 February 2007, accessed 1 February 2018, http://www.nytimes.com/2007/02/11/education/11phoenix.html.
6. They are, rather, non-profit but legally private entities which receive considerable amounts of public funding, and so are often considered to be part of the 'public' sector. On the complex relation between public and private, see the discussion in chapter two.
7. Josh Halliday, 'Prevent Scheme "Fosters Fear and Censorship at Universities,"' *The Guardian*, 28 August 2017, accessed 1 February 2018, http://www.theguardian.com/uk-news/2017/aug/29/prevent-scheme-fosters-fear-and-censorship-at-universities-just-yorkshire. A report published by JUST Yorkshire, funded by the Open Society Foundations, reveals the disturbing Islamophobic and racist underpinnings of Prevent (Bano Murtuja and Waqas Tufail, 'Rethinking Prevent: A Case for an Alternative Approach,' [Rotheram: JUST Yorkshire, 2017]; also online, *Rethinking Prevent*, accessed 1 February 2018, http://rethinkingprevent.org.uk/wp-content/uploads/2017/09/Rethinking-Prevent-A-Case-for-an-Alternative-Approach-v1.04.pdf.).
8. Kojin Karatani, 'Non-Cartesian Cogito or Cogito as Difference,' trans. Sabu Kohso, *Karatani Forum*, 1994, http://www.karataniforum.org/non.html (no longer online, archived at Archive.org).
9. Kojin Karatani, 'On the "Thing-in-Itself",' trans. Sabu Kohso, *Karatani Forum*, 1993, http://www.karataniforum.org/on.html (no longer online, archived at Archive.org); Kojin Karatani, *Transcritique*, trans. Sabu Kohso (Cambridge: The MIT Press, 2003), 1.
10. Karatani, *Transcritique*, 34.

178 NOTES TO INTRODUCTION

11. As far as I have been able to establish, there are only two pieces of secondary literature on Karatani in English which give some explicit attention to this aspect of his thought. The first is: Bryan Klausmeyer, 'Transcritical Encounters in Lacanian Psychoanalysis' (BA Thesis, University of Michigan, 2009). The second is an interview with Karatani conducted by the radical geographer Joel Wainwright, in which the latter questions the former as to whether Marx's value form theory can be understood as 'an explicit reiteration of Kant's triadic structure' (Kojin Karatani and Joel Wainwright, '"Critique Is Impossible without Moves": An Interview of Kojin Karatani by Joel Wainwright,' *Dialogues in Human Geography* 2/1 [2012], 33).

12. Karatani, 'Non-Cartesian Cogito'; Karatani, 'On the "Thing-in-Itself".'

13. Karatani links the Freudian ego, super-ego and id to the Kantian categories of understanding, reason and sensibility (Karatani, 'Non-Cartesian Cogito'). He also posits that the Lacanian Imaginary, Symbolic and Real correspond to the Kantian idea (that is, semblance or illusion, *Schein* in German), phenomenon (or form) and thing-in-itself (Karatani, *Transcritique*, 34). However, for the purposes of this book, the psychoanalytic dimension that these correlations potentially open up will not be explored.

14. Karatani, 'On the "Thing-in-Itself".'

15. Karatani. 'On the "Thing-in-Itself".'

16. Karatani, *Transcritique*, 217; Kojin Karatani, *The Structure of World History*, trans. Michael K. Bourdaghs (Durham and London: Duke UP, 2014), 233.

17. Karatani, *The Structure of World History*, 233.

18. Karatani, *The Structure of World History*, 224.

19. Karatani, 220–1. Karatani's point is clearly inspired by the Transcendental Deduction in the first edition of Kant's First Critique, where imagination mediates between sensibility and understanding (Immanuel Kant, *Critique of Pure Reason*, trans. Paul Guyer and Allen W. Wood [Cambridge: CUP, 1998], sec. A124). It is also notable that in interpreting the theoretical moves of Herder and Hegel he conflates reason (*Vernunft*) and understanding (*Verstand*) (Karatani, *The Structure of World History*, 221). This can be explained by the fact that Hegel's does not follow Kant's strict distinction between the two as distinct faculties of the mind with separate domains but rather assigns them separate tasks within his conception of the mind as a living, organic unity, with understanding concerned with apprehending parts and reason with grasping the whole (Christopher J. Berry, *Hume, Hegel, and Human Nature*, International Archives of the History of Ideas [The Hague: MNijhoff Publishers, 1982], 131–4).

20. Ivan Illich, *The Rivers North of the Future: The Testament of Ivan Illich* (House of Anansi Press, 2005), 147.

21. Kojin Karatani, 'Thing as Other,' in *Anything* (New York: Rizzoli, 2000), 258.

22. Karatani, *Transcritique*, 114.

23. Craig Calhoun, 'Evicting the Public,' *Possible Futures* (blog), 11 November 2011, accessed 1 February 2018, http://www.possible-futures.org/2011/11/19/evicting-the-public-why-has-occupying-public-spaces-brought-such-heavy-handed-repression/.
24. Donato Paolo Mancini, 'Occupy LSE Handed Eviction Notice,' *London Student* (blog), 29 April 2015, http://www.lsnews.co.uk/occupy-lse-handed-eviction-notice/ (no longer online); Calhoun, 'Evicting the Public.'
25. Charles Dickens, *Hard Times* (Ware: Wordsworth, 1995), 18.

Chapter One

1. Egon Bondy, *The Consolation of Ontology: On the Substantial and Nonsubstantial Models*, trans. Benjamin B. Page (Lanham, MD: Lexington Books, 2001), 217.
2. Stefan Collini, *What Are Universities For?* (London: Penguin, 2012), 140–1.
3. It should be noted that this definition of instrumentalism differs slightly from the more conventional formulation in social theory of what is termed 'instrumental rationality' or 'reason.' Instrumental reason is generally defined as a mode of thought which focuses on finding the best means to a certain end, without enquiring into the value of that end. In *Eclipse of Reason*, Max Horkheimer excoriated a particular version of this form of rationality, arguing that in it 'reason has become completely harnessed to the social process. Its operational value, its role in the domination of men and nature, has been made the sole criterion' (Max Horkheimer, *Eclipse of Reason* [New York: Bloomsbury Academic, 2013], 13). His specific critique here can be generalized to other forms of instrumental reason by simply replacing 'the social process' and 'the domination of men and nature' with whatever end is chosen. The difference between this conception of instrumental reason and the definition of instrumentalism in this book is that the former focuses on the relationship between and relative importance of means and ends, whereas the latter is more concerned about how a particular policy or set of practices is evaluated. In other words, while a critic of instrumental reason might propose, as an alternative, a system of rationality in which both means and ends must be evaluated, or indeed (as Gandhi argued) brought into harmony, this is somewhat tangential to the related question of *what* the *measure* of a *particular policy* should be.
4. Bill Readings, *The University in Ruins* (Cambridge: Harvard UP, 1996), 17.
5. Readings, *The University in Ruins*, 3.
6. Readings, *The University in Ruins*, 3–4.
7. Readings, *The University in Ruins*, 13, italics in original.
8. Readings, *The University in Ruins*, 23.

9. Readings, *The University in Ruins*, 24, italics in original.
10. Bob Dylan, *Subterranean Homesick Blues*, 7-inch single, Bringing It All Back Home (Columbia, 1965).
11. A. H. Halsey, *Decline of Donnish Dominion: The British Academic Professions in the Twentieth Century*, (Oxford: Clarendon Press, 1995), 108.
12. Maurice Kogan and Stephen Hanney, *Reforming Higher Education* (London and Philadelphia: Jessica Kingsley Publishers, 2000), 45–8.
13. Roger Brown and Helen Carasso, *Everything for Sale? The Marketisation of UK Higher Education* (Milton Park, Abingdon, Oxon; New York: Routledge, 2013), 3. This was the logical end point of the initial step which seriously called into question the 'value of an overseas student presence,' namely the introduction by the Labour government of higher (but still partially subsidized) fees for overseas students between 1966–7 (J. M. Lee, 'Overseas Students in Britain: How Their Presence Was Politicised in 1966–1967,' *Minerva* 36/4 [1998], 320.)
14. Various historians of British politics have explored this post-war consensus, but its classic statement can be found in Samuel H. Beer's *Modern British Politics*, see Samuel H. Beer, *Modern British Politics: A Study of Parties and Pressure Groups* (London: Faber & Faber, 1965). Other monographs which deal with the subject include Samuel H. Beer, *Britain Against Itself: Political Contradictions of Collectivism* (New York: Norton, 1982); Dennis Kavanagh and Peter Morris, *Consensus Politics from Attlee to Major*, 2nd ed. (Oxford: Blackwell, 1994); Paul Addison, *The Road To 1945: British Politics and the Second World War*, 2nd revised ed. (London: Pimlico, 1994); David Marquand, *The Unprincipled Society* (London: Fontana, 1988); Kenneth O. Morgan, *Britain Since 1945: The People's Peace* (Oxford: OUP, 2001).
15. The words 'truly' and 'i.e. popular' are inserted here as a gloss to indicate some divergence from Charles's enduring faith in the concept of the public as a rallying point for a radical vision of the university.
16. Matthew Charles, 'Of Course … However,' *Radical Philosophy* 172 (March/April 2012), 56, italics in original.
17. The other four 'great evils' were Want, Disease, Squalor and Idleness.
18. William Henry Beveridge Beveridge, *Social Insurance and Allied Services: Report*, Cmd. (Great Britain. Parliament); 6404 (London: HMSO, 1942), para. 456.
19. John Carswell, *Government and the Universities in Britain: Programme and Performance 1960–1980* (Cambridge: CUP, 1985), 14.
20. Michel Foucault, *Security, Territory, Population: Lectures at the Collège de France 1977–1978*, ed. Michel Senellart, trans. Graham Burchill (Basingstoke: Palgrave Macmillan, 2009), 117.
21. Michael Shattock, *Making Policy in British Higher Education 1945–2011* (Maidenhead: Open University Press, 2012), 7.
22. W. A. C. Stewart, *Higher Education in Post-war Britain* (Basingstoke: Macmillan, 1989); Malcolm Tight, *The Development of Higher Education in*

the United Kingdom since 1945 (Maidenhead: Society for Research into Higher Education & Open University Press, 2009). Stewart's book, published in 1989, sets out to give 'an historic sequence of developments which have taken place in universities, colleges of education and institutions of technical education in [the United Kingdom] particularly since 1945' as well as offer 'some reasons for the changes and the present position ... and [try] in some measure to look ahead' (Stewart, *Higher Education in Post-war Britain*, ix). Chapters are organized in a chronological order, considering one decade after 1945 at a time (e.g. 'the 1950s,' 'the 1960s,' etc.), and Stewart asserts in his preface that his is the first book of its kind (Stewart, *Higher Education in Post-war Britain*, ix). Malcolm Tight's 2009 book, *The Development of Higher Education in the United Kingdom since 1945*, positions itself specifically as 'an accessible, up-to-date, comprehensive, single-volume guide to the development of higher education in the UK since 1945,' an undertaking which Tight considers to not have resulted in any publication since Stewart's 1989 monograph (Tight, *Development of Higher Education*, 1). In contrast to the latter, however, Tight organizes his chapters according to themes, such as 'policy and funding,' 'research and knowledge,' and 'the student experience.' This is a method clearly influenced by the four-volume *A History of the University in Europe*, edited by Hilde de Ridder-Symeons and Walter Rüegg, which Tight himself praises in his *Researching Higher Education* (Tight Malcolm, *Researching Higher Education* [Maidenhead: Open University Press, 2012], 125). It would be fair to say that although the time period examined in this book, i.e. 'since 1945,' is akin to that which was dealt with by Stewart and Tight in their respective books, the overall methodology adopted here is far less empirical and more conceptual and critical. If pushed to categorize this book under Tight's classifications of recent higher education research on 'system policy' in *Researching Higher Education* (117–131), the work presented here would probably fall between 'the policy context,' 'national policies' and 'historical policy studies,' although its Karatanian methodological foundations is a distinctive characteristic.

23. Ken Loach, *The Spirit of '45*, Documentary (Dogwoof, 2013).

24. Donald Clarke, 'Ken Loach's Spirit and Direction Has Lost None of Its Revolutionary Spark,' *Irish Times*, 14 March 2013, accessed 1 February 2018, http://www.irishtimes.com/culture/film/ken-loach-s-spirit-and-direction-has-lost-none-of-its-revolutionary-spark-1.1324618.

25. Loach, *The Spirit of '45*, 1:08:35–38.

26. 'An ideal type is formed by the one-sided *accentuation* of one or more points of view and by the synthesis of a great many diffuse, discrete, more or less present and occasionally absent *concrete individual* phenomena, which are arranged according to those one-sidedly emphasized viewpoints into a unified *analytical* construct' (Max Weber, '"Objectivity" in Social Science and Social Policy,' in *The Methodology of the Social Sciences* (New York: The Free Press, 1949), 90.

27. Loach, *The Spirit of '45*, 26:06–18.

28. David Howell, *Attlee* (Haus Publishing, 2006), 130–2; Nicklaus Thomas-Symonds, *Attlee : A Life in Politics* (London: IBTauris, 2010), 15; Frank Field, 'Introductory Essay: A Social Democrat in Action,' in *Attlee's Great Contemporaries: The Politics of Character*, ed. Frank Field (Bloomsbury Publishing, 2009), xli.
29. John Maynard Keynes, 'The End of Laissez Faire–II,' *The New Republic* 48/613 (1926), 41.
30. Friedrich Wilhelm Nietzsche, *On the Genealogy of Morals* (New York: Vintage Books, 1967), 45.
31. Friedrich Wilhelm Nietzsche, *On the Genealogy of Morality*, trans. Carol Diethe (Cambridge: CUP, 2007), 26.
32. Robert B. Pippin, *Nietzsche, Psychology, and First Philosophy* (Chicago: University of Chicago Press, 2010), 75–6.
33. Pippin, *Nietzsche*, 78.
34. The approach taken here is indebted to an article by Cui Zhiyuan which draws from Pippin's reading of Nietzsche to justify an analysis of the Chongqing Experiment—a novel approach to urban and rural development that was pioneered in the direct-controlled municipality of Chongqing from the mid-2000s to 2012—according to the theories of Henry George, James Meade and Antonio Gramsci. In his words: 'It does not mean that the participants have deliberately followed these theories, only that their deeds are consistent with the theories' (Zhiyuan Cui, 'Partial Intimations of the Coming Whole The Chongqing Experiment in Light of the Theories of Henry George, James Meade, and Antonio Gramsci,' *Modern China* 37/6 (2011), 648, https://doi.org/10.1177/0097700411420852.
35. Martin Francis, *Ideas and Policies Under Labour, 1945–51: Building a New Britain* (UK-Manchester; New York: Manchester University Press, 1997), 38.
36. Ben Jackson, 'Property-Owning Democracy: A Short History,' in *Property-Owning Democracy: Rawls and Beyond*, ed. Martin O'Neill and Thad Williamson (Chichester: Wiley-Blackwell, 2012), 33–52. It should be noted, however, that Keynes was not the Almighty fount of all that has become associated with his name. For example, David Vines has argued that Meade had a significant role in the development of Keynes's ideas in *The General Theory of Interest, Employment and Money* through the former's involvement in the circle of younger economists who were gathered around Keynes at Cambridge, known as the 'Circus,' and who in the early 1930s were debating Keynes's 1930 *Treatise on Money* (David Vines, 'James Meade,' *Oxford Department of Economics Discussion Paper Series*, June 2007, accessed 1 February 2018, http://www.economics.ox.ac.uk/materials/working_papers/paper330.pdf). It is important, thus, to recognize even in early Keynesianism a school of thought originating from Keynes but not completely tied to him as a single, atomized individual.
37. Noel W. Thompson, *Political Economy and the Labour Party: The*

Economics of Democratic Socialism 1884–2005, 2nd ed. (London: Routledge, 2006), 139–42.

38. Thompson, *Political Economy and the Labour Party*, 4.

39. Although Keynes was not seen as a natural ally due to his ideological differences with the Labour Party over essential matters—we should remember that Keynes was a Bloomsbury Set elitist who had a generally negative perception of the working class, whom he regarded as 'boorish' (Gilles Dostaler, 'The Formation of Keynes's Vision,' *History of Economics Review* 25 [1996], 14–31)—it was the filtration of his ideas through more overtly left-wing writers such as Hobson that made it palatable to Labourites. In Peter Clarke's words, 'it was Keynes with a Hobsonian twist [which] remedied the scientific deficiencies of Hobson's analysis and the ideological deficiencies of Keynes's (Peter Clarke, *Liberals and Social Democrats* [Cambridge, CUP, 1981], 274). It should, however, be noted that among the influential interventions in Labour debates in the 1930s were books written by James Meade and Douglas Jay which were very clearly Keynesian in inspiration: J. E. Meade, *An Introduction to Economic Analysis and Policy* (Oxford: Clarendon Press, 1936); Douglas Jay, *The Socialist Case* (London: Faber and Faber, 1937).

40. John Maynard Keynes, 'Does Unemployment Need a Drastic Remedy?' in *The Collected Writings of John Maynard Keynes: vol. 19: Activities 1922–1929: The Return to Gold and Industrial Policy* (Cambridge: CUP, 1981), 219–223.

41. John Maynard Keynes, *The General Theory of Employment, Interest and Money* (London: Macmillan, 1936), 322. It is perhaps instructive to note that during the period of the Great Depression which Keynes wrote some of his most enduring works, a journal article in the *Psychological Review* attempted to explain the cycle of boom and bust as being akin to 'a patient suffering from a manic-depressive psychosis, in which the boom period parallels the manic phase and the subsequent slump parallels the depressive phase' (J. J. B. Morgan, 'Manic-Depressive Psychoses of Business,' *Psychological Review* 42/1 [1935], 91–107, https://doi.org/10.1037/h0059138.)

42. Keynes, 'The End of Laissez Faire–II,' 40.

43. Keynes, 'The End of Laissez Faire–II,' 40.

44. John Maynard Keynes, 'Am I a Liberal?,' in *The Collected Writings of John Maynard Keynes: vol. 9: Essays in Persuasion* (Cambridge: CUP, 1972), 295–6, italics added.

45. Annie Besant, 'Industry Under Socialism,' in *Fabian Essays in Socialism*, ed. George Bernard Shaw and H. G. Wilshire (New York: The Humboldt Publishing Co., 1891), II.2.10.

46. Sidney Webb, *The Difficulties of Individualism* (London: Fabian Society, 1896), 5.

47. Rod O'Donnell, 'Keynes's Socialism: Conception, Strategy and Espousal,' in *Keynes, Post-Keynesianism and Political Economy: Essays in Honour of Geoff Harcourt: Vol 3.*, ed. Claudio Sardoni and Peter Kriesler

(London; New York: Routledge, 1999), 158.

48. Herbert Morrison, *Socialisation and Transport: The organization of Socialised Industries with Particular Reference to the London Passenger Transport Bill* (London: Constable, 1933).

49. It should be noted that another alternative which was put forward in the 1920s to resolve the opposition between state socialism and *laissez-faire* capitalism was the guild socialism of writers such as G. D. H. Cole, who advocated a decentralized system of industry and enterprise which would be characterized by workers' control in organization and management (G. D. H. Cole, *Guild Socialism Re-Stated* [London: Leonard Parsons, 1920]). Keynes, of course, was not persuaded by anything of the sort due to his lack of faith in the capacities of the ordinary worker. Cole's vision, in its essence, was of a type which fell foul of Keynes general critique of socialisms other than his own, as it 'preferred the mud to the fish [and] exalts the boorish proletariat above the bourgeois and the intelligentsia who, with whatever faults, are the quality in life and surely carry the seeds of all human advancement' (John Maynard Keynes, 'A Short View of Russia,' in *Essays in Persuasion* [London: Macmillan, 1931]).

50. Our Special Correspondent, 'Managing Public Concerns: Mr. Keynes's Suggestions,' *The Manchester Guardian*, 1 August 1927.

51. John Maynard Keynes, 'A Managed Currency: Socialism of the Future,' *The Times*, 26 March 1925, sec. Letters to the Editor.

52. Keynes, 'A Managed Currency.'

53. Robert Skidelsky, 'Keynes's "Concluding Notes,"' in *A 'Second Edition' of The General Theory*, ed. G. C. Harcourt and P. A. Riach, vol. 1 (London: Routledge, 1997), 434.

54. Keynes, 'A Managed Currency.' In this Keynes was, in a sense, on the same side as the Fabians, who believed that the mergers of private enterprises into large trusts was part of a process of socialization. The difference, of course, was that for the Fabians the creation of these large firms was merely a stepping stone to full public nationalization—in Annie Besant's words, 'centrali[zation] for us by capitalists, who thus unconsciously pave the way for their own supersession' (Besant, 'Industry Under Socialism,' II.2.10)—whereas for Keynes such a step was anathema as he understood socialization in terms of *investment*, that is, in the gradual transformation in the managerial culture of large joint-stock companies from being focused on shareholder profits to a more public ethos as a result of a sense of accountability to the wider society. Neither managed to foresee the endurance and further development of the contemporary multi-national and transnational corporations in the latter half of the twentieth century, larger than any great centralized industry preceding it, and much further from any notion or actuality of socialization, whether that of formal ownership in the Fabian sense or of investment in Keynes's sense.

55. Keynes, 'A Managed Currency,' italics added.

56. Michael Shattock, *The UGC and the Management of British Universities* (Buckingham: Society for Research into Higher Education & Open

University Press, 1994), 3.

57. Tom Owen, 'Financing University Education' (Unpublished manuscript, 1981); quoted in Shattock, *The UGC and the Management of British Universities*, 1.

58. Owen, 'Financing University Education'; quoted in Shattock, *The UGC and the Management of British Universities*, 1.

59. Robert O. Berdahl, *British Universities and the State* (London: CUP, 1959), 201–2.

60. The Barlow Report was only one of several official reports commissioned and published at the time on post-secondary education, but it had by far the greatest impact upon post-war university expansion. These other reports included the 1943 Luxmore Report on agricultural education, 1944 McNair Report on teacher training, the 1944 Goodenough Report on medical education, the 1945 Percy Report on higher technical education, and the 1946 Loveday Report on veterinary education.

61. Alan Barlow, *Scientific Man-Power: Report of a Committee Appointed by the Lord President of the Council* (London: HMSO, 1946), 3.

62. Parliamentary and Scientific Committee, *Universities and the Increase of Scientific Manpower* (London, PSC, 1946), para. 1(13).

63. Barlow, *Scientific Man-Power*, 8.

64. Barlow, *Scientific Man-Power*, 16–17. The former recommendation of the Committee for at least one new university to be established was not, in the end, taken up. The latter recommendation, on the other hand, was implemented, and all five university colleges mentioned were granted university charters within just over a decade, beginning with Nottingham in 1948 and ending with Leicester in 1957.

65. A detailed account of the events that led to the UGC's creation can be found in Eric Hutchinson, 'The Origins of the University Grants Committee,' *Minerva* 13/4 (1975), 583–620.

66. Christine H. Shinn, *Paying the Piper: The Development of the University Grants Committee 1919–1946* (Lewes: The Falmer Press, 1986); Christine H. Shinn, 'The Beginnings of the University Grants Committee,' *History of Education* 9/3 (1980), 234, https://doi.org/10.1080/0046760800090305.

67. Hutchinson, 'The Origins of the University Grants Committee,' 587.

68. University Grants Committee, *The University Grants Committee: Terms of Reference, Brief History and Membership* (London: University Grants Committee, 1985), 1.

69. Barlow, *Scientific Man-Power*, 21.

70. Barlow, *Scientific Man-Power*, 21.

71. *Hansard Parliamentary Debates*, 5th ser., vol. 426 (1946), col. 129, italics added.

72. University Grants Committee, *University Development from 1935–1947* (London: HMSO, 1948), 82.

73. Liberal Industrial Inquiry, *Britain's Industrial Future: Being the Report*

of the Liberal Industrial Inquiry (London: Benn, 1928), 64–5.
74. Brian Harrison, *Seeking a Role: The United Kingdom, 1951–1970* (Oxford: OUP, 2011), 305.
75. Shattock, Making Policy in British Higher Education, 122–4.
76. Campaign for the Public University, 'Manifesto for the Public University,' *Campaign for the Public University*, 2010, accessed 1 February 2018, http://publicuniversity.org.uk/manifesto/.
77. Christopher Newfield, *Unmaking the Public University: The Forty-Year Assault on the Middle Class* (Cambridge, MA: Harvard University Press, 2008), 3.
78. Gary S. Becker, *Human Capital: A Theoretical and Empirical Analysis, with Special Reference to Education*, 2nd ed. (New York: National Bureau of Economic Research, 1975).
79. Berdahl, British Universities and the State, 201.
80. *Hansard Parliamentary Debates*, 5th ser., vol. 516 (1953), cols. 96–7.

Chapter Two

1. Slavoj Žižek, *The Sublime Object of Ideology* (London: Verso Books, 2008), 69.
2. John Henry Newman, *The Idea of a University*, ed. Frank M. Turner (New Haven; London: Yale University Press, 1996). It is worth noting, however, that many commentators sidestep a key element of Newman's argument, namely his stress upon the importance of theology to the university, see 'Discourses II–IV' in Newman, *The Idea of a University*, 25–58.
3. Bill Readings, *The University in Ruins* (Cambridge, MA: Harvard University Press, 1996).
4. Jacques Derrida, 'The University Without Condition,' in *Without Alibi*, trans. Peggy Kamuf (Stanford: Stanford University Press, 2002).
5. Karatani, *Transcritique*, 90.
6. There are also programmatic ideals which at first glance appear to be a strand of idealism, but which are based not on rational construction but rather a conservative inclination towards what has served the institution well in times gone by, and which is then advocated for preservation. In their 1971 work, *The British Academics*, the sociologists A. H. Halsey and Martin Trow identified what they considered to be a unifying 'idea of a university' in the British system of higher education. This idea or ideal consists of 'certain normative criteria': 'First, it should be ancient; second it should draw its students, not from a restricted regional locality, but from the nation and internationally; third, its students, whatever their origins, should be carefully selected as likely to fit into and maintain the established life and character of the university; fourth, those who enter should be offered (to use a Victorian distinction) 'education' and not merely 'training.' This end necessitates, fifth, a small-scale residential community affording close contact of teachers with taught in a shared domestic

life and, sixth, a high staff-student ratio for individualized teaching' (A. H. Halsey and Martin A. Trow, *The British Academics* [London: Faber and Faber, 1971], 67). It is clear that this ostensible 'idealism' is in fact an example of a community-centred approach, that is, closer to a plea for a specific form of life, albeit one which is an apologia for a former or vanishing *status quo*.

7. In some translations of Karatani's work into English, most notably *The Structure of World History*, the Japanese term *kōseiteki* is mistranslated as 'constructive' rather than 'constitutive,' the latter being the correct term given the Kantian foundation of Karatani's arguments (Elena Louisa Lange, 'Exchanging without Exploiting,' *Historical Materialism* 23/3 [2015], 197, https://doi.org/10.1163/1569206X-12341425.)

8. Karatani, *The Structure of World History*, 233.

9. Karl Marx, *The German Ideology* (Amherst, NY: Prometheus Books, 1998), 57, italics in original.

10. Karatani, *Transcritique*, xi–xii.

11. George Molnar, 'Conflicting Strains in Anarchist Thought,' *Anarchy* 4 (1961), 125.

12. George Woodcock, 'Nurturing the Positive Trends,' *Freedom* 27 (1956), 4. It is instructive to note that the distinction between Molnar and Woodcock's respective views mirrors that of two of the five different strategies that H. Richard Niebuhr argues Christians have taken in relation to the wider culture. Molnar's recommendation is akin to the perspective of 'Christ against culture,' where 'the sole authority of Christ over the Christian' is affirmed while 'culture's claims to loyalty' are rejected (H. Richard Niebuhr, *Christ and Culture* [San Francisco: Harper, 2001]), 45. Woodcock's position, on the other hand, is analogous to that of 'Christ transforming culture,' whereby the Christian believes that the conversion of the culture to the Christian way is possible. This, of course, requires 'a more positive and hopeful attitude' (Niebuhr, *Christ and Culture*, 191). At the end of the day, the anarchist and the rigorously non-conformist Christian are both opposed to mainstream culture, which the tradition of the latter terms simply 'the world.' For this reason, any person or movement desiring to contest elements of the hegemonic way of the world can find useful resources in both the anarchist and the radical Christian traditions, which in fact overlap at points, for example in the Christian anarchism of Leo Tolstoy and the Catholic Worker movement.

13. Colin Ward, 'Anarchism and Respectability,' *Freedom* 2 (1961), 3.

14. Murray Bookchin, *Social Anarchism or Lifestyle Anarchism: An Unbridgeable Chasm* (Edinburgh: AK, 1995); Stuart White, 'Social Anarchism, Lifestyle Anarchism, and the Anarchism of Colin Ward,' *Anarchist Studies* 19/2 (2011), 102.

15. White, 'Social Anarchism ... and the Anarchism of Colin Ward,' 97.

16. Karatani, *The Structure of World History*, xiv.

17. Robert Skidelsky, writing about Keynes's ideas of the public, argues that it 'has its roots in a mediaeval past, when property was invested

with both private and public functions' (Skidelsky, 'Keynes's "Concluding Notes",'434). In his *Summa Theologica*, Aquinas explains the theological aspect of property through a broad distinction between 'the power to procure and dispense' these external things and the power to use them (Thomas Aquinas, '*Summa Theologica,*' *New Advent*, accessed 1 February 2018, http://www.newadvent.org/summa/3066.htm, sec. 66) Bede Jarrett OP glosses this passage by explaining that within the Christian theology of the medieval era, 'the possession of property belongs to the individual, but ... that the use of it is not limited to him' (Bede Jarrett, *Mediaeval Socialism* [London: TC & EC Jack, 1914], 81.) It can be argued that the British university obeyed this principle up until the post-war period. Despite being private bodies which possessed private property, the use of such property was open to those outside the university. According to John Carswell, for instance, the universities were always seen as 'public' given their 'public' character of providing museums, parks and so on, even before they were publicly funded (Carswell, *Government and the Universities in Britain*). By contrast, the completely publicly funded model of higher education is, in a sense a reversal of this medieval principle. Public property in the form of taxes fall into the private 'use' of individual students. This is analogous, interestingly, to the form of possession and use within the monastic tradition. Nevertheless, we should note that Jarrett argues that 'the economics of a religious house are hardly of such a kind, thought the mediaevalists, as to suit the ways and fancies of this workaday world' (Jarrett, *Mediaeval Socialism*, 82).

18. 'Universities "Ripe for Nationalization",' *Times Educational Supplement*, 24 June 1966.

19. John Holmwood, 'The Idea of a Public University,' in *A Manifesto for the Public University*, ed. John Holmwood (London: Bloomsbury Academic, 2011), 8.

20. Holmwood, 'The Idea of a Public University,' 14.

21. Holmwood, 'The Idea of a Public University,' 3.

22. Gareth Williams, 'Will Robbins Ride Again?' *Times Higher Education*, 17 October 2013.

23. Holmwood, 'The Idea of a Public University,' 8.

24. The turbulent economic period of the 1970s led to a series of policies which gradually reduced government expenditure on higher education, leading to a matching gradual reduction of the target for full-time and sandwich places in higher education by 1980/1981 from 750,000 in December 1972 when the White Paper 'Education: A Framework for Expansion' was published (somewhat ironically by Margaret Thatcher, then Secretary of State for Education and Science) to a mere 500,000 by March 1980 (Clive Booth, 'DES and Treasury,' in *Resources and Higher Education*, ed. Alfred Morris and John Sizer [Guildford, Society for Research into Higher Education, 1982], 36–7). A more generous interpretation of a 'golden age' for 'public' British higher education would date its beginning to the immediate post-war period. This is

the view that was expressed, for example by Lord Swann in his opening of the debate in the House of Lords on the Croham Review on the UGC. He opined that the 'golden age for universities' lasted 'from just after the war until 1973,' and in this period 'society valued them, governments of every shade valued them, new universities were founded, morale was high and it was a time of great enthusiasm and creativity' (*Hansard Parliamentary Debates*, 5th ser., vol. 485 [1987], col. 1426).

25. Brian Simon, *Education and the Social Order 1940–1990* (London: Lawrence & Wishart, 1991), ch. 5. Indeed, if we wanted to be generous, we could begin this 'long decade' of mass higher education expansion in 1961 when Sussex, the first of the 'plate-glass universities,' opened its doors.

26. Simon, *Education and the Social Order*, 262, 426.

27. John Brennan, 'Higher Education Outside the Universities: The UK Case,' in *Non-University Higher Education in Europe*, ed. James S. Taylor (Berlin: Springer Science & Business Media, 2008), 233.

28. Eric Robinson, *The New Polytechnics* (Harmondsworth: Penguin, 1968).

29. Peter Scott, 'Robbins, the Binary Policy and Mass Higher Education,' *Higher Education Quarterly* 68/2 (2014), 147–63, https://doi.org/10.1111/hequ.12040.

30. It is noteworthy that Richard Layard, who was Senior Research Officer for the Robbins Committee, has stated that the emerging work on human capital by Gary Becker, 'identifying education as a major factor in economic performance and showing that there were quite good returns to higher education as an investment,' was an important influence on the Report (Richard Layard, 'What Was the World like Then? The Context in 1963,' in *Shaping Higher Education: 50 Years After Robbins*, ed. Nicholas Barr [London: London School of Economics, 2014], 14.)

31. Steve Fuller, 'Intellectual Fruit of Neoliberal Seedbed,' *Times Higher Education*, 24 October 2013.

32. Fuller, 'Intellectual Fruit of Neoliberal Seedbed.'

33. Simon, *Education and the Social Order*, 202.

34. Lionel Robbins, *An Essay on the Nature & Significance of Economic Science* (London: Macmillan, 1932), 125. It is worth noting the obvious fact that the report was a policy document on higher education rather than a work of scientific economics. Therefore it could be argued that in this context social utility was not a postulate which would be 'entirely foreign' and unavailable to Robbins in writing the report. Nevertheless, what Robbins produced clearly bears the marks of a conservative economist, and there is ultimately nothing in the Report which contradicts his neoliberal economic views.

35. Lionel, *Report of the Committee Appointed by the Prime Minister under the Chairmanship of Lord Robbins 1961–63* (London: HMSO, 1963), sec. 31, italics added.

36. Robbins, *Higher Education: Report*, sec. 32, italics added.

37. The term economic utilitarianism is used here to denote the form of instrumentalism which focuses upon economic goals and aims, that is, economic utility. This can be distinguished from the classical utilitarianism of Jeremy Bentham and John Stuart Mill which takes the advancement of pleasure or happiness to be the measure of the utility of a particular thing. In Bentham words: 'By utility is meant that property in any object, whereby it tends to produce benefit, advantage, pleasure, good, or happiness' for the party concerned, whether an individual or a community (Jeremy Bentham, *An Introduction to the Principles of Morals and Legislation* [Kitchener: Batoche Books, 2000], 14–15). Henceforth, whenever the term 'utility' is used in this book, it is economic and not classical (i.e. hedonistic) utility that is being referred to.

38. Robbins, *Higher Education: Report*, sec. 33.

39. Margaret Schabas, 'The Jevonian Revolution Re-Appraised,' in *Contributions to the History of Economic Thought: Essays in Honour of R.D.C. Black*, ed. Antoin Murphy and Renee Prendergast (London: Routledge, 2000).

40. Maurice Dobb, *Theories of Value and Distribution since Adam Smith: Ideology and Economic Theory* (Cambridge: CUP, 1973), chap. 7.

41. Dobb, *Theories of Value and Distribution since Adam Smith*, 167, italics added.

42. Lionel Robbins, 'The Place of Jevons in the History of Economic Thought,' *The Manchester School* 7/1 (1936), 4, https://doi.org/10.1111/j.1467-9957.1936.tb01430.x, italics added.

43. Elizabeth Gibney, 'Robbins: 50 Years Later,' *Times Higher Education*, 24 October 2013, accessed 1 February 2018, http://www.timeshighereducation.co.uk/features/robbins-50-years-later/2008287.article.

44. Here it is important to note that the Barlow Committee did resort to a similar logical procedure when it relied on research on 'the distribution of intelligence' to allay traditional fears that university expansion would mean a reduction in standards. Tests conducted by psychologists of the time concluded that five percent of the population possessed intelligence on a level with the upper half of Scottish and Manchester university students. Based on this research, the committee argued that the fact that the upper half of university students nation-wide constituted only one percent of the population meant that only one in five potential university graduates were being recruited (Barlow, *Scientific Man-Power*, 8–9). The key difference between the Barlow Report and the Robbins Report, however, is that Robbins's argument rested completely upon supply side calculations, while the Barlow Committee utilized such arguments merely to assert that there was sufficient talent for its proposed doubling of the number of students recruited by the universities.

45. Department for Business Innovation and Skills, *Higher Education: Students at the Heart of the System*, June (London: HMSO, 2011).

46. David Willetts, *Robbins Revisited: Bigger and Better Higher*

Education (London: The Social Market Foundation, 2013).
47. Willetts, *Robbins Revisited*, 67.
48. Willetts, *Robbins Revisited*, 17.
49. In her biography of Robbins, Susan Howson writes that the first lecture that Robbins attended at the London School of Economics was very likely that of the director, Sir William Beveridge, 'opening the session on the first day of the Michaelmas term, Monday 4 October 1920,' in which the latter 'expatiated on the virtues of "Economics as a liberal education".' Beveridge 'defined the objects of a liberal education as twofold—"*The training of the mind*" and "*The understanding of one's environment so as to be in harmony with it*"—both of which the study of economics and the other social sciences, especially in the form of a broad degree such as the BSc(Econ), could easily provide' (Susan Howson, *Lionel Robbins*, Historical Perspectives on Modern Economics [Cambridge: CUP, 2011], 69). She goes on to say that 'Robbins was involved in several future reforms of the BSc(Econ) and tended to look back on the degree he took as a model to be preserved or recreated' (Howson, *Lionel Robbins*, 69). With this knowledge, it is unsurprising that Robbins continued to believe whole-heartedly in the value of a liberal education, and expressed such sentiments in the report he wrote, even if they did not sit easily with the strongly instrumentalist tenor of his economic and political views. Here we have a classic case of the tension in British conservatism between radical neoliberalism and older forms, e.g. that of Disraeli and the One Nation Toryism which descends from him. The latter strand, while still believing in the free market, is less ebullient about its virtues due to a greater emphasis on 'preserving and safeguarding the old, the familiar, the beloved, the well-tried' (F. J. C. Hearnshaw, *Conservatism in England: An Analytical, Historical, and Political Survey* [London: Macmillan & co, 1933], 7). This often leads to a conservatism which is marginally less instrumentalist in the economistic sense we are most concerned with.
50. David Marquand, 'Beyond Social Democracy,' *The Political Quarterly* 58/3 (1987), 246–7, https://doi.org/10.1111/j.1467-923X.1987.tb00739.x, italics added.
51. Chesterton's original statement concerned 'the *Christian* ideal,' see G. K. Chesterton, *What's Wrong With the World* (Empire Books, 2011), 19.
52. Once again, it should be noted that the conservative pattern of Oxbridge described by Halsey and Trow, although put forward as a unified ideal, in fact developed incrementally rather than according to a 'rational' blueprint, and should be treated as a species of community, see Halsey and Trow, *The British Academics*, 67.
53. Žižek, The Sublime Object of Ideology, 60–77.
54. Franz Kafka, *The Complete Short Stories of Franz Kafka* (London: Minerva, 1992), 433. Aside from this most basic premise of constructing a tower to the heavens, the versions in the Hebrew scriptures and Kafka differ significantly.

55. Kafka, *Complete Short Stories*, 433.
56. Kafka, *Complete Short Stories*, 434.
57. Kojin Karatani, *Architecture as Metaphor: Language, Number, Money*, trans. Sabu Kohso (Cambridge, MA: MIT Press, 1995), xxxv.
58. Marx, *The German Ideology*, 57, italics in original.
59. Karatani, *The Structure of World History*, 233.
60. Kant, *Critique of Pure Reason*, sec. A689.
61. One commits the genetic fallacy when one conflates the 'causal origins of a belief with its justification,' see Ted Honderich, *The Oxford Companion to Philosophy* (Oxford: OUP, 1995), 306.
62. Karatani, *Transcritique*, 281, italics added.
63. Hilaire Belloc, *Augustan Books of Modern Poetry: Hilaire Belloc* (New York: Frederick A. Stokes, 1925), 28.

Chapter Three

1. Sigmar Groeneveld, Lee Hoinacki, and Ivan Illich, 'Declaration on Soil,' 6 December 1990, http://illich.org/texts-about-illich/declaration-on-soil/view (no longer online).
2. Kojin Karatani, 'Notes on Communicative Space,' in *Anywhere* (New York: Rizzoli, 1992), 137.
3. In the history of modern Western philosophy, these two figures of city and village can be represented by Königsberg and Todtnauberg, the favoured dwelling spaces of, respectively, Immanuel Kant and Martin Heidegger. Könisberg was an important port by the Baltic Sea, the multicultural capital of the Kingdom of Prussia. Todtnauberg was and is a tiny village in the Black Forest, remote and scenic. Kant was a theoretician of cosmopolitanism founded on reason, Heidegger of home (*Heimat*) and rootedness based on a certain spiritual sentiment. We find here in the correspondence of biography and thought what Richter calls a '"homology" of life and thinking' (Steffi Richter, 'Review of Karatani, "The Structure of World History,"' *H-Asia*, April 2015, accessed 1 February 2018, https://networks.h-net.org/node/22055/reviews/67387/richter-karatani-structure-world-history-modes-production-modes.) Furthermore, Karatani points out that the inward-facing elements of Heidegger's philosophy and life led him to read the Pre-Socratics Heraclitus and Parmenides as focused on *being* rather than recognizing their worldly position of being *'in between* communities' (Karatani, *Transcritique*, 99).
4. Ferdinand Tönnies, *Community and Civil Society*, Cambridge Texts in the History of Political Thought (Cambridge: CUP, 2001).
5. Tönnies, *Community and Civil Society*, 18.
6. The full verse runs: 'If a man say, I love God, and hateth his brother, he is a liar: for he that loveth not his brother whom he hath seen, how can he love God whom he hath not seen?' While it may seem odd to liken the stranger or alien to God, what they share is a radical otherness which is unruly

and unpredictable. Depending on one's theology and social framework, both God and the outsider may be rumoured to be good or bad (or, to use more traditional language on the theistic question, benevolent or wrathful), or even both (whether a mixture or equally at the same time), thus one or all of faith, reason and/or experience is required for an assessment to be made and a conviction to be formed.

7. Karatani, 'Non-Cartesian Cogito or Cogito as Difference.'
8. In a 1997 lecture, Karatani stated that he 'felt almost suffocated in Japan during the 1980s,' during the generalized euphoria created by the triumph of Japanese capitalism (Kojin Karatani, 'Japan Is Interesting Because Japan Is Not Interesting,' *Karatani Forum*, 1997, www.karataniforum.org/jlecture.html, [no longer online, archived at Archive.org]). Carl Cassegard has pointed out that during this period, Karatani's trenchant opposition to 'the closed, amorphous system of Japanese power' led him to describe 'the global market in positive terms as a liberating and deconstructive tool that undermined the autonomy and closure of national communities,' although he did so 'not because he saw the market as good in itself but because he hoped that the collapse of the Japanese model would liberate buried alternative traditions' (Carl Cassegard, 'Exteriority and Transcritique: Karatani Kōjin and the Impact of the 1990s,' *Japanese Studies* 27/1 [2007], 11, https://doi.org/10.1080/10371390701268612). This interiority-phobic aspect of his thought has not subsided in recent years, as his 2014 conversation with Kim Uchang demonstrates. There, Karatani argues that the Japanese tradition of avoiding open discussion and dissensus is 'not universal' and 'cannot work outside Japan' (Uchang Kim and Kojin Karatani, 'Conversation on East Asian Civilization, Past and Present,' trans. Jeon Seung-Hee, *Azalea: Journal of Korean Literature & Culture* 7/1 [2014], 179, https://doi.org/10.1353/aza.2014.0003).
9. It is worth noting the centrality of the conception and practice of friendship within Illich's thought, which has led to the use of the term 'friends' for his circle of collaborators and interlocutors. A concise treatment of his understanding of friendship can be found in Ivan Illich, *The Rivers North of the Future*, ch. 11.
10. Groeneveld, Hoinacki, and Illich, 'Declaration on Soil.'
11. Tönnies, Community and Civil Society, 18.
12. Karatani, *Architecture as Metaphor*, 140, italics added.
13. Karatani, 'On the "Thing-in-Itself".'
14. Karatani, *Transcritique*, 134.
15. Karatani, *The Structure of World History*, 105.
16. Given that any sense of common belonging is necessarily inchoate and partial, it may be questioned whether the figure of community as a force of overpowering conformism is in fact a straw man erected by its critics. It is true that the ideology of identitarian community, in certain contexts, has been and continues to be a divisive, retrograde force, providing fuel for nationalist and even fascist movements. Nevertheless, to tar all forms of community with the

brush of incipient fascism is to take a particular phenomenon and generalize it for a much wider category, simply by virtue of the same word being invoked. Instead of performing this elision (which can considered a form of the 'hasty generalization' fallacy), we should carefully distinguish between different forms of community.

17. Jose Harris, 'General Introduction,' in Tönnies, *Community and Civil Society*, xxviii.

18. Roberto Esposito, 'Community, Immunity, Biopolitics,' trans. Zakiya Hanafi, *Angelaki* 18/3 (2013), 83, https://doi.org/10.1080/09697 25X.2013.834666. In *Communitas*, Esposito makes a similar argument but includes alongside these three strands of theory 'the communist tradition … despite quite a different categorical profile' (Roberto Esposito, *Communitas: The Origin and Destiny of Community* [Stanford: Stanford University Press, 2010], 2).

19. Esposito, 'Community, Immunity, Biopolitics,' 83, italics added.
20. Esposito, 'Community, Immunity, Biopolitics,' 83, italics added.
21. Jean-Luc Nancy, *The Inoperative Community* (Minneapolis, MN; Oxford: University of Minnesota Press, 1991), 11, italics in original.
22. Esposito, *Communitas*, 7.
23. Kojin Karatani, 'Architecture and Association,' *Thesis: Wissenschaftliche Zeitschrift Der Bauhaus-Universität Weimar* 3 (2003), 23.
24. Nancy, *The Inoperative Community*, 1–3.
25. It should also be noted that although each of these texts has its own specificities and nuances, and thus it may to some seem audacious—and perhaps even ironic, given their critique of commonality as a property—to bundle them all up into a common unit, it is certainly the case that what they all share, as Marita Vyrgioti has pointed out, is an affirmation that 'community does not constitute any "wider subjectivity," and neither does it bear any objective, material elements, apart from one: "it cannot be objectified"' (Marita Vyrgioti, 'Community beyond Identity: Rethinking Radical Politics with Nancy, Agamben, and Esposito,' *The International Journal of Civic, Political and Community Studies* 13/3 [2015], 2). Vyrgioti's article explores the deep resonances between the respective texts of Nancy, Agamben and Esposito, but it can also be said that underlying the divergences between Nancy and Blanchot is an agreement on the originary 'absence of community,' see Ian James, 'Naming the Nothing: Nancy and Blanchot on Community,' *Culture, Theory and Critique* 51/2 (2010), 177, https://doi.org/10.1080/14735784.20 10.496594.

26. Alan Watts, *Behold the Spirit: A Study in the Necessity of Mystical Religion* (London: J. Murray, 1947), 8.

27. D. E. Nineham, *The Use and Abuse of the Bible: A Study of the Bible in an Age of Rapid Cultural Change*, (London: Macmillan, 1976), 227.

28. Friedrich Wilhelm Nietzsche, *Untimely Meditations*, (Cambridge: CUP, 1997), 95.

29. Shattock, *Making Policy in British Higher Education*, 157.
30. 'Increased Fees for Overseas Students,' *Minerva* 5/3 (1967), 461, https://doi.org/10.1007/BF02388585.
31. Lee, 'Overseas Students in Britain,' 318.
32. Shattock, *Making Policy in British Higher Education*, 157.
33. In the British context, it is instructive that the state still funds the bulk of higher education by providing loans to students for fees and living costs, even if the loan portfolio or 'student loanbook' may be sold, part by part, to private parties in order for the government to transfer the risk of 'the growing portfolio of Income-Contingent Repayment student loans on the Government's balance sheet' to the private sector (HM Government, *Operational Efficiency Programme: Asset Portfolio* [HM Treasury Publishing Unit, 2009], 68, available at *National Archives*, accessed 1 February 2018, http://webarchive.nationalarchives.gov.uk/+/http:/www.hmg.gov.uk/media/52715/oep-assetportfolio.pdf). Andrew McGettigan has examined this and other intricacies of the post-2010 student finance system in detail, see Andrew McGettigan, *The Great University Gamble: Money, Markets and Higher Education* (London: Pluto Press, 2013), ch. 13–14. A third stream of university funding comes from partnerships with profit-making (i.e. in our time, capitalist) institutions as well as some public sector bodies.
34. Hastings Rashdall, *The Universities of Europe in the Middle Ages*, Vol. 1 (Oxford: Clarendon Press, 1895), 210.
35. Hilde de Ridder-Symoens, ed., *A History of the University in Europe: Volume 1, Universities in the Middle Ages* (Cambridge: CUP, 2003), 48.
36. Rashdall, *The Universities of Europe in the Middle Ages*, Vol. 1, 163–164.
37. Alan B. Cobban, 'Student Power in the Middle Ages,' *History Today* 30/2 (1980), online at *History Today*, accessed 1 February 2018, https://www.historytoday.com/alan-b-cobban/student-power-middle-ages.
38. Rashdall, *The Universities of Europe in the Middle Ages*, Vol. 1, 167.
39. Ridder-Symoens, *A History of the University in Europe*, 48.
40. Alan B. Cobban, 'Medieval Student Power,' *Past & Present* 53/1 (1971), 35, https://doi.org/10.1093/past/53.1.28.
41. Rashdall, *The Universities of Europe in the Middle Ages*, Vol. 1, 211.
42. Rashdall, *The Universities of Europe in the Middle Ages*, Vol. 1, 212.
43. Cobban, 'Student Power in the Middle Ages.'
44. Paulo Freire, *Pedagogy of the Oppressed* (New York: Continuum, 2003), 56.
45. The Who, '*Won't Get Fooled Again*,' on *Who's Next*, compact disc (Track Records, Decca Records, 1971).
46. Rashdall, *The Universities of Europe in the Middle Ages*, Vol. 1, 197–9.
47. Michel Foucault, *Discipline and Punish*, trans. Alan Sheridan (London: Allen Lane, 1977), 156.

48. Freire, *Pedagogy of the Oppressed*, 56.
49. Freire, *Pedagogy of the Oppressed*, 56.
50. Rashdall, *The Universities of Europe in the Middle Ages*, Vol. 1, 212–13.
51. Cobban, 'Medieval Student Power,' 48.
52. Department for Business Innovation and Skills, *Higher Education: Students at the Heart of the System.*
53. Cobban, 'Medieval Student Power,' 33.
54. The proposed Teaching Excellence Framework would strengthen this tendency. For a cogent critique of the recent White Paper, *Success as a Knowledge Economy*, which sets out this planned development and other related mechanisms, see Woodcock and Toscano, 'On the Poverty of Student Choice,' *The Sociological Review Blog*, 19 July 2016, accessed 1 February 2018, https://www.thesociologicalreview.com/blog/on-the-poverty-of-student-choice.html
55. Jacques Le Goff, *Time, Work & Culture in the Middle Ages* (Chicago ; London: University of Chicago Press, 1980), 146.
56. Rashdall, *The Universities of Europe in the Middle Ages*, Vol. 1, 170.
57. Cobban, 'Medieval Student Power,' 66.
58. Although *gemeinschaft* and *gesesllschaft* are normally translated into English as 'community' and 'society,' it may be also helpful to draw from a distinction the theologian and social critic Giles Fraser has made between 'thick community' and 'thin community.' In the former configuration of social ties 'people look after each other and have a high degree of civic pride,' but are 'often not good at dealing with difference, or with outsiders' (Giles Fraser, 'Diversity Is a Boon—but We're Losing Our Sense of Community,' *The Guardian*, 6 October 2016, accessed 1 February 2018, https://www.theguardian.com/commentisfree/belief/2016/oct/06/diversity-is-a-boon-but-were-losing-our-sense-of-community). In the latter situation, 'you can be as different as you like. Nobody cares,' and so although what exists 'isn't really much of a community at all' (Fraser, 'Diversity Is a Boon'), it is nevertheless a *variety* of community, even if a rather heterodox one.
59. Taylor defines the term in the following manner: 'By social imaginary, I mean something much broader and deeper than the intellectual schemes people may entertain when they think about social reality in a disengaged mode. I am thinking, rather, of the ways people imagine their social existence, how they fit together with others, how things go on between them and their fellows, the expectations that are normally met, and the deeper normative notions and images that underlie these expectations' (Charles Taylor, *Modern Social Imaginaries* (Durham, N.C.; London: Duke University Press, 2004), 23.)
60. Michael Rustin, 'Flexibility in Higher Education,' in *Towards a Post-Fordist Welfare State?*, ed. Roger Burrows and Brian Loader (London: Routledge, 1994), 190–1.
61. Rustin, 'Flexibility in Higher Education,' 191. This latter development,

of course, would not have been possible without technological innovations which allow for increasingly disembodied learning which can be done at any place or time, e.g. with lectures that one could watch on a tablet or smartphone on public transport. In a 1996 interview, Ivan Illich comments that 'hospitality requires a threshold over which I can lead you and TV, internet, newspaper, [and] the idea of communication [has] abolished the walls and therefore also the friendship, the possibility of leading somebody over the door' ('Ivan Illich with Jerry Brown: We The People, KPFA—March 22, 1996,' *We The People*, accessed 1 February 2018, http://www.wtp.org/archive/transcripts/ivan_illich_jerry.html). It can likewise be said that communications technology has abolished the walls of the university, for both good and ill.

62. Hastings Rashdall, *The Universities of Europe in the Middle Ages*, Vol. 3 (Oxford: Clarendon Press, 1895), 662.

63. Various, 'Weaponise the Corpse! Anti-privatization Struggle at Sussex University,' *Mute*, accessed 17 February 2016, http://www.metamute.org/editorial/articles/weaponise-corpse-anti-privatization-struggle-sussex-university.

64. Solidarity Federation, 'The Pop Up Union: A Postmortem,' *Solidarity Federation*, 10 November 2014, accessed 1 Feburary 2018, http://www.solfed.org.uk/brighton/the-pop-up-union-a-postmortem.

65. Solidarity Federation, 'The Pop Up Union: A Postmortem.'

66. Mark Bergfeld, 'New Struggles, New Unions? On the Pop-Up Union at Sussex University,' *Ceasefire Magazine* (blog), 18 April 2013, accessed 1 February 2018, https://ceasefiremagazine.co.uk/struggles-unions-pop-up-union-sussex-university/.

67. Solidarity Federation, 'The Pop Up Union: A Postmortem.'

68. Richard Braude, 'Crisis in the Cleaning Sector,' *Mute*, 18 December 2013, accessed 1 February 2018, http://www.metamute.org/editorial/articles/crisis-cleaning-sector.

69. Braude, 'Crisis in the Cleaning Sector.'

70. Braude, 'Crisis in the Cleaning Sector.'

71. In the UK, the 'bedders' of Cambridge (the equivalent term at Oxford being 'scouts'), domestic workers who cleaned the residential rooms of students appear to have been acknowledged in a university edict in 1635 which forbade women under fifty 'to make any beds or perform any other service within any scholars' chambers' (Frank Stubbings, *Bedders, Bulldogs and Bedells: A Cambridge Glossary* (Cambridge: CUP, 1995), 12).

72. George Caffentzis, *In Letters of Blood and Fire: Work, Machines, and the Crisis of Capitalism* (Oakland, CA: PM Press, 2013), 26–7.

73. Even those in the perceived 'upper tier' of non-academic staff such as senior library personnel are not exempt from being at least occasionally perceived as a structurally important yet secondary appendage of the body of the university. Although not a few academics regularly acknowledge the role of librarians in contributing to their research, the situation appears rather different among students. Research at the University of Sheffield

'showed that most students were unable to distinguish different groups of staff, were unaware of their departmental librarian and did not recognize the academic role of librarians' (Rachel Bickley and Sheila Corrall, 'Student Perceptions of Staff in the Information Commons: A Survey at the University of Sheffield,' *Reference Services Review* 39/2 [2011], 223, https://doi.org/10.1108/00907321111135466.)

74. Alia Al Ghussain, '4 Reasons the Privatization of Sussex University Services Affects Us All,' Novara Wire, February 19, 2014, accessed 1 February 2018, http://wire.novaramedia.com/2014/02/4-reasons-the-privatization-of-sussex-university-services-affects-us-all/, italics added.

75. Chartered Institute of Personnel and Development, 'Over-Qualification and Skills Mismatch in the Graduate Labour Market' (London: CIPD, August 2015), 15.

76. Rebecca Gumbrell, *Unions in Western Europe: Hard Times, Hard Choices* (Oxford: OUP, 2013), 2.

77. Karatani, *Transcritique*, 134.

78. Karatani, 'On the "Thing-in-Itself",' 1993.

79. René Descartes, *A Discourse on the Method of Correctly Conducting One's Reason and Seeking Truth in the Sciences*, (Oxford: OUP, 2006), 27.

80. Descartes, 'Descartes, *A Discourse on the Method*,' xi. The original French reads: '*Je n'y confidere pas autrement les hommes que i'y voy, que je ferois les arbres qui se rencontrent en vos forests, ou les animaux qui y paissent*,' (René Descartes, *Oeuvres de Descartes*, vol. 1 [Paris: Léopold Cerf, 1897], 203).

81. A case can certainly be made that the degree to which what is created from academic activity can be attributed to a single person or small group is largely an illusion, given the many 'inputs' into the process from various sources and directions. Stefano Harney and Fred Moten, for example have argued persuasively for an understanding of the 'sociality' of academic labour (Stefano Harney and Fred Moten, 'Doing Academic Work,' in *Chalk Lines: The Politics of Work in the Managed University*, ed. Randy Martin [Durham, NC: Duke UP, 1998], 170–2). In a somewhat different direction, theorists of Actor-Network Theory have explored the connections between human researchers and non-human 'actants' in the material environments of laboratories and other spaces of research (Bruno Latour, *Laboratory Life: The Social Construction of Scientific Facts*, Sage Library of Social Research [Beverly Hills: Sage, 1979]; Bruno Latour, *Reassembling the Social : An Introduction to Actor-Network-Theory*, [Oxford: OUP, 2005]). Nevertheless, the illusion is primarily an exaggeration—even if in some cases a gross exaggeration—rather than a complete fiction, for there is a sense in which even the broadest understanding of academic work cannot erase the aspects of solitary, personal labour which is involved, especially on an existential level. Moreover, what is certainly far from a fiction is the system of academic measurements and rewards which favour single-authored pieces, and thus less collaborative work.

82. Roger Smith, *Mind and Nature: A History of Psychology* (London: Reaktion Books, 2013), 18.
83. Gary L. Herstein, 'Independent Scholars: Return of the Modern?,' *The Quantum of Explanation* (blog), 14 January 2016, accessed 1 February 2018, http://garyherstein.com/2016/01/14/independent-scholars-return-of-the-modern/.
84. Rashdall, *The Universities of Europe in the Middle Ages*, Vol. 1, 4.
85. Desmond M. Clarke, *Descartes: A Biography* (Cambridge: CUP, 2006), 218.
86. Clarke, *Descartes: A Biography*, 229, 241.
87. Clarke, *Descartes: A Biography*, 179–80.
88. Clarke, *Descartes: A Biography*, 180.
89. The village, located on the coast of the North Sea, 'was so isolated that it took eight days for letters to reach him from Leiden' (Clarke, *Descartes: A Biography*, 277). It goes without saying that Descartes would not have participated in any serious way in the elements of *gemeinschaft* which would have existed there.
90. A convincing argument has been made that such is the case in the sphere of the wider economy, where post-war Fordism and Keynesianism in the Western world has to be regarded as an exception or aberration to the more long-standing and global condition of precarity (Brett Neilson and Ned Rossiter, 'Precarity as a Political Concept, Or, Fordism as Exception,' *Theory, Culture & Society* 25/7–8 (2008), 51–72, https://doi.org/10.1177/0263276408097796.)
91. Alexander W. Astin, 'Higher Education and the Concept of Community,' in *Fifteenth David Dodds Henry Lecture* (Urbana: Office of Publications University of Illinois, 1993), 8.
92. Astin, 'Higher Education and the Concept of Community,' 8, italics in original.
93. Russell L. Friedman, *Intellectual Traditions at the Medieval University: The Use of Philosophical Psychology in Trinitarian Theology among the Franciscans and Dominicans, 1250–350*, (Leiden: Brill, 2013).
94. A. Rupert Hall, *Philosophers at War : The Quarrel between Newton and Leibniz* (Cambridge: CUP, 1980).
95. Doug Henwood, 'Explaining What Goes on in the World: In Memory of Bob Fitch' *LBO NEWS from Doug Henwood*, 22 May 2012, accessed 1 February 2018, http://lbo-news.com/2012/05/22/explaining-what-exists-in-memory-of-bob-fitch/.
96. Astin, 'Higher Education and the Concept of Community,' 9.
97. Decca Aitkenhead, 'Peter Higgs: I Wouldn't Be Productive Enough for Today's Academic System,' *The Guardian*, 6 December 2013, accessed 1 February 2018, https://www.theguardian.com/science/2013/dec/06/peter-higgs-boson-academic-system.
98. Roger Burrows, 'Living with the H-Index? Metric Assemblages in the Contemporary Academy,' *The Sociological Review* 60/2 (2012), 356.

99. Burrows, 'Living with the H-Index?', 357, italics in original.
100. Burrows, 'Living with the H-Index?', 359.
101. Burrows, 'Living with the H-Index?', 368.
102. Rosalind Gill, 'Breaking the Silence: The Hidden Injuries of Neoliberal Academia,' in *Secrecy and Silence in the Research Process: Feminist Reflections*, ed. Róisín Flood and Rosalind Gill (London: Routledge, 2009).
103. Gill, 'Breaking the Silence,' 235.
104. Gill, 'Breaking the Silence,' 235, italics added.
105. One notable exception is, of course, certain forms of research—primarily empirical, but existing in not just in the sciences, but also the social sciences and humanities—which is highly collaborative in practice, but which is still influenced by the individualistic tendencies of contemporary academia. On the other hand, Mark Olssen has argued that the present system 'not only ... place[s] too much emphasis on research productivity and performativity,' but 'encourages dubious research tactics and strategies for maximizing publications, citations and team-based research' (Mark Olssen, 'Neoliberal Competition in Higher Education Today: Research, Accountability and Impact,' *British Journal of Sociology of Education* 37/1 [2016], 135, https://doi.org/1 0.1080/01425692.2015.1100530.)
106. Eileen A. Joy, 'Nothing Has Yet Been Said: On the Non-Existence of Academic Freedom and the Necessity of Inoperative Community,' *Punctum Books* (blog), 1 May 2015, accessed 1 February 2018, https://punctumbooks.com/uncategorized/nothing-has-yet-been-said-on-the-non-existence-of-academic-freedom-and-the-necessity-of-inoperative-community/.
107. Costas Douzinas, 'A Short History of the British Critical Legal Conference Or, the Responsibility of the Critic,' *Law and Critique* 25/2 (2014), 189, https://doi.org/10.1007/s10978-014-9133-9.
108. BABEL Working Group, 'About BABEL,' *BABEL Working Group*, accessed February 10, 2016, http://babel-meeting.org/.
109. Joy, 'Nothing Has Yet Been Said,' italics in original.
110. Costas Douzinas, 'Oubliez Critique,' *Law and Critique* 16/1 (2005). 66, 68–9, https://doi.org/10.1007/s10978-005-4907-8.
111. Roberto Esposito and Jean-Luc Nancy, 'Dialogue on the Philosophy to Come,' *The Minnesota Review* 2010/75 (2010), 81, https://doi.org/10.1215/00265667-2010-75-71.
112. Kojin Karatani, 'Thing as Other,' in *Anything* (New York: Rizzoli, 2000), 259.
113. Cassegard, 'Exteriority and Transcritique,' 11.
114. Kanishka Goonewardena, 'Theory and Politics in Karatani Kōjin's The Structure of World History,' *Journal of Japanese Philosophy* 4/ 4 (2016), 77–105.
115. Karatani, *The Structure of World History*, 3.
116. Karatani, *The Structure of World History*, 5.
117. Karatani, *The Structure of World History*, 5–6.

118. Karatani, *The Structure of World History*, 8.
119. Kojin Karatani, 'An Introduction to Modes of Exchange' trans. Michael K. Bourdaghs, *Kojin Karatani Official Web Site*, 2017, accessed 1 February 2018, http://www.kojinkaratani.com/en/pdf/An_Introduction_to_Modes_of_Exchange.pdf. Mode U is a recent development in Karatani's thought. Previously he held that Mode D was the return of a form of the repressed Mode A.
120. Karatani, *The Structure of World History*, 8.
121. Charles P. Loomis and John C. McKinney, Introduction to *Community and Society*, by Ferdinand Tonnies (Mineola, N.Y: Dover Publications Inc., 2003), 3.
122. Karatani, *The Structure of World History*, 225.
123. Karatani, *Architecture as Metaphor*, 146.
124. Karatani, *Architecture as Metaphor*, 146.
125. Karatani, *Transcritique*, 105.
126. Kojin Karatani, 'Beyond Capital-Nation-State,' *Rethinking Marxism* 20/ 4 (2008), 585.
127. Karatani, 'An Introduction to Modes of Exchange,' 15; Karatani, *Transcritique*, 303.
128. Equally, any attempt to return to a state of affairs where Mode B-style redistribution was more prominent simply reconfigures the parts while maintaining the deeply unjust whole. Here Karatani's observation that 'more often than not, social democracy functions as chauvinistic nationalism' should be borne in mind (Karatani, 'Beyond Capital-Nation-State,' 591). It should not be forgotten that British citizens (and subsequently EU citizens) enjoyed highly subsidized higher education for forty-four years after fees were dramatically raised for non-citizens. The generality of this phenomenon can also be seen in a central video message for the unsuccessful campaign for Bernie Sanders to be the 2016 presidential nominee of the Democratic Party, which has as its background music Simon & Garfunkel's 'America.' Although Sanders's definition of what America stands for was far wider than all of the other candidates seeking the nomination of the two major parties, the fact remains that in order to campaign for social democratic policies, the most effective tool was to invoke a national consciousness, in order to gain the support of the 'all [who have] come to look for America' (Simon & Garfunkel, '*America*,' on *Bookends*, compact disc, [Columbia Records, 1968]). Another example is British Prime Minister Theresa May's disavowal of anti-state Thatcherism in the wake of the Brexit vote, in which she stated, 'It's time to remember the good that government can do,' while resurgent nationalism provided the backdrop ('Theresa May: I'll Use Power of State to Build Fairer Britain,' *BBC News*, 5 October 2016, accessed 1 February 2018, http://www.bbc.co.uk/news/uk-politics-37556019.)
129. Indeed, already in *Architecture as Metaphor* he acknowledges that 'capitalism itself is deconstructive,' see Karatani, *Architecture as Metaphor*, 71.

130. Karatani, 'An Introduction to Modes of Exchange,' 25.
131. Karatani, *The Structure of World History*, xii.
132. Giles Fraser, 'The Fantasy of the Beautiful Nomad Is Morally Bankrupt,' *The Guardian*, 15 September 2016, accessed 1 February 2018, https://www.theguardian.com/commentisfree/belief/2016/sep/15/the-fantasy-of-the-beautiful-nomad-is-morally-bankrupt.
133. For an extended discussion of global or digital nomads, see Päivi Kannisto, 'Global Nomads: Challenges of Mobility in the Sedentary World' (Tilburg University, 2014), accessed 1 February 2018, https://pure.uvt.nl/portal/files/3511053/Kannisto_Global_18_06_2014.pdf.
134. Richter, 'Review of Karatani, "The Structure of World History".'
135. Karatani, *The Structure of World History*, 127.
136. Karatani, *The Structure of World History*, 145.
137. Karatani, *The Structure of World History*, 145.
138. Karatani, *The Structure of World History*, 145.
139. Karatani, *The Structure of World History*, 146–7.
140. Tobias Jones, *Utopian Dreams: In Search of a Good Life* (London: Faber, 2008), 5.
141. David Cayley, 'Introduction,' in Illich, *The Rivers North of the Future*, 24–25.
142. Groeneveld, Hoinacki, and Illich, 'Declaration on Soil.'
143. Esposito and Nancy, 'Dialogue on the Philosophy to Come,' 82, italics added.
144. Illich, *The Rivers North of the Future*, 47.
145. Kojin Karatani, Brian Hioe, and Houston Small, 'There Is No Such Thing as Japanese Marxism: An Interview with Kojin Karatani,' *Platypus Review* 71 (2014), 3.
146. Esposito, *Communitas*, 4.
147. Esposito, *Communitas*, 4.
148. Karatani, *The Structure of World History*, 35.
149. Illich, *The Rivers North of the Future*, 52.
150. Illich, *The Rivers North of the Future*, 52.
151. Illich, *The Rivers North of the Future*, 54.
152. Illich, *The Rivers North of the Future*, 54.
153. Karatani, 'Beyond Capital-Nation-State,' 593.
154. Karatani, *Transcritique*, 134.
155. Charles Taylor, *A Secular Age* (Cambridge, MA; London: Belknap Press of Harvard University Press, 2007), 793.
156. Karatani, *The Structure of World History*, 259.
157. Karatani, *The Structure of World History*, 306–7.
158. Rob Lucas, 'Socialism as a Regulative Idea?', *New Left Review*, II/94 (2015), 123–4; Harry Harootunian, 'Philosophy of History's Return,' *History and Theory* 54/1 (2015), 104–5, https://doi.org/10.1111/hith.10743. The first practical attempt to give institutional form to Mode D, the New Associationist

Movement (NAM) was founded by Karatani and others in Japan in 2000, but came to an end a mere two years later. Karatani attributes NAM's demise to the confluence of two developments, both of which called into question NAM's primarily economic strategies to counter-act Capital-Nation-State. The first was the September 11 attacks, which led to the deployment of Japanese troops in Iraq, and the second was the realization that that the alternative economy they were engaged in building up could only be successful with 'the support and regulation of national and local government' (Kojin Karatani, 'Abstract: Toward World Republic—Beyond Capital-Nation-State' [University of Chicago, 2006]) This realization spurred Karatani to dig deeper into understanding the dynamics behind state and nation, and his writing from the mid-2000s onwards reflect this research, most notably *The Structure of World History*. Having interrogated the histories and workings of Modes A and B more intimately, his present research project is, as was mentioned above, focused upon grasping Mode D in greater detail.

Chapter Four

1. Karatani, *Transcritique*, 106.
2. William Blake, *Collected Poems*, Routledge Classics (London: Routledge, 2002), 167.
3. Robert Browning, *The Works of Robert Browning* (Ware: Wordsworth Poetry Library, 1994), 439.
4. Kojin Karatani, 'The Irrational Will to Reason,' in *Literary Mischief: Sakaguchi Ango, Culture, and the War*, ed. James Dorsey and Douglas Slaymaker (Lanham, Md: Lexington Books, 2010), 25. Sakaguchi Ango was the writer's pen name, arranged in the traditional Japanese format whereby Sakaguchi is the surname and Ango the first name. Against the usual practice, however, he has come to be known by the first name of his pen-name, including in scholarly articles, and hence here we observe this irregularity.
5. Sakaguchi, 'Kongo No Jiin Seikatsu Ni Taisuru Shikō (My Thoughts on the Future of Temple Life),' in *Sakaguchi Ango Zenshū (The Complete Works of Sakaguchi Ango)*, ed. Kojin Karatani and Sekii Mitsuo, Vol. 1 (Tokyo: Chikuma shobō, 1999); quoted in Kojin Karatani, *History and Repetition* (New York: Columbia University Press, 2012), 196.
6. Sakaguchi, 'Kongo No Jiin Seikatsu Ni Taisuru Shikō (My Thoughts on the Future of Temple Life),' 25, italics added.
7. Sakaguchi, 'Kongo No Jiin Seikatsu Ni Taisuru Shikō (My Thoughts on the Future of Temple Life)'; quoted in Karatani, *History and Repetition*, 196, italics added. Lippit translates 'aiyoku' as 'sexual desire,' but the word is in fact made up of the words for love ('ai' or 愛) and desire ('yoku' or 欲), and so means, literally, 'desire of love.' I am indebted to Michiko Oki for this explanation, and for the other points about the Japanese language in this section.

8. Karatani, *Transcritique*, 102.
9. Karatani, *Transcritique*, 51. The etymology of *specio* ('to see') and *spes* ('hope'), although distinct in many respects, are both united in a concern with sight. This leads to deriatives such as, from the former, *conspicere*, 'to catch sight of, discern' as well as, from the latter, *sperare*, 'to hope, look forward to' (Michiel Arnoud Cor de Vaan, *Etymological Dictionary of Latin and the Other Italic Languages*, Leiden Indo-European Etymological Dictionary Series, Vol. 7 [Leiden: Brill, 2008]). In other words, the modern use of 'spec' as 'bet' is in harmony with its ancient root, given that any well-considered bet requires an adequate degree of of *discernment* and *foresight*.
10. Kant, *Critique of Pure Reason*, 686.
11. Kant, *Critique of Pure Reason*, 686.
12. Kant, *Critique of Pure Reason*, 687.
13. Just as linguistics recognizes singular collective nouns such as 'council' and 'team,' by treating collective actors as singularities and not as mere aggregations of individuals (as in methodological individualism) we are affirming the concept of group personality, a key tenet of political pluralism in the English tradition as developed by thinkers such as J. N. Figgis, Harold Laski, G. D. H. Cole, and F. W. Maitland. This theory of group personality holds that 'social groups are real entities which have a life and being which is something more than the sum of their individual members,' and it is crucial to note that its legal consequences are not simply fictive but 'rooted in social facts' (David Nicholls, *The Pluralist State: The Political Ideas of J.N. Figgis and His Contemporaries*, 2nd ed. [Basingstoke: Macmillan in association with St Antony's College, Oxford, 1994], 56).
14. Weslati's daring hypothesis, drawing from the published recollections of various figures who were in close contact with Kojève at the time and her interpretation of various comments in his writings about the potential tyrant-philosopher relationship between Napoleon and Hegel which did not come to pass, is that Kojève's recently rediscovered Russian manuscript from 1940–1, a copy of which was deposited in the Russian embassy in Paris at the time in rather shadowy circumstances, was intended as nothing less than a 'letter' to Stalin which he hoped would inaugurate such a relationship between the Soviet dictator and himself (Hager Weslati, 'Kojève's Letter to Stalin,' *Radical Philosophy* 184 [2014], 7–18).
15. Karatani, *Transcritique*, 100–112.
16. William James, *Pragmatism: And Four Essays from The Meaning of Truth* (New York: Meridian Books, 1955), 20.
17. James, *Pragmatism: And Four Essays from The Meaning of Truth*, 20.
18. Louis Althusser, *Lenin and Philosophy, and Other Essays* (New York: Monthly Review Press, 1998), 173–4.
19. The male pronoun is used throughout to remain consistent with the historical context of the example.
20. Karatani, *Transcritique*, 100, italics in original.

21. Immanuel Kant, *The Critique of Judgement*, trans. James Creed Meredith (Oxford: OUP, 1986), 52–53; Karatani, *Transcritique*, 38.
22. Karatani, *Transcritique*, 38.
23. Steven Shaviro, 'Transcritique (part 1: Kant),' *The Pinocchio Theory* (blog), 9 November 2005, accessed 1 February 2018, http://www.shaviro.com/Blog/?p=455 Kojin.
24. Karatani, *Transcritique*, 105.
25. Karatani, *Transcritique*, 103–4.
26. The Romantic idea that the nation is the ground and context for all being (not least of all being-with) and becoming has, of course, a much older provenance. We can find a prototype of its modern form in the Greek idea of *ethnos*, which Agamben translates elegantly as a 'national collectivity based upon descent and homogeneity' (Giorgio Agamben, *The Kingdom and the Glory: For a Theological Genealogy of Economy and Government*, trans. Lorenzo Chiesa [Stanford: Stanford University Press, 2011], 257). Illich has explored the primitive Christian disruption of the Platonic conception of friendship. For Plato, the possibility of love or *philia* is premised upon a shared conception of virtue upon which is built an ethics or *ethos*, which is itself formulated within the context of a certain *ethnos* or people (Illich, *The Rivers North of the Future*, 147). This particularistic conception is challenged in the Gospels, symbolized in the Lukan parable of the Good Samaritan, which we discussed analogically in our previous chapter, whereby the Palestinian outsider 'acts as a friend towards a beaten-up Jew' (Illich, *The Rivers North of the Future*, 147).
27. Peter Hallward, 'The Singular and the Specific,' *Radical Philosophy* 99 (2000), 8.
28. Hallward, 'The Singular and the Specific,' 8.
29. Hallward, 'The Singular and the Specific,' 8–9.
30. Hallward, 'The Singular and the Specific,' 8.
31. Hallward, 'The Singular and the Specific,' 8.
32. Immanuel Kant, *Toward Perpetual Peace and Other Writings on Politics, Peace, and History*, ed. Pauline Kleingeld, trans. David L. Colclasure, (New Haven; London: Yale University Press, 2006), 19.
33. Among the examples which Kant gives are citizens who are bound to pay their taxes, officers who are obliged to comply with the orders of their superiors and clergy who are to teach the catechism and instruct their congregations according to their respective church traditions, see Kant, *Toward Perpetual Peace*, 19–20.
34. Kant, *Toward Perpetual Peace*, 19.
35. Charles Gore, *The Incarnation of the Son of God* (London: John Murray, 1891), 157–8.
36. This dynamic can also be linked to what Charles Taylor, in his work on secularity, has called 'excarnation.' Writing in the context of religion, Taylor points out that the movements of Reform in Latin Christendom resulted in 'the

transfer of our religious life out of bodily forms of ritual, worship, practice, so that it comes more and more to reside 'in the head" (Taylor, *A Secular Age*, 613). As a consequence of this, 'embodied feeling is no longer a medium in which we relate to what we recognize as rightly bearing an aura of the higher; either we do recognize something like this, and we see reason as our unique access to it; or we tend to reject this kind of higher altogether, reducing it through naturalistic explanation' (Taylor, *A Secular Age*, 288). To transpose Taylor's argument into the terms we have been using in this book, the Reformation marks a turn to thought-centricism and a concomitant denigration of feeling-centricism, which also results in a simultaneous transformation of the sphere of acting.

37. Karatani, *Transcritique*, 104.
38. Karatani, *Transcritique*, 100, italics added.
39. Karatani, *The Structure of World History*, 236.
40. Karatani, *The Structure of World History*, 143.
41. Karatani, *Transcritique*, 117.
42. Blake, *Collected Poems*, 167.
43. The Italian feminist Adrian Cavarero has argued against the blanket application of the poststructuralist axioms of difference and anti-essentialism to the field of sexual difference, pointing out that 'feminine sexual difference is a corporeal difference,' and that this 'banality' nevertheless 'asks for a meaning, the returning of a meaning' (Adriana Cavarero and Elisabetta Bertolino, 'Beyond Ontology and Sexual Difference: An Interview with the Italian Feminist Philosopher Adriana Cavarero,' *Differences* 19/1 (2008), 143–4). The Blake proverb likewise grounds its meaning upon the banality of differences in the physical world. It is far more contentious whether human persons are distinct in such 'banal' ways, but the bare fact of physical and physiological differences, both external and internal, which lead to differences in basic abilities such as dexterity and strength, do indicate that although the human person is arguably more adaptable and malleable than the apple tree, there are distinct *limits* to her degree of self-creation.
44. Anton Schütz, '"Legal Critique": Elements for a Genealogy,' *Law and Critique* 16/1 (2005), 85.
45. In their zeal to abolish as many elements of the *ancien régime* as possible, the French revolutionaries adopted a new decimalized calendar which had twelve months, each divided into three weeks of ten days length. The months were renamed with neologisms referring to the season, such as Fructidor (a combination of the Latin word for fruit, *fructus*, and the Greek word for gift, *doron*), see Matthew Shaw, *Time and the French Revolution: The Republican Calendar, 1789–Year XIV* (Boydell & Brewer Ltd, 2011), 43.
46. Charlton Thomas Lewis and Charles Short, *A Latin Dictionary: Founded on Andrews' Edition of Freund's Latin Dictionary* (Oxford: Clarendon Press, 1879).
47. Henry George Liddell and Robert Scott, *A Greek-English Lexicon*,

ed. Henry Stuart Jones and McKenzie, 9th Edition (Oxford: Clarendon Press, 1940).

48. For reasons of space and argumentative cohesiveness, we shall constrain our *textual* discussion to the Judeo-Christian tradition, given that it is the central source for the Western idea of vocation which we are most concerned with here. It is unfortunately beyond the scope of this chapter to investigate concepts within non-Western civilizations and pre-Christian Western Antiquity which are similar to the Christian and/or secular notions of vocation which have arisen in the West in the Common Era. This is not to downplay the significance of these alternative discourses, but rather simply to recognize their less prominent role in constructing the sphere of the British university and indeed Anglo-American discourse more generally.

49. Walter Brueggemann, *Genesis*, Interpretation: A Bible Commentary for Teaching and Preaching (Atlanta: John Knox Press, 1982), 46.

50. Of course, the Adamic naming of the animals in the creation narrative pertains to a particular and not a singular reality, for as Karatani points out, the sphere of the singular is that of the proper name, such as with a dog named Taro, rather than the generic name, as with the genus *Canis* to which the dog named Taro belongs on a taxinomic level, see Karatani, *Architecture as Metaphor*, xxiii.

51. David Dawson, *Allegorical Readers and Cultural Revision in Ancient Alexandria* (University of California Press, 1991), 85.

52. James Strong, *Strong's Exhaustive Concordance of the Bible*, 6th edition (Nashville, TN: Abingdon, 1890).

53. M. C. Howatson, *The Oxford Companion to Classical Literature*, ed. M.C. Howatson, 3rd ed. (Oxford: OUP, 2013), 528.

54. M. M. Austin, *Economic and Social History of Ancient Greece: An Introduction* (Berkeley: University of California Press, 1980), 22–3.

55. Neil Elliott, *Liberating Paul: The Justice of God and the Politics of the Apostle* (USA: Fortress Press, 2005), 33. In the words of Karl Barth, the Swiss proponent of 'dialectical theology,' this calling is 'the act of the call of God issued in Jesus Christ by which a man is transplanted into his new state as a Christian, is made a participant in the promise … bound up with this new state, and assumes the duty … corresponding to this state' (Karl Barth, *Church Dogmatics: The Doctrine of Creation*, ed. G. W. Bromiley and Thomas F. Torrance, Vol. III.4 [Edinburgh: T&T Clark, 1961], 600).

56. Indeed, much of the language used by early Christians to refer to Christ and his Kingdom could be seen as plagiarized from imperial terminology. To give just a few examples, the 'good news' of Emperor Augustus's birthday became the Christian *euangélion* or gospel, the inscription referring to Julius Caesar as 'God made manifest' was transposed into the Christian understanding of the Incarnation, and the word for the Second Coming of Christ, *parousia*, was originally used to describe the Emperor's visit to a city (Frances M. Young, 'Prelude: Jesus Christ, Foundation of Christianity,' in *Cambridge History of*

Christianity, ed. Margaret M. Mitchell and Frances M. Young [Cambridge: CUP, 2006], 14–15.

57. Giorgio Agamben, *The Time That Remains: A Commentary on the Letter to the Romans* (Stanford: Stanford University Press, 2005), 19.

58. William C. Placher, *Callings: Twenty Centuries of Christian Wisdom on Vocation* (Grand Rapids, Michigan: Wm. B. Eerdmans Publishing, 2005), 6–7.

59. Jane Dawson, 'A History of Vocation: Tracing a Keyword of Work, Meaning and Moral Purpose,' *Adult Education Quarterly* 55/3 (2005), 223.

60. The Plowshares Movement began in 1980 when eight antiwar activists broke into the General Electric Nuclear Missile facility in King of Prussia, Pennsylvania, damaged nose cones of nuclear warheads and poured blood onto various documents. The name of the movement comes from a passage in the biblical Book of Isaiah: 'They shall beat their swords into plowshares, and their spears into pruninghooks: nation shall not lift up sword against nation, neither shall they learn war any more' (Isa. 2:4, KJV). Over seventy-five similar actions have taken place around the world since the first action, primarily but not exclusively by religious activists (Mary Anne Muller and Anna Brown, 'The Plowshares Eight: Thirty Years On,' *Waging Nonviolence* [blog], 2010, accessed 1 February 2018, http://wagingnonviolence.org/feature/the-plowshares-8-thirty-years-on/).

61. Martin Luther, 'An Open Letter to The Christian Nobility Concerning the Reform of the Christian Estate,' trans. C. M. Jacobs, *Project Wittenberg*, accessed 1 February 2018, http://www.iclnet.org/pub/resources/text/wittenberg/luther/web/nblty-03.html.

62. Luther, 'An Open Letter to The Christian Nobility.'

63. Martin Luther, 'Temporal Authority: To What Extent It Should Be Obeyed,' in *Martin Luther's Basic Theological Writings*, ed. Timothy F. Lull (Minneapolis: Fortress Press, 1989), 429.

64. Luther, 'An Open Letter to The Christian Nobility.'

65. Luther, 'An Open Letter to The Christian Nobility.'

66. Placher, *Callings*, 205–6.

67. Martin Luther, 'The Gospel for the Early Christmas Service,' in Placher, *Callings*, 214.

68. Luther would probably not have accepted this claim, given his interesting thought experiment in the sphere of political theory, one which he considers analogical to the priesthood of all believers. He sketches a situation where 'ten brothers, all king's sons and equal heirs' decide upon 'one of themselves to rule the inheritance for them all,' and argues that in such a situation 'they would all be kings and equal in power, though one of them would be charged with the duty of ruling' (Luther, 'An Open Letter to The Christian Nobility.') An enthusiastic democrat may see Luther's image as an apologia for popular sovereignty, and even link it to the claims that an 'ascending' theory of government—to use Walter Ullmann's term—was the

practice of medieval Germanic tribes, who elected their rulers (Walter Ullmann, *Principles of Government and Politics in the Middle Ages*, 4th ed. [London: Methuen, 1978], 22). However, as even Ullmann recognizes, the king could only be elected those from deemed to be of royal blood. Frode Horvik has pointed out that this 'royal blood-right' was considered to be sacral; thus, the plausibility of claiming a strong element of democracy—whether in the classical or modern sense—among these tribes is rather low (Frode Hervik, 'The Nordic Countries,' in *Edinburgh Companion to the History of Democracy: From Pre-History to Future Possibilities*, ed. Benjamin Isakhan [Edinburgh: Edinburgh University Press, 2012], 144.) Luther's enthusiastic cooperation with the various princes in the Holy Roman Empire, moreover, makes any claim for a pronounced democratic impulse in him rather difficult, at least in the secular kingdom of Law. Furthermore, to return to the question of levelling up or down in the spiritual kingdom of Grace, if we take priesthood as being something that is 'added' to 'bare humanity' upon one's embrace of the Christian faith, Luther's concomitant proviso that practical order requires the office of priest to be exercised by specific people means that in his attempt to raise all Christians to the status of priesthood, Luther ironically reduces all to the position of the laity. This may not be a bad thing for some, particularly anti-institutionalists and anti-clericalists whether formally within the sphere of Christianity (such as the Quakers or the Japanese Non-Church Movement) or outside it, but ultimately Luther's claim that ten heirs may select one of their number to rule and yet be all kings equally is nonsensical, for to be a king is to be a monarch, and the very meaning of *monarchos* is 'sole ruler.'

69. Elliott, *Liberating Paul*, 36.

70. Gerhard Kittel and Gerhard Friedrich, *Theological Dictionary of the New Testament*, trans. G. W. Bromiley, Vol. III (Grand Rapid, Michigan: Eerdmans, 1966).

71. Luther, 'The Gospel for the Early Christmas Service,' 214.

72. Society of the Sacred Mission, *Principles* (Kelham, Newark-on-Trent: Society of the Sacred Mission, 1909), sec. xii. Beyond this occupational indifference, however, Luther's translation of *klesis* as *Beruf* has gradually led to an even nastier turn in the intepretation of the subsequent verse in the chapter. As S. Scott Bartchy has shown, *Beruf* gradually morphed in some translations into words even further from the original meaning of *klesis* such as *Stand* or, in English, condition. Hence in the New Revised Standard Version, published in 1989, verses 20 and 21 are translated as follows: 'Let each of you remain in the condition in which you were called. Were you a slave when called? Do not be concerned about it. *Even if you can gain your freedom, make use of your present condition now more than ever*' (1 Cor. 7:20–21, NRSV, italics added). Thus Paul's ruminations about the calling to embrace the way of Christ have evolved monstrously into a justification for slaves to remain in slavery (S. Scott Bartchy, 'Paul Did Not Teach 'Stay in Slavery': The Mistranslation of Κλῆσις in 1 Corinthians,' in *Combined Session of the African-American Hermeneutics*

and *Paul and Politics Sections of the Society of Biblical LIterature* [Boston, MA, 2008], available online, accessed 1 February 2018, http://media.patheos.com.s3.amazonaws.com/Media/PaulDidNotTeachforSBL_Nov-2008.pdf).

73. S. Scott Bartchy, 'Paul Did Not Teach 'Jeder Soll in Seinem Stand Bleiben': Luther's Mistranslation of 'Κλῆσις' in 1 Corinthians,' in *Guest Lecture at Augustuna Theologische Hochschule* (Neuendettelsau, Germany, 2009), online at *Bibel in gerechter Sprache*, accessed 1 February 2018, http://www.bibel-in-gerechter-sprache.de/wp-content/uploads/paul-did-not-teach.pdf.

74. David Phillips, *Investigating Education in Germany: Historical Studies from a British Perspective* (Routledge, 2015), 219. I am indebted to Félix Krawatzek for this distinction between the two terms.

75. Max Weber, *The Protestant Ethic and the Spirit of Capitalism*, Routledge Classics (London: Routledge, 2001), xiii.

76. William Perkins, 'A Treatise of the Vocations,' in The Works of That Famous and Worthy Minister of Christ in the University of Cambridge, Mr. William Perkins, Vol. I (Cambridge: John Legatt, 1626), 752, 754.

77. It is true that the doctrine of limited atonement is a later formulation and does not itself occur in the writings of Calvin or other early Calvinists, although some argue that it and the other four of the 'five points' of Calvinism can be traced back to the Synod of Dort between 1618–19, which was convened in response to the rise of Arminianism, with its belief in what was subsequently termed unlimited atonement, namely the notion that Christ died for all and not just for the elect, although some may choose not to believe and thus not be saved (James B. Torrance, 'The Incarnation and 'Limited Atonement,'' *The Evangelical Quarterly* 55/2 [1983], 83). The historical theologian Richard A. Muller has cast doubt on these claims, noting that not only is atonement an English word which was not used by Calvin or any of the sixteenth and seventeenth century Calvinist theologians who wrote in Latin, the theological debates of their time were very different from those that erupted in the Anglo-American world from the nineteenth century, and the 'five points' of Calvinism are a distillation of the tradition which occurred in that spatial-temporal context (Richard A. Muller, *Calvin and the Reformed Tradition: On the Work of Christ and the Order of Salvation* [Grand Rapids, MI: Baker Academic, 2012], 59–60.

78. Andrew Ballitch, '"Not to Behold Faith, But the Object of Faith": The Effect of William Perkins's Doctrine of the Atonement on His Preaching of Assurance,' *Themelios* 40/3 (2015), 452.

79. William Perkins, *A Christian and Plaine Treatise of the Manner and Order of Predestination and of the Largenes of Gods Grace*, trans. Francis Cacot and Thomas Tuke (London: William Weley, 1606), 18, italics added.

80. Perkins, 'A Treatise of the Vocations,' 758.

81. Weber, *The Protestant Ethic and the Spirit of Capitalism*, 40.

82. Perkins, *A Christian and Plaine Treatise*, 758.

83. It is true that the predominant metaphor used by such Christian

writers to describe the Christian community—or, in a few cases, society as a whole—is an organic one, i.e. a human body, and in this they follow St Paul. However, it has been discerned that the conception or paradigm of a living creature which they worked with was influenced by the philosophies of mechanism in thinkers such as Descartes and Hobbes who were their contemporaries. The literary theorist George C. Herndl, for instance, detects mechanistic strands in Perkins's sermons and tracts (George C. Herndl, *The High Design: English Renaissance Tragedy and the Natural Law* [Lexington: The University Press of Kentucky, 1970], 154).

84. Hence, one finds in Evelyn Waugh's 1945 novel *Brideshead Revisited* the fifteen-year old Cordelia Flyte, a devout Roman Catholic, explaining to the Anglican-raised protagonist, Charles Ryder, what it would mean for her to have a vocation: 'A vocation means you can be a nun. If you haven't a vocation, it's no good however much you want to be; and if you have a vocation, you can't get away from it, however much you hate it' (Evelyn Waugh, *Brideshead Revisited: The Sacred and Profane Memories of Captain Charles Ryder* [London: Penguin Books, 2000], 213).

85. Weber, *The Protestant Ethic and the Spirit of Capitalism*, 39.

86. Pope Leo XIII, Rerum Novarum: Encyclical on the Rights and Duties of Capital and Labour (London: Catholic Truth Society, 2002), sec. 5.

87. Walter Rauschenbusch, *Christianity and the Social Crisis in the 21st Century: The Classic That Woke Up the Church*, ed. Paul Rauschenbusch (New York: HarperOne, 2007), 263.

88. Rauschenbusch, *Christianity and the Social Crisis in the 21st Century*, 253.

89. Rauschenbusch, *Christianity and the Social Crisis in the 21st Century*, 290.

90. Jacques Ellul, 'From the Bible to a History of Non-Work,' trans. David Lovekin, *CrossCurrents* 35/1 (1985), 43.

91. Jacques Ellul, 'Work and Calling,' *Katallagete* 4/ 2–3 (1972), 8.

92. Stanley Eugene Fish, *Versions of Academic Freedom: From Professionalism to Revolution* (Chicago: The University of Chicago Press, 2014).

93. Fish, *Versions of Academic Freedom*, 7.

94. Literary critic Evan Kindley, in a review of Fish's book, points out that Fish is 'being disingenuous: there is in fact a large class of professionals within the university who tend to hold just such a view—the view that professors are, at the end of the day, just employees, with no special rights or privileges that don't attach to other kinds of employees. They're called administrators' (Evan Kindley, 'The Calling,' *Dissent Magazine*, accessed 25 July 2016, https://www.dissentmagazine.org/article/the-calling-academic-freedom-stanley-fish).

95. Fish, *Versions of Academic Freedom*, 10.

96. Fish, *Versions of Academic Freedom*, 3.

97. The 1915 Declaration certainly describes the task of the academic

in lofty terms, including as a 'high calling' which 'our profession may prove unworthy of' (American Association of University Professors, 'Appendix I: 1915 Declaration of Principles on Academic Freedom and Academic Tenure,' in *AAUP Policy & Documents*, 10th edition [Washington, D.C.: American Association of University Professors, 2006], 300.)

98. Fish, *Versions of Academic Freedom*, 10.

99. Nonetheless, there is a residue of religiosity here, for it was St Paul who summarized the entirety of the law in one single duty, namely to love one's neighbour (Gal. 5:14).

100. American Association of University Professors, 'Appendix I.'

101. American Association of University Professors, 'Appendix I.'

102. Fish, Versions of Academic Freedom, 11.

103. Fish, Versions of Academic Freedom, 11–12, italics in original.

104. Fish, Versions of Academic Freedom, 12.

105. Fish, Versions of Academic Freedom, 13.

106. Fish, Versions of Academic Freedom, 13.

107. Fish, Versions of Academic Freedom, 13.

108. Henry A. Giroux, *Against the Terror of Neoliberalism: Politics Beyond the Age of Greed* (Boulder, CO: Routledge, 2008), 128.

109. An analogue from the history of Christianity is the *devotio moderna* movement which flowered in the fourteenth and fifteenth centuries in Germany and the Low Countries. The central idea behind this movement was that it was possible to live a rigorous and devoted Christian life in the world without formally embracing the institutional framework of the religious orders (Bernard McGinn, *The Varieties of Vernacular Mysticism (1350–1550)*, Vol. 5 [New York: Crossroad Publishing Company, 2012], 97.

110. Fish, *Versions of Academic Freedom*, 11.

111. The basic structure of this triangular diagram is adapted from one in Donald F. Durbaugh's study, *The Believers' Church: The History and Character of Radical Protestantism*, in which he maps out the various Christian churches and sects according to the Trinitarian poles of Word, Spirit and Tradition (Donald F. Durnbaugh, *The Believers' Church: The History and Character of Radical Protestantism* [Scottdale, PA: Herald Press, 1985], 31).

112. In his aforementioned review of the book, Kindley asserts that 'there are left[-wing] and right[-wing] versions of all of the positions [Fish] describes' (Kindley, 'The Calling').

113. Fish, *Versions of Academic Freedom*, 7.

114. David Harvey, *The Condition of Postmodernity: An Enquiry into the Origins of Cultural Change* (Cambridge, MA; Oxford; Victoria: Blackwell Publishing, 1990), 22.

115. An example of this would be a critical scholar who decides to enter the world of representative politics. Instances of this in the critical legal world include Roberto M. Unger in Brazil and, more recently, Costas Douzinas in Greece.

116. It is important to note that this new synthesis is itself often an instance of creativity and novelty, rather than simply a piecing together of elements previously considered to be contradictory. The fruit of integration is a new thing, akin to a chemically bonded compound rather than just a mixture.

117. Julia Kristeva, *Desire in Language : A Semiotic Approach to Literature and Art* (New York: Columbia University Press, 1980), 36.

118. M. M. Bakhtin, *The Dialogic Imagination: Four Essays* (Austin: University of Texas Press, 1981), 272–3.

119. M. M. Bakhtin, *Problems of Dostoevsky's Poetics* (Minneapolis: University of Minnesota Press, 1984), 287.

120. Bakhtin, *Problems of Dostoevsky's Poetics*, 287.

121. James, *Pragmatism: And Four Essays from The Meaning of Truth*, 20.

122. Gerhard Kittel and Gerhard Friedrich, *Theological Dictionary of the New Testament*, trans. G. W. Bromiley (Grand Rapids, Michigan: Eerdmans, 1985).

123. A fairly recent example of this exceptional confluence of singularity and particularity in the religious sphere is that of Mother Teresa and her Missionaries of Charity.

124. Obtained via personal correspondence with Professor Bartchy on 7th July 2016.

125. Manuel DeLanda, 'Ontological Commitments,' *Speculations: A Journal of Speculative Realism* IV (2013), 71.

126. An additional objection to the deployment of the concept of *charismata*, from a secular perspective, is that speaking of gifts presupposes a giver, which in the Christian references here is assumed to be God. Indeed, as Angus McDonald has pointed out in an exploration of 'Critique as Avocation,' the same can be said about the idea of vocation as a calling, for historically speaking the one who calls the human being to a certain thing was also a divine being (Angus McDonald, 'Critique as Avocation,' unpublished *Plenary* of the Critical Legal Conference 2012). Nevertheless, this protest does not in any significant way challenge the use to which we have put Pauline concepts such as *klesis* and *charismata*, for although they may have a religious origin, the empirical matters which they deal with—namely stirrings towards particular and singular tasks and the certain capacities which tend to accompany them—are indisputable, even if they often resist easy explanation.

127. Karatani, *The Structure of World History*, 185–9.

128. Some more recent translations have interpreted Luther's famous statement in a manner which stress its propositional element. For instance, in the collection edited by Henry Scowcroft Bettenson, we find the first phrase translated as 'On this I stand' (Bettenson 1967, 201). The traditional, and more literal, translation from the German *Hie stehe ich* is here preferred for its spatial connotations.

129. Karatani, *Transcritique*, 23.

130. Slavoj Žižek, 'The Parallax View,' *New Left Review* 25 (2004), 129.

131. Theodor W. Adorno, *Minima Moralia: Reflections from Damaged Life* (London: Verso, 2005), 50.

132. G. K Chesterton, *Lunacy and Letters* (London; New York: Sheed and Ward, 1958), 129.

133. One source of inspiration for this formulation is a text by the Tiqqun collective, first published in 2001, see Tiqqun, *How Is It to Be Done?* (Inoperative Committee, 2008), https://tarnac9.files.wordpress.com/2009/01/how-is-it-to-be-done.pdf (no longer online).

134. Kojin Karatani, *Transcritique*, trans. Sabu Kohso (Cambridge: The MIT Press, 2003), 41.

135. It should be noted, however, that these questions of *how* and *why* are most worthy of closer examination by those who wish to take them up. Even those who are the most disdainful of psychologisms or sociologisms in such an area cannot deny the everyday experience, whether banal or profound, of being more attracted to particular directions in thought, feeling, and action.

136. Karatani, *Architecture as Metaphor*, xlii. In an interview with Joel Wainwright, published in 2012, Karatani responds to a question on whether 'Marx's value form theory' can be regarded 'as an explicit reiteration of Kant's triadic structure' by first gesturing toward his bringing together of the Kantian and Lacanian triads, before stating that commodities can be considered as akin to the real, value-form to the symbolic and money to the imaginary (Kojin Karatani and Joel Wainwright, '"Critique Is Impossible without Moves": An Interview of Kojin Karatani by Joel Wainwright,' *Dialogues in Human Geography* 2/1 (2012), 33.

137. Karatani, *Architecture as Metaphor*, xliii.

138. Kant, *Critique of Pure Reason*, 466.

139. The Italian Neoplatonic philosopher Marsilio Ficino is regarded as the first to distill this tripartite formulation of the transcendentals from the discord of debates through the centuries. In *The Philebus Commentary*, published in 1496, he writes, 'So the action of the intelligence is directed to some end. For in so far as it understands, its end is the truth; in so far as it wills, its end is the good; in so far as it acts, its end is the beautiful' (Marsilio Ficino, *Marsilio Ficino: The Philebus Commentary* [Berkeley; London: University of California Press, 1975], 78.) Although Ficino uses the word 'acts' to describe the activity of the intelligence with regard to the beautiful, we should understand this less as an instance of physical activity in the world, and more in the generic sense in which aesthetics is concerned with judging impressions which have a sensuous dimension. Kant himself, in a 1772 letter to his student, Marcus Herz, spoke of 'the universal principles of feeling, taste, and sensuous desire' (Kant, *Critique of Pure Reason*, 47).

140. Uchang Kim and Kojin Karatani, 'Conversation on East Asian Civilization, Past and Present,' trans. Jeon Seung-Hee, *Azalea: Journal of Korean Literature & Culture* 7/1 (2014), 182, https://doi.org/10.1353/aza.2014.0003.

141. Kim and Karatani, 'Conversation on East Asian Civilization, Past and

Present,' 182.

142. Kim and Karatani, 'Conversation on East Asian Civilization, Past and Present,' 182.

143. Karatani's thinking-centred leanings are evident in his consistent advocacy of universality and singularity over communal (i.e. subjectivist and particular) perspectives. However, it can be argued that his primary approach is an action-centric one, which can be discerned from his recurring emphasis on the ethical as well as politics. In his dialogue with Kim Uchang, for instance, he laments the historical bias towards aesthetics (i.e. feeling-centricism) in Japan and appears to admire the political stance of contemporary Koreans, opining: 'We need to become more political in Japan' (Kim and Karatani, 'Conversation on East Asian Civilization, Past and Present,' 187).

144. Karatani, *Transcritique*, 35.

145. Immanuel Kant, *Practical Philosophy*, trans. Mary J. Gregor (Cambridge: CUP, 1996), 178.

146. It is important to note, however, that in *The Metaphysic of Morals*, Kant distinguishes between what he calls the *juridical* and the *ethical* aspects of morality. The former is 'directed merely to external actions and their conformity to law' whereas the latter 'also require[s] that they (the laws) themselves be the determining grounds of actions' (Immanuel Kant, *The Metaphysics of Morals*, [Cambridge: CUP, 1991], 42). In this manner Kant reserves the term *juridical* for the sphere of external laws. Bearing this distinction of his in mind, as we shall see, his repeated invocation of legal words and phrases can nevertheless be said to provide what we term here a 'pseudo-juridical flavour' to his philosophical system.

147. Kant, *Critique of Judgement*, 16–17.

148. Angelica Nuzzo, *Kant and the Unity of Reason*, (West Lafayette, Ind: Purdue University Press, 2005), 127.

149. Talal Asad, 'Free Speech, Blasphemy, and Secular Criticism,' in *Is Critique Secular?: Blasphemy, Injury, and Free Speech*, ed. Talal Asad, Wendy Brown, Judith Butler, and Saba Mahmood (Berkeley, CA: Townsend Center for the Humanities, 2009), 50.

150. Asad, 'Free Speech, Blasphemy, and Secular Criticism,' 49–50.

151. Cornel West and Bill Brown, 'Beyond Eurocentrism and Multiculturalism,' *Modern Philology* 90 (1993), 163.

152. Asad, 'Free Speech, Blasphemy, and Secular Criticism,' 50, italics in original.

153. It is crucial to note, however, that Kant does not use the word 'aesthetics' for the domain of sensuous beauty which we are discussing here, preferring the term 'taste.' In a footnote in the First Critique he states that 'the Germans are the only ones who now employ the word "aesthetics" to designate that which others call the critique of taste' (Kant, *Critique of Pure Reason*, 156). Instead, he reserves the word 'aesthetics' for its etymological and classical sense, that is, for sensuous perception.

154. Kant, *Critique of Judgement*, 56, italics in original.
155. Karatani, *Transcritique*, 38.
156. Michael Wayne, *Red Kant: Aesthetics, Marxism and the Third Critique* (London; New York: Bloomsbury Academic, 2014), 96.
157. Karatani, *Architecture as Metaphor*, xxxii, xxxv.
158. Karatani, 'Beyond Capital-Nation-State,' 593.
159. Morris Berman, *Wandering God: A Study in Nomadic Spirituality* (Albany, NY: State University of New York Press, 2000), 208–9.
160. Berman, , *Wandering God*, 211–12.
161. Karatani, *Transcritique*, 34.
162. Michel Foucault, *Technologies of the Self: A Seminar with Michel Foucault*, ed. Luther H Martin, Huck Gutman, and Patrick H Hutton (Amherst: University of Massachusetts Press, 1988), 9.
163. Peter Maurin, 'The Purpose of the Catholic Workers' School,' in *Easy Essays* (Eugene, OR: Wipf and Stock Publishers, 2010), 37.

Appendix A

164. Karatani, *Origins of Modern Japanese Literature*, ed. and trans. Brett de Bary (Durham, NC: Duke UP, 1993).
165. ANY was an acronym for Architecture New York, but also a playful reference to undecidability, with conference titles such as Anyone, Anywhere, Anything and Anybody. Collected excerpts from the proceedings of each conference were published. Karatani's papers were: Kojin Karatani, 'The Status of an Individual,' in *Anyone* (New York: Rizzoli, 1991); Kojin Karatani, 'Notes on Communicative Space,' in *Anywhere* (New York: Rizzoli, 1992); Kojin Karatani, 'On the Thing-in-Itself,' in *Anyway* (New York: Rizzoli, 1993); Kojin Karatani, 'Architecture and Earthquakes,' in *Anywise* (New York: Rizzoli, 1995); Kojin Karatani, 'Architecture's Impurity,' in *Anyhow* (New York: Rizzoli, 1997); Kojin Karatani, 'Thing as Other,' in *Anything* (New York: Rizzoli, 2000).
166. Karatani, *Architecture as Metaphor*, xlvi.
167. Kojin Karatani, *Transcritique*, trans. Sabu Kohso (Cambridge: The MIT Press, 2003).
168. Slavoj Žižek, *The Parallax View* (Cambridge, MA: The MIT Press, 2006).
169. New Associationist Movement, *Principles of the New Associationist Movement (NAM)*, Revised Version, 2001, http://www.nam21.org/english/principles.html (No longer online).
170. Karatani, *History and Repetition*; Karatani, *The Structure of World History*; Kojin Karatani, *Nation and Aesthetics*, trans. Hiroki Yoshikuni, Jonathan E. Abel, and Darwin E. Tsen (New York: OUP, 2017); Kojin Karatani and Joseph A. Murphy, *Isonomia and the Origins of Philosophy* (Durham, NC: Duke University Press, 2017); Kojin Karatani, 'World Intercourse:

A Transcritical Reading of Kant and Freud,' *UMBR(a): A Journal of the Unconscious Semblance* (2007); Kojin Karatani, 'Revolution & Repetition,' *UMBR(a)* Utopia (2008), 133–46; Kojin Karatani, 'Beyond Capital-Nation-State,' *Rethinking Marxism* 20/4 (October 2008), 569–95.

171. Karatani, 'Thing as Other,' 259.

172. Eduardo Mendieta, 'On Left Kantianism: From Transcendental Critique to the Critical Ontology of the Present,' *Foucault Studies* 18 (2014), 246–7.

173. Jonathan E. Abel, Preface to *Nation and Aesthetics*, by Kojin Karatani, trans. Hiroki Yoshikuni, Jonathan E. Abel, and Darwin E. Tsen (New York: OUP, 2017).

174. Yamoi Pham, 'Book Review: Karatani's "The Structure of World History,"' *Journal of World-Systems Research* 20/ 2 (2014), 330.

175. Sabu Kohso, 'Translator's Remarks,' in Karatani, *Architecture as Metaphor*, xviii.

176. Arata Isozaki, 'Introduction: A Map of Crises,' in Karatani, *Architecture as Metaphor*, vi.

177. Indeed, it is noticeable that in the published excerpts from the panels during the Any conferences, the participants addressed very few questions to Karatani, and rarely made references to his papers.

Appendix B

1. Michel Foucault, 'Nietzsche, Genealogy, History,' in *Language, Counter-Memory, Practice: Selected Essays and Interviews*, ed. Donald F. Bouchard (Ithaca: Cornell UP, 1977); Wendy Brown, *Politics Out of History* (Princeton: Princeton University Press, 2001), 100.

2. Brown, *Politics Out of History*, 100.

3. Modifying slightly the method propounded by the Cat in the Hat in the Dr Seuss children's video The Lorax: 'The way to know a certain something is to find out what it's not.' Or to quote a more distinguished source, in Oscar Wilde's essay 'The Artist as Critic,' he states that 'the primary aim of the critic is to see the object as … it really is not' (Oscar Wilde, *The Soul of Man Under Socialism and Selected Critical Prose*, ed. Linda Dowling, New Ed edition [London; New York: Penguin Classics, 2001], 240).

4. Brown, *Politics Out of History*, 100.

5. Karatani, *Origins of Modern Japanese Literature*.

6. Jonathan E. Abel, Preface to *Nation and Aesthetics*, xi.

7. Jonathan E. Abel, Preface to *Nation and Aesthetics*, xii.

8. Karatani, *Origins of Modern Japanese Literature*, xii.

9. The Foucauldian scholar Clare O'Farrell even wrote a book-long exploration of this issue, see Clare O'Farrell, *Foucault: Historian or Philosopher?* (Basingstoke: Macmillan, 1989).

10. Brown, *Politics Out of History*, 95.
11. This point and the quotes in the rest of the paragraph are drawn from O'Farrell, see Clare O'Farrell, *Michel Foucault* (London; Thousand Oaks, Calif: Sage Publications UK, 2005), 71–72.
12. Michel Foucault and Jeremy Carrette, 'Who Are You, Professor Foucault?,' in *Religion and Culture* (Manchester: Manchester University Press, 1999), 91.
13. Foucault, *Discipline and Punish*, 31.
14. Michel Foucault, 'What Our Present Is,' in *Foucault Live: Interviews 1961–1984*, ed. Sylvere Lotringer, 2nd ed. (New York: Semiotext(e), 1996), 411.
15. Foucault, 'Nietzsche, Genealogy, History,' 146.
16. Foucault, 'Nietzsche, Genealogy, History,' 146.
17. Foucault, *Discipline and Punish*, 31.
18. Kojin Karatani, 'Beyond Capital-Nation-State,' *Rethinking Marxism* 20/4 (2008), 570.
19. Karatani, 'Beyond Capital-Nation-State,' 570.
20. Andre Glucksmann, 'Michel Foucault's Nihilism,' in *Michel Foucault: Philosopher*, ed. Timothy J. Armstrong (New York: Routledge, 1992), 336–9. Although Glucksmann does not mention it in his piece, it is quite certain that he adopted the term 'intolerable' from the language of the Group for Information on Prisons (GIP) that Foucault co-founded in 1971, declaring in a questionnaire that: 'The situation in the prisons is intolerable. Prisoners are being treated like dogs' (David Macey, *The Lives of Michel Foucault*, [London: Vintage, 1994], 262).
21. Glucksmann, 'Michel Foucault's Nihilism,' 337.
22. Karatani, *Transcritique*, ix.
23. Karatani, *The Structure of World History*, xiii.
24. O'Farrell, *Michel Foucault*, 72.
25. Foucault, 'Nietzsche, Genealogy, History,' 143. Foucault's reference gives the source of the quote by Nietzsche as aphorism 3 of *The Wanderer and His Shadow*. The text is actually what is sometimes published these days as Part Two of Volume II of *Human, All Too Human*. The aphorism in the R. J. Hollingdale translation reads as follows: '"*In the beginning*". To glorify the origin—that is the metaphysical aftershoot that breaks out when we meditate on history and makes us believe that what stands at the beginning of all things is also what is most valuable and essential' (Friedrich Wilhelm Nietzsche, *Human, All Too Human: A Book for Free Spirits*, trans. R. J. Hollingdale [Cambridge: CUP, 1996], 302), italics in original.
26. Foucault, 'Nietzsche, Genealogy, History,' 140.
27. Michel Foucault, 'Truth and Juridical Forms,' in *Power: Essential Works of Michel Foucault, 1954-1984, Vol. 3*, ed. James D. Faubion (New York: The New Press, 2000), 6–7.
28. Karatani, *Origins of Modern Japanese Literature*, 193, italics in

original.
29. Karatani, *Origins of Modern Japanese Literature*, 2.
30. Foucault, 'Nietzsche, Genealogy, History,' 146.
31. For an examination of the medieval European university, see Ridder-Symoens, *A History of the University in Europe*, 8. However, it should be noted that what we can learn from examining the earlier days of the university is how seemingly bygone elements can resurface in more recent times as a matter of contingency which nevertheless appears as a (singular) repetition. We see this to be the case in chapter three when we compare certain aspects of the university at present with that of the medieval and early modern periods.
32. Michel Foucault, *The Birth Of Biopolitics: Lectures At The College De France, 1978–1979*, ed. Lawrence D. Kritzman (Basingstoke: Palgrave Macmillan, 2010), 3.
33. Michel Foucault, *Security, Territory, Population: Lectures at the Collège de France 1977–1978*, ed. Michel Senellart, trans. Graham Burchill (Basingstoke: Palgrave Macmillan, 2009), 239.
34. Gustav Landauer, 'Weak Statesmen, Weaker People!,' in *Revolution and Other Writings* (Oakland, CA: PM Press, 2010), 214. Among those who regarded the state as an institution was Landauer's fellow anarchist Peter Kropotkin (Peter Kropotkin, *The State: Its Historic Role* [London: Freedom Press, 1946], sec. X).
35. Foucault, *Security, Territory, Population*, 239.
36. Louis Althusser, *Lenin and Philosophy, and Other Essays* (New York: Monthly Review Press, 1998), 166.
37. Althusser, *Lenin and Philosophy*, 143.
38. Warren Montag, *Althusser and His Contemporaries* (Durham, NC: Duke University Press, 2013), 161–9.
39. Montag, *Althusser and His Contemporaries*, 164.
40. Similarly, in 'Questions of Method,' he asserts that in *Discipline and Punish*, 'the target of analysis wasn't "institutions," "theories," or "ideology" but practices—with the aim of grasping the conditions that make these acceptable at a given moment; the hypothesis being that these types of practice are not just governed by institutions, prescribed by ideologies, guided by pragmatic circumstances—whatever role these elements might actually play—but, up to a point, possess their own specific regularities, logic, strategy, self-evidence, and "reason." It is a question of analyzing a "regime of practices"—practices being understood here as places where what is said and what is done, rules imposed and reasons given, the planned and the taken-for-granted meet and interconnect' (Michel Foucault, 'Questions on Method,' in *Power*, 225, italics in original).
41. See for instance, Karatani, 'Beyond Capital-Nation-State,' 575.
42. Foucault, *The Birth Of Biopolitics*.
43. Michel Foucault et al., 'Considerations on Marxism, Phenomenology and Power. Interview with Michel Foucault; Recorded on April 3rd, 1978,'

Foucault Studies 14 (2012), 109.

44. Michel Foucault, *Society Must Be Defended: Lectures at the Collège de France, 1975-1976* (New York: Picador, 2003), 52, italics added.

45. Michel Foucault, 'Truth and Power,' in *Power*, 126–127.

46. Mark Olssen, *Michel Foucault: Materialism and Education*, (Westport, Conn.; London: Bergin & Garvey, 1999), 65.

47. Karatani, *Transcritique*, xii.

48. Examples of secondary literature which bring out Foucault's oppositional tendencies include C. G. Prado, *Foucault's Legacy*, (London: Continuum, 2009), 2–3; Barry Smart, *Foucault, Marxism, and Critique* (London: Routledge & Kegan Paul, 1983), 135; Mark Poster, *Foucault, Marxism and History: Mode of Production versus Mode of Information* (Cambridge: Polity, 1984). However, for a reading of Foucault as a 'radical reformist,' cf. Colin Koopman, *Genealogy as Critique: Foucault and the Problems of Modernity* (Bloomington: Indiana University Press, 2013), 143. The terms 'micro-political' and 'macro-political,' strictly speaking, originate from Deleuze and Guattari rather than Foucault, but the distinction is one which is apposite for the purpose of distinguishing Foucault from other leftist thinkers of his time.

49. Kanishka Goonewardena, 'Theory and Politics in Karatani Kōjin's The Structure of World History,' *Journal of Japanese Philosophy* 4/4 (2016), 92, italics added.

Index

American Association of University Professors (AAUP) 133–4
anarchy 56–7, 132, 168
Anarchy 56
Ancient Greece 124
Astin, Alexander W. 97–9
Attlee, Clement 35–41, 44–5, 47, 51–2, 173

Bakhtin, Mikhail 141–2, 213
Barlow Report 37, 47–8, 51, 64–5, 185, 190
Berman, Morris 156, 216
Beruf 128–9, 131–2, 134, 136, 138–9, 143,
Bologna 85–7, 167
bracketing 28, 151, 167
Bracketing xi, 26, 28
Braude, Richard 91–2
Browne Review 66
Brueggemann, Walter 123
Buddhism 110–11
Burrows, Roger 98–9

Calhoun, Craig 29
capitalism 36, 40, 42, 46, 58, 73, 103–5, 130–1, 165, 167
charismata 114, 140, 143–6, 149–50, 175
Chesterton, G. K. 69, 150
Christianity 117, 120–3, 125–32, 134, 136, 145–7
  Bible 123, 125, 127, 129, 132, 139, 143
  Calvinism 130
  Catholic 127, 131–2, 135–6, 158
  St Paul 114, 119, 122, 125, 127–8, 144–6, 169, 175

Vatican 131, 135
Churchill, Winston 52
collegia doctorum 85
Collini, Stefan 31–2, 179
community 13, 21, 25–6, 28, 32, 35, 51, 55, 58, 70, 73–83, 87–90, 94–7, 99–109, 112–13, 119–20, 126, 133, 135, 139, 146, 151, 172, 174–5
constitutive idea 56–8, 69, 72, 108, 173
constitutive ideal 57
Counter-Reformation 131, 135
Critical Legal Conference 100–1

deconstruction 81, 101–2
Descartes, René 94–6, 100
Dobb, Maurice 65, 190

equality 58, 62, 64–5, 119
Esposito, Roberto 79–81, 101, 106–7, 194, 200, 202

Fabianism 41
Fichte 23
Fish, Stanley 53, 132–6, 138–40, 143, 147
Foucault, Michel 17, 19, 37, 86, 157, 160, 162–71
founding myth 58
Fuller, Steve 63

Gemeinschaft 76–80, 83–4, 88–90, 93, 95, 100, 102–4, 106
German Idealists 23
German Romantics 24, 117–18

222 INDEX

Gesellschaft 76, 78–84, 89, 94–6, 100, 102–4, 106
Gill, Rosalind 99

Hegel, GWF 24–5, 112, 117
Holmwood, John 61
Humboldt, Alexander von 33, 55, 118
Husserl 28

idealism 13, 21, 24–6, 43, 51, 53, 55, 57–8, 67, 74, 82, 108–9, 112, 148, 151, 153, 172–5
Idealism xi, 23
Illich, Ivan 26, 76–8, 106–8
instrumentalism xi, 13, 21–6, 31–5, 44–7, 50–3, 58, 67–70, 72, 74, 82, 87, 89, 108–9, 112, 138–9, 148–9, 151, 153, 172–5

Judaism 120, 125

Kafka, Franz 70–1, 174
Kant, Immanuel 18–25, 28, 55–6, 72, 112–13, 117, 119–21, 150–7, 159–60, 164–5, 173, 178
Karatani, Kojin 76–9, 81–2, 89–90, 94, 102–5, 107–8, 162–7, 169–71
  Capital-Nation-State 57, 82, 104, 160, 171
  Modes 103–9, 120, 158, 160
  Transcritique 18–19, 73, 94, 103–4, 116, 120, 159–60, 165
Keynes / Keynesianism 35, 39–46, 50, 60
klesis 114, 123–6, 128–30, 132, 134, 136, 139–40, 143–7, 149–50
Kojève, Alexandre 114
Kristeva, Julia 141

Labour Party 39, 41–2
laissez-faire 42–4
liberty 43, 50, 58, 62, 86
Loach, Ken 38–9
Luther, Martin 127–31, 134, 136, 139, 148

market rationality 35
Marquand, David 68
Marx 18, 24, 40, 56, 78, 102–3, 152, 159, 164–5
Murdoch, Rupert 46

Nancy, Jean-Luc 79–81, 100–1, 106
nationalization 37–8, 41–2, 44–5, 60
National Student Survey 47, 88
National Universities Board 45
neoliberalism 62, 73
Nietzsche 40, 83, 152, 162, 164, 166

parallax 26, 28–9, 51, 159
post-war consensus 36, 41–2, 45, 50, 72
precarity 91, 94–6
privatization 20, 35, 39, 58, 60, 91, 93
Protestant Reformation 95, 124
psychoanalysis 19, 22

Rashdall, Hastings 86, 88, 90–1, 195–7
rationalism 22, 24, 119, 156
Readings, Bill 33–4, 55, 100
regulative idea 56–7, 72, 108–9
Research Assessment Exercise (RAE) 46, 98
Robbins Report xi, 61–7, 69, 72, 76, 84, 173

Schütz, Anton 122, 126
singularity-universality 111, 115–16, 119–21
Skidelsky, Robert 45, 60
socialism 39–43, 45–6, 50, 60, 68, 81, 122
social justice 42–3, 61, 134, 136, 139
Socrates 71, 75, 124
studium 85, 92

Thatcher, Margaret 35–6, 39, 50, 173
Tönnies, Ferdinand 76–8, 103, 174
totalitarianism 57, 146, 170
transcendental 19–22, 24, 26, 55, 72,

78, 81, 102, 108, 118, 160, 162–3, 166

universitas 85–9, 92, 113, 167
University (British)
  graduates 65–6
  Middlesex viii, 14, 113
  neoliberal 36, 99, 173
  non-academic staff 76, 82–3, 90–1, 93–4, 133, 174
  post-war 13, 21, 34, 36–8, 44, 47, 51, 54, 69–70, 72, 76, 87, 113, 120, 148, 153, 167, 169, 175
  public 23, 35–6, 49, 51–2, 54, 57–8, 60–2, 65–6, 68–73, 76, 173–4
  student 93
  Sussex 91, 93, 197–8
  University Grants Committee (UGC) 48–52

vocation 26, 77, 110, 114, 117, 121–36, 143–4, 146–7, 150, 169, 174–5

Willetts, David 46, 66–7, 84

Žižek, Slavoj 26, 70, 122, 150, 159

www.ingramcontent.com/pod-product-compliance
Lightning Source LLC
Chambersburg PA
CBHW071341080526
44587CB00017B/2919